THE FIERCE

Praise for *The Fierce*

'Judy Piercey expertly captures the remarkable and complicated relationship between David Whitelaw and his mother Judith. An inspiring story that reminds us what it means to be human and the responsibility we all have to make the world around us a better place.'

Barbara Smith, best-selling author

'A groundbreaking portrayal of the trauma and burden imposed on the children of Holocaust survivors. Teenager David Whitelaw was a force of nature that inspired his government to seek justice for the unspeakable crimes unleashed against innocent people.'

Phil Blazer, founder of Jewish Life Television

'Author Judy Piercey shines a brilliant light into this dark corner of post-war history, one that has been concealed for too long. You'll find yourself cheering for the Jewish teenager who struggled to bring down one of the worst Nazi killers in history, sickened by the crimes this mass murderer committed, and aghast that he was protected by the United States government. Meticulously researched and skilfully written, this book provides a significant contribution to our body of historical knowledge about the Holocaust.'

Elinor Florence, author of *Bird's Eye View*

EVERY
GOLIATH
HAS A
DAVID

THE FIERCE

The Untold Story
of the Teenager Who
Took On the Worst
War Criminal Living
in America

JUDY PIERCEY

The
History
Press

In memory of Phil Blazer
Journalist, activist and dear friend

Front cover images: Jasenovac Memorial Site; UPI/Alamy Stock Photo.

First published 2023

The History Press
97 St George's Place, Cheltenham,
Gloucestershire, GL50 3QB
www.thehistorypress.co.uk

© Myth Merchant Films, 2023
Fierce definition © Oxford University Press, 2023

British Library Cataloguing in Publication Data.
A catalogue record for this book is available from the British Library.

ISBN 978 1 80399 115 3

Typesetting and origination by The History Press
Printed and bound in Great Britain by TJ Books Limited, Padstow, Cornwall.

Trees for Life

Contents

Andrija Artuković
in his Ustasha
uniform. (Jasenovac
Memorial Site)

David Whitelaw
as an 18-year-old
member of the Jewish
Defense League
in 1974. (David
Whitelaw/Myth
Merchant Films)

Foreword

fierce, definition
1. Savage predatory and violent aggressiveness.
2. A powerful and passionate heartfelt intensity.

Oxford Languages

It was the second definition that struck me the first time I met David Whitelaw in 2018. I'd been warned that he was an intense and passionate character. Still, I wasn't prepared for the slightly dishevelled man who walked into the room, barely taking the time to acknowledge me, before thrusting his hand into a plastic shopping bag and, with a flourish, pulling out a stapled sheaf of paper. He threw it on the desk. 'You've heard of Schindler's list?' he asked fiercely. 'This is Whitelaw's list.'

Whitelaw's list, typewritten on paper faded and yellowed by time, contains the names of his seventy-six relatives murdered in the Holocaust.

It was a gripping moment, one that set the scene for the story that he was about to share with a stranger for the first time. The story, with its many dramatic and fateful twists and turns, would always come back to this truth: the crushing misery inflicted upon three generations of one family by the Holocaust. One family, their lives a vignette, a microcosm of the worst genocide in our time.

The Whitelaw family suffered from two traumas: the Holocaust and parental abandonment. The story resonated with me, especially since my own family was shaped by parental abandonment that echoed David's father's. On a deeply personal level, I understood that particular inter-generational trauma. It had shaped me, too. It had also, perhaps unconsciously, drawn me onto my professional path. As a young journalist, I found my niche in telling stories that focused on Indigenous people in Canada. They told me stories about their own inter-generational trauma, the legacy of residential schools that stole their language, culture, dignity and all too often the lives of their loved ones. The crimes against them were sanctioned by government and executed in church-run schools.

The theme of crimes committed in the name of religion, one that has run through narratives since time immemorial, is a central theme of this story, too. David Whitelaw's faith in the belief that he could create a better world led him to take on a war criminal, a true-life David-and-Goliath story that could have cost him his life. He acted in the belief that he was obeying God.

As I got to know David better, I was struck again by another parallel: the Goliath to his David was a man uncannily like himself. As a child, Andrija Artuković stood out for his intelligence. Like David Whitelaw, he excelled at school. Both young men aspired to become physicians. Both abandoned careers in medicine because they couldn't stand the sight of blood. Both men were student activists engaged in fights fuelled by their faith. The identities of both David Whitelaw, a Jew, and Andrija Artuković, a Roman Catholic, were rooted in their religion. Both were fervent, even militant, in their religious beliefs. Both committed crimes in the name of God. Artuković became known as the 'Butcher of the Balkans' for his role in the murder of 770,000 people in Croatia's death camps during the Second World War.

Both Whitelaw and Artuković were fierce men, serving organisations that invoked the first definition of fierce: savage predatory and violent aggressiveness.

Both the Jewish Defense League (JDL), which attracted 17-year-old David Whitelaw, and the Ustasha, which Andrija Artuković joined as a young man, were far-right movements that boasted about their violence. Both were terrorist organisations. Many Jews recoiled at the JDL's tactics, just as many Croatians were repulsed by the Ustasha. My own perceptions about the organisations were informed by FBI files. As I pored through hundreds of pages of FBI reports, I learned that the FBI had been keeping tabs on Croatian American organisations even before the Second World War and were watching the JDL since its inception in 1968. As the Cold

War set in, the FBI focused on JDL protests against the Soviet Union and on Andrija Artuković as a person with firsthand knowledge of communism. During my research, I also read firsthand accounts of witnesses and survivors who swore affidavits to support Artuković's prosecution. Their accounts were poignant and chilling, especially since I had known little about the atrocities in Croatia. Some of those accounts were later disputed, as were the number of people murdered in the genocide. Depending on the source, some of which deny the genocide or claim that its number was vastly exaggerated, between 350,000 and 770,000 people were murdered. Since the true number can never be verified, I chose to stay with 770,000, the number cited by Yugoslavia in its prosecution against Artuković and reported in the media from the 1950s to 1980s. The numbers may be disputed but the horrors are not. I discovered how thoroughly the brutality of the Ustasha was documented when I started reading historical records and newspaper coverage spanning the Second World War and the 1980s, when Andrija Artuković was finally brought to justice.

Conducting research from my home in Canada proved challenging, despite the wealth of online resources. As a result, I split my time evenly between Edmonton and Los Angeles for a three-year period. In Los Angeles, I was able to visit the locations where this story took place and reflect upon the historical material cited here. I also examined archival court records and conducted 300 hours of interviews with David Whitelaw, his family, friends and supporters. I approached the Artuković family and requested interviews but received no reply.

I've always been a voracious reader, and as I read dozens of books about the Holocaust, I pondered the similarities with our world today. Antisemitism and white supremacism are on the rise globally. An appalling number of people believe the Holocaust didn't happen or that the number of Jews murdered was considerably less than six million.

With *The Fierce*, I hope to shine a light on the danger of dogma and show how it fosters hatred. The tragic historical period of the Holocaust reminds us how hatred escalates and becomes normalised, a message that I believe is more important today than ever before.

'I Felt the Spirit of the Warsaw Ghetto Fighters'

2 a.m., Sherman Oaks, Los Angeles, 29 January 1975

Focusing intently on his mission, David Whitelaw rolled down the car window and took a deep breath. Inhaling the air of the Smog Capital of the World was preferable to the stink of gasoline wafting from the back seat.

David listened for the familiar whir of the police helicopters in the sky. Nothing. But he could not afford to be lulled into a false sense of security because the Los Angeles Police Department's helicopters could swoop in out of nowhere. He flipped on the AM radio to hear if any police blotter news had erupted. The last thing they needed was to happen upon some bone-headed crime that might draw attention to their own cargo in the back seat.

Traffic was mercifully light. He glanced over at the driver, Mike Schwartz, and thought the airhead ought to be paying more attention to the speed limit. If the cops happened to stop them for speeding along Sunset Boulevard, they'd be screwed.

Transporting the gasoline in the back seat had been a last-minute decision. But now David's Boy Scout training sent a question flickering through his mind about the safety of carrying incendiary devices inside the car for the forty-five-minute drive to the San Fernando Valley.

Nothing in his entire nineteen years of existence had prepared him to even think of challenging authority. David practically grew up in Disneyland, which had opened down the road in neighbouring Anaheim on 17 July 1955, less than a week before his birth. Never one to seek the thrill of the adrenaline rush, David always preferred the tamest rides, making him an unlikely candidate for this mission. But as Bob Dylan sang, 'The Times They Are A-Changin''.

It was a fitting anthem for the chaos of his adolescent years: the Vietnam War, the Kent State Massacre, Watergate and the daily news footage of protests, bombings or hijackings. David couldn't relate to the Black Panthers; or Patti Hearst, the rich kid who joined her kidnappers; or the IRA. His own mission was specific, with a single target. His goal was to expose the evil, once and for all, that had been allowed to live, even thrive, thanks to powerful protectors. After their mission tonight, the world would learn about the worst war criminal in America. Not only did he pray that no one would get hurt, but he was also keenly aware that causing any injury at all might blemish the moral rightness of their cause. When the mission was complete, David wanted to hold his head high and celebrate that he was able to accomplish what even the US government was unable to do: bring down the mass murderer living quietly on a California beach.

But as soon as David stepped out of the car, he sensed danger. Instinctively, he knew something was wrong. His shoulders tensed, eyes darting around. A shiver crawled up his spine, and he regretted not wearing a jacket. The temperature had dropped to 37°F since he'd slipped out of the house around dinner time, avoiding his mother's inevitable questions about where he was going. To his relief, the wind that gusted earlier in the afternoon had settled down, and now the air was still. There was a full moon, and he could clearly see the 1974 Ford Mustang 11 parked in the carport, just as it had been the night before when he did a reconnaissance.

Next to the carport was a garage. Next to that was a sprawling two-storey house clad in typical California stucco but upgraded with brick trim on the lower half. The inside of the house was pitch black except for a night light in what he guessed was the kitchen of 16011 Meadowcrest Road.

David's eyes quickly scanned the rest of the street. The windows were dark in every house.

Meadowcrest Road was a winding, dead-end street at the top of a hill in the leafy suburb of Sherman Oaks. The home of John Artukovich, the wealthy owner of a construction business, was one of the last houses on the upscale street, almost at the top of the hill.

David's stomach rumbled, reminding him of the nerves that had prevented him from eating since lunch. His eyes took in the car parked down the street. It wasn't as fancy as the cars that belonged in this neighbourhood. He wondered briefly if there were people inside it? Lovers making out?

He gauged the distance from the parked car to the Mustang. Less than 50 feet. Too close. It didn't look as if anyone was in the car. But what if there was? Feeling the bile rise in his throat, he repressed the desire to jump back into the car and urge Schwartz to put the pedal to the metal and get the hell out of there.

The teenager swallowed hard, trying to shake the unsettling feeling that had sent his senses into overdrive. Unconsciously, he reached for his neck and fingered the pendant hanging on a cheap metal chain. It was an amulet, a prized possession that he had bought proudly with his own hard-earned money to wear on only the most special occasions. The Star of David medallion made from hammered black metal was admittedly a bit gaudy, big enough to cover half his hand. But that was the whole point. To be labelled. To stand out and be identified as a proud Jew.

Since David had started earning his own money, collecting Judaica had become a hobby, and perhaps an obsession. He cherished his small purchases from the Jewish gift shops on Fairfax Avenue, the beating heart of Jewish Los Angeles. Even his job in a factory, the night shift of boxing and labelling eight-track tapes, brought an intense feeling of connection with his people. The popular songs on the tapes, while not specifically Jewish, resonated with the moody teenager. Pink Floyd's *Dark Side of the Moon* reinforced fighting for justice, and Black Sabbath's *Sabbath Bloody Sabbath* conjured up images of evil and ghosts. Listening to the dark music on his car's eight-track stereo, how could he not think of the six million Jews murdered? Of the evil that had robbed him of a family? Evil, as his mother reminded him every day of his life, had led to the unspeakable horrors of the Holocaust. The ghosts of the seventy-six members of his family murdered by Hitler haunted his mother's every waking moment. For as long as he could remember, the evil had plagued him, too, disrupting his nightly sleep with terrifying nightmares.

Tonight, finally, was his chance to seek justice.

The opportunity had come out of the blue just two nights ago.

David wished that he'd had more time to plan, but after two years of wasted effort, he had to concede that time was not his friend. In the last forty-eight hours he'd created a plan, one that he shared with only one other person, Mike Schwartz. From the moment he started planning, David began thinking of himself and Schwartz as members of a cell, a Jewish Defense League fighting unit.

In the driver's seat, Schwartz slipped his hands into a pair of rubber gloves and stuck to the plan of leaving the engine running and the doors open. As David watched his accomplice slide out and stride around the car, he experienced a surge of sensory overload. His ears, hidden by long curly brown hair, pricked up at the sound of Schwartz opening the door to the back seat of their borrowed 1965 Chevy Nova. The overwhelming smell of the gasoline filled his nose. Despite his parched mouth, he could even taste it. His skin tingled under the loose-fitting, black cotton sweatshirt and jeans chosen carefully earlier that evening. Dark clothing for camouflage, in fabrics less likely to cling and burn his flesh in case of a fire. But he was not prepared for the uneasy sensation of his sixth sense. The apprehension that something was lurking in the bushes.

He took a calming breath as he watched Schwartz strut around the car and lean into the back seat. He was about David's height, but skinny, and when he lifted the gasoline can, it was heavy enough that he needed to use both hands.

Dressed as usual in cowboy boots, jeans and western-style shirt, Schwartz exuded an aura of confidence. He was 21, only two years older than David, but he was living on his own, having made his way from Houston to Los Angeles for reasons that he had never disclosed.

Schwartz had barely said a word all evening, not that he was what you'd call a world-class conversationalist anyway. David hardly knew the guy, having only met the Texan a few times after being introduced by the JDL's California leader, Irv Rubin. Charismatic, with a wit that sharpened the bite of his militancy, Rubin had a wise-cracking grin that practically absorbed his wisp of a moustache. He no longer looked like the US soldier that he had once been, having grown his reddish-brown hair shaggily close to his collar. David, admittedly conceited about his own rich curls, empathised with Rubin's vanity, especially since Rubin's hair was already starting to thin at the age of 29. Rubin was tall, about 6ft 3in, and he enjoyed the attention of the ladies. David thought that maybe Rubin enjoyed female company a little too much since he was married to a nice woman from a well-off and respectable family. Nonetheless,

David admired Rubin's easy manner with women, whereas David himself seemed to be forever disappointing girls who wanted more from him than he had to give. At this point in his life, David was more focused on his mission with the JDL than going steady with a girl in junior college, no matter how cute she might be.

David, like Schwartz and the other young men hanging around the shabby offices of the JDL, was fond of putting his feet up on a desk and affecting a cocky air. Unlike David, Schwartz neither had a job nor went to school. He was a pimply faced drifter who seemed to spend most of his time schmoozing Rubin. David suspected that Schwartz looked up to Rubin as a father figure, seeking to fill an emotional void, a need that David understood. His own father was away at sea most of the time, and David had seen him infrequently since his parents' divorce.

Hard-working and a straight-A student, David was far from impressed by Schwartz's lack of ambition, but he was mollified by Schwartz's enthusiasm for the JDL. Schwartz, now striding purposefully toward the Mustang parked in the carport, certainly seemed to know what he was doing.

Silently reassuring himself that he was just suffering a case of nerves, David picked up one of the quart-sized beer bottles sitting under the back seat. He checked to make sure the rags were stuffed firmly inside the bottles and still soaked in gasoline. Holding a Molotov cocktail in each hand, he summoned the spirit of the Warsaw Ghetto fighters. They were his heroes, those young people who risked their lives to resist the Nazis. For three days, they kept the Germans at bay, fighting with nothing more than their bare knuckles and Molotov cocktails.

David held the bottles close to his heart. The Molotov cocktail had been his heroes' weapon of last resort. It was his weapon of choice, offered in their blessed memory.

He silently offered a prayer for them as his hands clenched the bottles. Just as they fought evil, so would he. The monster lurking inside the picture-perfect suburban Los Angeles home had gotten away with horrific murders for nearly thirty years, satisfied in the knowledge that no one would ever come for him.

It was time to shatter his peace. The JDL had him in its sights.

And David Whitelaw relished his role as a soldier.

6 a.m., Pico-Robertson District, Los Angeles, 29 January 1975

Judith Whitelaw awoke early and prepared her usual small continental breakfast. Vigilant about her size-five figure, the former homecoming queen stirred a packet of artificial sweetener and a little cream into the one cup of instant coffee she rationed herself each day. She carried her breakfast tray to her bedroom for her morning ritual of eating while listening to the news.

The roar of traffic coming off the freeway and onto La Cienega Boulevard was starting to pick up as Judith opened the curtains on the barred windows of her modest bungalow. It took her a moment to absorb the fact that something wasn't quite right with the scene before her. She peered at the patch of lawn, the rosebushes that lined the fence, all of which usually brought a smile to her face. The wrought iron fence, custom-made with a Star of David design between each post and the gate, was her pride and joy. It was a luxury for which she had scrimped and saved, proudly showcasing her Jewish identity to her mostly Christian neighbours. The house at 1772 South Crescent Heights was the first house that Judith owned, the first that bore her name and her name only on its deed. And the Star of David design in the fence was both a symbol and a reminder of the childhood home she had lost. The one the Nazis stole from her.

The sun was just coming up; in the morning light, Judith could see what was missing from the picture. David's van was not parked in its usual spot on the street. Was it possible that her son had not come home last night?

Frowning, Judith walked down the hall and into his bedroom. The room was just as he'd left it after dinner the night before: his bed neatly made, his guitar tucked into the corner, his radio and toy replica of a ship occupying a prominent bookshelf, and – in contrast to the orderly room – his desk overflowing with books and paper. The room was a reassuring reflection of David, her sensible, sensitive and studious middle son, the only one of her three sons that she could boast about as a 'nice Jewish boy'.

Never before had David stayed out late without calling to let her know where he was. Even if he was working late, he always called. Of course, Judith had demanded that all of her sons let her know where they were going and when they'd be home. But only David was considerate enough to obey her.

David, who'd bought the beat-up old van with his own money so that he could commute to his part-time factory job, was hard-working. Solid. Reliable. Once in a while, he'd complain when Judith asked him for extra money, but what teenager wouldn't complain? Her first-born son, Stephen, had never given her a penny and her youngest, Billy, was a drain on resources, albeit through no fault of his own. Billy, at the age of 14, was now in a psychiatric hospital, being treated for an undiagnosed condition that had led to a series of violent outbursts. If it weren't for David's support, both financial and emotional, Judith couldn't imagine how she would even begin to cope.

Although he tried not to show it, Judith knew that David felt burdened by the weight of her emotional needs. She could read it in his gorgeous brown eyes, the way he would look away when she would tell him how much she relied on him. Or the way that he closed himself off in his room, listening to the radio or playing his guitar. Once in a while he would even joke that she treated him more like a husband than a son. Judith didn't see the humour. The fact that her own husband, ex-husband for the past ten years, could not be relied upon was nothing to joke about.

'Who am I supposed to rely on, if not you?' Judith retorted to David's jibe. 'Certainly not your father. And certainly not your brother. And need I remind you that we don't have any family.' She sighed, and her voice softened. She smiled and cocked her head to one side, daring to see if she could get away with the special German pet name he no longer liked to hear. '*Mein Puppele*, there is no one else. You're it.'

Her risk paid off. David rewarded her with a quick hug. Judith patted him on the back and tried not to cling too tightly.

Judith closed her eyes and took a deep breath as she remembered the moment. When had she become so clingy? It didn't seem so long ago that she was the one wrapping men around her little finger, fighting off suitors, instead of begging for attention. At 54, Judith could still turn heads. But the men she was attracting were a far cry from the wealthy, educated men of the past. High-quality men like Rudy Sternberg, who fell in love with her when they were teenagers back in Germany. Rudy, elegant and handsome with his earnest brown eyes and sensuous mouth, was drawn to Judith as a mirror of himself. Her dark hair, soulful eyes and wide, Cupid-bow lips had always captivated men, and Rudy was no exception. Their romance seemed destined to bloom, but it had barely gotten past the flirtation stage before the Nazis came. Before Judith and Rudy could even begin to understand what lay ahead.

Like so much else in her life, Judith saw no point in contemplating 'what if' about her romance with Rudy. They had been forced to flee for their lives, Judith to Guatemala and Rudy to England.

Rudy had risen high in the world. He had used his chemical engineering degree to build one of Europe's biggest petrochemical companies, the Sterling Group, which made Bakelite, the first plastic made from synthetic components. Judith couldn't have been prouder when he was knighted by Queen Elizabeth in 1970.

And now another honour. Just one day ago, Judith had read in the newspaper that Rudy was named Baron Plurenden of Plurenden Manor in the County of Kent. She rushed to share the news with David that her old boyfriend had been awarded a life peerage.

A shadow had crossed her son's face as he looked up from the book he was studying. But seeing her excitement, he managed a smile and started his customary teasing. 'So, what are you telling me, Mom? If you'd married him, wouldn't we be practically royalty? He's a lord. What would that make me? Like I told you a million times, you should have married him, Mom.'

Judith smiled, letting David get away with this harmless, well-worn joke. Rudy had become a friend. Whatever might have been was forty years in the past. But still. Judith's romance with Rudy was another example of what the Nazis had stolen from her. Her home. Her family. Everything about her life in Breslau, her city. Germany itself, her country that she loved. Judith would never forgive, never forget. Could never forgive. Could never forget.

Her destiny had changed forever on the night of 9 November 1938. Kristallnacht.

Her mother, Klara, had shaken Judith awake at 3 a.m., agitated and demanding that she rush into the kitchen. They stood at the window, watching in disbelief as the flames from burning Jewish businesses and synagogues seemed to scream as they shot into the heavens. As the fires grew, Klara took 18-year-old Judith by the hand to descend the stairs of their elegant five-storey building. They made their way to the square where, over the next two days, the glass of broken windows glittered like crystal in the flames. A couple of days earlier, Klara's intuition had warned her that something evil was about to happen when she saw trucks loaded with cans of gasoline driving through the streets. For months, she'd been pleading with her parents to leave Germany. Even before that, as far back as 1935, she and her husband, Sigmund, had discussed getting away from the Nazis. But Sigmund had died two years ago and now, watching the Nazis toss the synagogue's holy books into the fire, Klara made a decision. She turned to Judith and said: 'We're getting out of here.'

Judith stared at her mother, wide-eyed in disbelief. Leave their home? Their apartment building wasn't just their home. It was their business. Some of Breslau's finest people were their tenants. Judith knew other Jews who had packed up and left, but she never dreamed her mother would consider abandoning their home, their business, their beloved country, everything they knew.

Klara, her mind made up, was adamant. 'Honey, in a couple of years, there'll be nothing left.'

Once again, Klara implored her family to flee. This time, her parents and five other relatives agreed to go. Klara, Judith and her brother, Walter, packed as fast as they could. One suitcase each. Judith ignored her mother's disapproving looks as she sorted through her most sentimental possessions. She could not bear to leave behind the things that meant most to her father: his Iron Cross, which the Kaiser himself had pinned on his chest, the battlefield photograph with his regiment. If she was forced to leave her father behind in his grave, Judith deserved something of his to cling to, and only after they were safely packed did she look for room for her book of sewing patterns, the drawings of dresses and suits illustrated in exquisite detail with her own artistic flair. Her mother, ever practical and without Judith's sentimental streak, found hiding places for money. Klara took her own most precious possession, her wedding ring, and inserted it into her vagina, thanking Sigmund for continuing to protect his family even after his death. It was thanks to her husband that they had a place to go. After the First World War, when Sigmund had proudly served the Fatherland, he seized an opportunity to invest with relatives in a banana plantation in Guatemala. And now, Klara was determined to bribe whomever it took to get the family safely to the land and house that Sigmund had bought.

The wisdom of their decision to leave was validated when their new passports were issued. Stamped with the letter 'J' in red ink to identify them as Jews, the passports were part of a new provision introduced a month earlier by the Reich Ministry of the Interior to begin separating Jews from other Germans. With nothing but their suitcases and the Reichsmark equivalent of $4 each, the family took the train to Hamburg on 26 November 1938, to board the MS *Cariba* to Guatemala.

As a property owner with relatives in Guatemala City, Klara was fortunate. She had a destination as a safe haven. Many of the 36,000 Jews who fled Germany and Austria after Kristallnacht were turned away from the New World. And many of those who sought refuge in Europe were rounded up and sent to concentration camps after the Nazis occupied western Europe in 1940. Of the relatives that Judith, Klara and Walter left behind, seventy-six went on to perish in Hitler's death camps.

Not a day went by that Judith did not think of her loved ones, of what their family had lost through their murders. Not a day passed without reminding her three sons of the injustice to their family and to their people. Of what had been stolen from them.

But even within the walls of her own home, Judith's anger and grief did not fully resonate. Her eldest son tuned her out. Her youngest paid no attention. But her middle son, David, took the message to heart. He felt her loss. It was he who nodded solemnly when Judith teared up, asking the question she could never answer: how much loss could one heart bear?

And this morning, David's bed was empty.

Her one good son hadn't come home last night. The unsettling thought crossed her mind that he might have spent the night with a girl. Judith had discouraged girlfriends, finding fault even with the girls that David claimed were 'just friends'. Her boy, so kind and sensitive, couldn't see through what Judith saw as clearly as if the girls were wearing their hearts on their sleeves. She recognised the longing in their eyes, heard the eagerness as they laughed at his jokes.

Judith never missed an opportunity to remind David that the 'just friends' wanted more from him. And what they wanted could hold him back from achieving his dream. She reminded him that he was a natural healer, born to be a doctor. He had been working toward this goal since his bar mitzvah when he declared his intention 'to build a better tomorrow'. Medical school was well within his intellectual reach, and he worked hard to keep his marks up. But medical school was expensive, far beyond the reach of Judith, a single mother who survived on the money she earned babysitting other people's children.

David couldn't afford to lose focus with the distraction of a girlfriend. Without straight As he'd never win the full scholarship needed to get through medical school. So far, David had listened to his mother, reassuring her that none of his friends would morph into girlfriends. Judith couldn't help but wonder if David understood on some deep intuitive level that she had another reason to fight against the very notion of a girlfriend. Judith needed David. He wasn't just her one good son; he was her sole emotional support. She clung to him as she clung to the memories of her lost family.

And last night he'd stayed out without calling to let her know where he was.

Judith feared she was losing David, too.

Present-day Croatia and Bosnia and Herzegovina. (Base map courtesy of d-maps.com/
carte.php?num_car=14895)

2

A Destiny to Serve God

Half a world away, in the last days of the nineteenth century, another boy was born, a prodigy who would also aspire to become a doctor. Like David Whitelaw, he would be moulded by a belief in the injustice created by wartime hatred. And like David Whitelaw, his destiny would be shaped by faith and religious identity.

Even his name predicted his destiny: Andrija, named for Saint Andrew, a disciple and messenger of Jesus, a name which means 'warrior' in the Croatian language.

Andrija Artuković was born on 29 November 1899 in Klobuk, Herzegovina. He was the eldest of fourteen children born to Raza Rasic and Marija Artuković, deeply religious Croat farmers whose lives were anchored by the Roman Catholic Church. In many ways, life was idyllic for peasants who raised enough cattle, corn, pomegranates and figs to create delicious meals for their families. They grew cash crops, such as the region's famous high-quality tobacco, to pay the bills and buy staples from local markets. For this, Roman Catholic families continuously expressed their gratitude through prayers, marking each juncture of the day with a blessing. They made the sign of the cross over their heads and hearts to greet the morning before they dressed, again over the bread they would break, and again with their bed-time prayers. Their gratitude was steeped in duty; their Catholic identity stamped in 1519 when Pope Leo X praised Croatia as a bulwark of Christianity for the bravery of Croatian soldiers fighting the Ottomans.

But as peaceful as life may have been on the farm, political strife from the outside world crept in. Croats in Bosnia and Herzegovina longed to be part of a Croatian homeland, a long-standing aspiration of Catholics living under Ottoman rule. Their Muslim rulers taxed Christians at a higher rate than Muslims and stifled many of their rights. Their dream of Croatian independence suffered another blow when the Austro-Hungarian Empire absorbed Croatia and placed it under Hungarian rule. In 1868, Austria-Hungary granted Croatia statehood but just how little power Croatia possessed became swiftly obvious. The Croatian Sabor, or parliament, tried to take back Bosnia and Herzegovina by arguing that it had been part of Croatia since medieval times. They failed to persuade Austria-Hungary. Croats were devastated; their grievance bolstered a growing nationalism.

Andrija's own parents grew up in this turbulent time. When they were children, Bosnia and Herzegovina's Muslim rulers tried to keep a lid on Croatian Catholics' resentment by allowing some communities to build their own churches and schools. But they also imposed a farm tax, which burdened peasants. When Christian farmers revolted in 1875, they were brutally repressed. In the coming decades, new tensions developed, fuelled in part by the increasing number of Serbians who had moved into Croatia, as well as Bosnia and Herzegovina. As Serbian numbers grew, so did their political voice. Croats referred to them as 'foreigners', a hostile word that would take on an ominous meaning in the future.

In 1908, when Andrija Artuković was nine years old, Austria-Hungary marched in and annexed Bosnia and Herzegovina. Croatian nationalism, already entrenched when his own parents were growing up, reached a feverish pitch. Whenever Croats gathered in churches and markets, the talk always turned to politics. A new railway and roads had been built and industry was developing in Bosnia and Herzegovina. But Croats had little stomach for any future under rulers they perceived as oppressors. The discussions grew hot with anger and frustration. Some of Andrija's relatives were talking about leaving. Everyone knew someone who had taken the train or caught a ride to travel down the new road, looking for a better future. Andrija's own cousins were dreaming about America, a place of equality, where they would be free to build a new life, where their hard work would lead to prosperity.

Young Andrija soaked it all up. But little did he know that his own future would be shaped by another Croat who lived just a couple of hours down the road. This boy, now a teenager, had grown up drinking in all of the heated discussions.

He was thriving in the hotbed of political unrest that was Bosnia and Herzegovina. And this teenager was not talking about leaving. He was planning to stay and put his mark on Croatia.

★ ★ ★

Andrija Artuković had always stood out from the other children in his family and at church. Even before he started school, the priests noticed his keen intelligence and devotion to God. Providence seemed to intervene when Andrija started parochial school. The bright little boy so impressed the Roman Catholic priests who taught him that they selected him for a higher calling than farming. They encouraged his parents to commit to greater education for Andrija, even though school attendance was not mandatory and it would mean sending their son away from the village to attend school. The church ensured that the Artuković family had the resources to send Andrija to a high school run by the Franciscan order.

He excelled as a student. In his last year of high school, the First World War broke out, but neither Andrija nor his spiritual mentors could have predicted that the war would bring about changes that further solidified the teenager's fate.

By the time he was 16, the priests had raised money for scholarships and Andrija was sent even further away to the University of Zagreb. He entered medical school and began working part time setting up pins in a bowling alley to subsidise his education.

However, he was not destined to become a physician. As a family member would later tell a journalist, Andrija 'didn't like all that blood' or the odour of cadavers in anatomy class. He and other medical students began smoking cigarettes to cope with the stench. By the time Andrija abandoned his ambition of a career in medicine, he'd developed a two-pack-a-day tobacco addiction.

Unsure of his path, Andrija considered the possibilities. He had an intellectual bent. He possessed a keen facility for languages and had learned to speak Greek, Bulgarian, Italian, French, German, Czech and Latin.

He settled on becoming a lawyer and the decision to attend law school proved life-changing. For Andrija, like students through the ages, the circle of acquaintances made on campus evolved into lifelong friends and a professional network that would alter his destiny.

One of those people was Ante Pavelić, who had graduated with a Doctor of Laws degree in 1915, the year that Andrija arrived as a freshman. Another was Mile Budak, a writer and poet whose work romanticised peasants like the Artuković family. Pavelić and Budak were emerging leaders who idolised peasants, placing them on a pedestal as pure and true Croatians. Andrija, with a foot in both worlds, must have seemed an attractive recruit.

The University of Zagreb, formed by the Jesuits in 1699, was a hotbed of political activism as the First World War came to an end. Croatia had suffered heavily in the war, losing 190,000 soldiers and civilians, and drought and famine had taken a toll, especially on children. The economy was struggling, and in 1918, the Spanish Flu pandemic further gutted the population.

In 1919, when the Treaty of Versailles was signed in Paris to officially end the war, Andrija had already been immersed in four years of student politics. The fallout from the war was a turning point for the promising 20-year-old student.

For eight centuries, ethnic hatred between Croats and Serbians had been held in check through the historical legacy of the Austro-Hungarian Empire to the north and the Ottoman Turks to the south. But now, thanks to the spoils of war, the lines of the old empires were dissolved. The Treaty of Versailles created a new country, the Kingdom of Serbs, Croats and Slovenes, in an attempt to unify southern Slavs under one federation. Croats were furious that they would be ruled by a Serbian king; they saw the new federation as a prize granted to Serbia for fighting with the Allies, and, by extension, as punishment to Croatians for fighting for the losing side.

As a devout Catholic, Andrija Artuković and other Croats both resented and feared the Serbs' Eastern Orthodox religion. Both sides considered the other heathen. The resentment against 'the other' encompassed two of the usual suspects that nurture identity politics: religion and language. Both were Christians and spoke the same language. But the Serbs wrote in Cyrillic script and the Croats in Latin script.

Outnumbered by the Serbs and with a Central European identity fostered under the rule of the Austro-Hungarian Empire, Croatians saw Serb domination as the writing on the wall. Three years later, when the new constitution eliminated Croatia's autonomy, they predicted that their culture and identity would go next. Stoking their fears were radical politicians. They revived an old dream, buried for eight centuries, that Croatia would once again be an independent country under a Roman Catholic pope. Nationalism soared as the Croatian Peasant Party gained popularity and political power.

Surprising opposition came from students at the University of Zagreb. Andrija Artuković and other young radicals were less than satisfied with the Croatian Peasant Party. The times were changing, and students felt that the establishment party was out of step, its nationalist message too meek to achieve Croatian dreams.

Ante Pavelić stepped in to offer a more appealing vision of a proud Catholic Croatia. He was a rising star in the ultra-nationalistic Croatian Party of Rights, or *Hrvatska stranka prava*. A charismatic leader, he was still connected to his friends on campus and young enough to share a beer at their drinking parties. By now, Pavelić was a practising lawyer in Zagreb and the president of the Croatian Law Society. Even if he hadn't been so politically connected, Pavelić was a good contact for an ambitious student like Artuković.

Andrija Artuković was a natural protégé. The sense of ambition instilled in him by his childhood priests had blossomed at law school. After graduation, he served an apprenticeship with the law court in Zagreb. He joined Pavelić's party and began using his legal skill to defend party members accused of political crimes.

Pavelić's influence continued to spread. He became a member of Zagreb's city council, taking on the role of Zagreb deputy for the Croatian Party of Rights. With a base that included the youth vote, the best and brightest from the University of Zagreb, Pavelić's party eroded support for the more moderate Croatian Peasant Party.

The nationalist sentiment that had been brewing for almost ten years boiled over in 1928. The inciting moment was dramatic, happening on the floor of the National Assembly, no less: a Serb brazenly walked onto the floor and assassinated the leader of the Croatian Peasant Party.

For Croatians, the blow was twofold. Not only had they lost a beloved advocate, but the assassination led to a Serbian crackdown. A few short months later, the Serbs centralised the government. They called the new country Yugoslavia, and it was ruled by a Serbian king, Alexander.

For Artuković, personally, the moment proved pivotal. His hatred of the Serbian king was so fierce and well known that for the rest of his life, rumours of that hatred would follow him. The rumours eventually ended up in police files, casting a cloud of suspicion over Artuković.

To an objective observer looking at the life of the farm boy who had made good, the rumours might have seemed a stretch. But police reports suggested that Andrija Artuković was the ringleader of a plot to assassinate the Serbian king.

Proud as he may have been of his roots, Andrija Artuković had moved well beyond the farm. Upon graduation from the University of Zagreb law school, he could add Doctor in front of his name. With his newly minted Doctor of Laws degree, Artuković hung out his shingle and began practising law in Gospić, a picturesque town in the highlands on the River Lika.

His circle had expanded to include an intellectual and political powerhouse soon to make their mark on Croatia. At the centre of their orbit was Ante Pavelić, who had become even more radicalised. In 1929, Pavelić was calling for an uprising. He created a new movement called the Ustaše, translated as Ustasha, a name stemming from the word *ustanak* or 'uprising'.

Andrija Artuković was one of the first to join up. For the young lawyer from a peasant family, joining the Ustasha must have felt like destiny since the movement held hard-working peasants in the highest esteem. But the more spiritual tug came from the Ustasha's deep-seated commitment to the Catholic faith. Taken under the wing of priests since his childhood and wrapped in fabric woven with the threads of faith and cultural identity, Artuković was a true believer. His own identity as a devout Catholic was steeped in the principles of Pavelić's new political movement: Croatians had a God-given duty to fight Orthodoxy and communism. Pavelić preached that the threat from godless communists would destroy Croatia's religion, and that the Serbs would impose their religion.

According to historian Rob McCormick, the Ustasha believed they had been called to fight a 'holy war'. In his book, *Croatia Under Ante Pavelić: America, the Ustaše and Croatian Genocide in World War II*, McCormick stresses the significance of religion:

Another key aspect of Ustaše ideology was an unmistakably close association with Catholicism. As a devout Catholic, Pavelić reckoned that the Croatian peoples had been chosen by God to defend Catholicism against assaults from both Orthodoxy and Communism. This religious zeal held by some Ustaše, which demanded no tolerance for Orthodoxy, helped give a mystical and almost Biblical quality to the Ustaše movement.

McCormick notes that Pavelić's spiritual fervour managed to successfully demonise Serbs and whip up antagonism against communists as 'mortal foes who had to be stopped'. It is no wonder then, that the ritual to become a member of the Ustasha was to take an oath of allegiance in a ceremony that included a crucifix, a revolver and a knife.

Andrija Artuković, championed from childhood by Catholic priests, took the oath. He swore allegiance to an independent Croatia with the Ustasha motto of *Za dom spremni*, which means 'For the homeland, ready'. The motto, accompanied by a salute, was like the *Sieg Heil* gesture adopted by the Nazi Party in Germany.

From the outset, the Ustasha was violent and revolutionary. And despite the intellectual prowess and elegant poetry of its leaders, the Ustasha only managed to attract ne'er-do-wells. Most Croatians were repulsed by the violent rhetoric and those with nationalistic leanings tended to remain loyal to the Croatian Peasant Party.

Ante Pavelić looked elsewhere for support, and he found it in Benito Mussolini. When Pavelić approached the Italian prime minister through his emissaries, Il Duce liked what he heard. Mussolini had political goals of his own, namely to cause the collapse of Yugoslavia and take the Dalmatian coast. He thought it would serve him well to nurture Croatian independence and he was confident that Pavelić's Ustasha would ultimately win. As a sign of his faith in the Ustasha, Mussolini supplied arms, money and training camps. With financial backing from Mussolini, Pavelić assigned Artuković to train his men for war. In short order, the Ustasha carried out 100 assassinations.

One of their first attacks was in 1932 on a police station in the Lika district of Gospić, where Artuković was practising law. The Velebit Uprising, as it was called, was not high in casualties, but it set off alarm bells in the Yugoslav capital. The government was concerned about Croatian unrest, and a warrant was issued for the arrest of Andrija Artuković.

Artuković escaped by fleeing to Venice, where Pavelić appointed him as an adjunct to the Ustasha commander for Italy. He stayed there for a couple of years before bouncing around Budapest, Vienna and London. He was living in London when the Yugoslav king was assassinated in an official motorcade procession while on a state visit to Marseilles. It was a sensational shooting: King Alexander's death, on 9 October 1934, was captured on film and produced into newsreels which played in theatres around the world. French Foreign Minister Louis Barthou, sitting beside the king, tried to protect him when two gunmen jumped onto the car's running board, but the bullets also hit him, and he died on the operating table a few hours later.

One of the gunmen was captured alive, the other shot dead by police. Pavelić, deemed to have given the order, was hunted by officials. An arrest warrant was also issued for Andrija Artuković, who was said to be the mastermind behind King Alexander's assassination. Artuković was arrested in Paris, where he remained in jail for three months before he was extradited to Yugoslavia.

In Belgrade, he spent more than a year in prison, awaiting trial. A judge reluctantly acquitted him because he couldn't find enough evidence for a conviction, but rumours persisted that Artuković was involved in planning King Alexander's assassination. Decades later, those rumours ended up in an FBI file.

The name of Andrija Artuković first came to the attention of American intelligence-gathering agencies in the 1930s. Informants reported that Artuković was one of several Ustasha members sent to the United States to raise money and support from expatriate Croatians in 1930.

Artuković's name also arose in 1939 following the arrest of Branimir Jelić, nicknamed 'Branko', at Ellis Island. Jelić, the medical doctor who had been Pavelić's student deputy at the University of Zagreb, was on a mission to solicit money and memberships from Croatians who had immigrated to the United States, a diaspora of already more than 100,000.

With the growing certainty of war in Europe, US authorities were keeping an eye on revolutionary groups at home. Immigration officials found that Jelić's passport was not in order; he was arrested and held at Ellis Island. At an immigration hearing on 20 February 1939, Jelić admitted that he'd entered the United States under a false name, Andrija Artuković. 'He admitted using the name Andrija Artuković in order to allow an individual of that name to obtain credentials for admission to the United States,' the informant said.

Years later, that piece of information would also end up in an FBI file.

As the National Socialist German Workers' Party took hold in Germany, Andrija Artuković made Berlin his home. The atmosphere of one of Europe's great cultural hubs was stimulating, and the ideals of the Nazis, who held peasants in the highest esteem, appealed to Artuković's own identity. Ironically, the man named for Saint Andrew – legendary for promoting the 'good news' message of Jesus – copied the message of hatred promoted by the Nazis. In exile from his beloved Croatia, Artuković took on the role of propagandist, using his skills at Ustasha headquarters to spread propaganda. The messages aimed to curry favour with the Nazis, strengthening the relationships that would help Croatia achieve independence.

Artuković had dedicated his life to achieving that goal since he was a teenager. More than twenty years had passed since he first took on the all-consuming intellectual pursuit. There was no question of his passion for Croatia; there had been little room in his life for anything but Croatia and God. But as he approached middle age, Artuković found romantic love. Ana Marija Heidler was as fervent in her Catholic faith as Artuković himself. Austrian-born, she was twenty-one years his junior, half his age, and the sister of his cousin's wife. They fell in love and married. In Ana, Artuković had found a steadfast partner, a woman who would stand with him in the turbulent years ahead.

Europe was at war. Artuković and his leader, Ante Pavelić, remained in exile. While Artuković was based in Berlin, Pavelić had been working from Italy to advance Croatia's cause. He had forged a deep connection with his benefactor, Mussolini. Il Duce held Pavelić in high enough regard that he had funded and armed the Ustasha. In the years leading up to the war, Mussolini was happy to help Pavelić facilitate the relationships that would eventually bring Croatia into the Axis alliance of Germany, Italy and Japan. Il Duce presented Pavelić to Adolf Hitler. The Führer trusted Mussolini's judgement on Pavelić and accepted him into the fold.

On 6 April 1941, Nazi tanks rode into Belgrade, followed by German bombs that destroyed much of the centre of the capital. Over the next few days, Yugoslavia suffered overwhelming losses of thousands of civilians and soldiers. On 13 April, the devastated military surrendered and on 17 April, the Nazis took over Yugoslavia.

The Nazi invasion of Croatia on 10 April went more smoothly. There was little resistance and many Croatians welcomed the Nazis as liberators.

Hitler took to the airwaves to broadcast the news and to urge Croatians to hang Croatian flags and German flags from their homes. 'It gives me special joy and satisfaction in this hour when the Croat people have received their long-sought independence,' he declared.

Pavelić was installed as 'Poglavnik', just as Hitler was known as 'Führer' and Mussolini as 'Duce'. One of Pavelić's first telegrams was to Mussolini, sent on 8 April 1941, effusively thanking him for his support:

> In this decisive hour, after 22 years of oppression for the Croatian people by the imposition of the Treaty of Versailles and the Serbian tyranny, I address to you the salute of all Croat Nationalists, of all combatant organizations and the entire Croatian people.
>
> All of Croatia rejoices at your glorious soldiers and all our nationalist forces, our organized and ready combatants will fight with them for the freedom of our people and for the independent state of Croatia for which we have for so long and so bloodily fought.
>
> We see in you the great friend of the oppressed and the founder of a new government of justice, and we stand ready to testify with our eternal gratefulness. I assure you to that, at this hour, and in the future we will always be with you.
>
> Long live the independent state of Croatia! Long live Italy!

But the Independent State of Croatia (NDH) fell far short of fulfilling the long-held dream of a homeland. Italy had also invaded, claiming most of the Dalmatian coast, which it called the Governorate of Dalmatia. It was a big price for Pavelić to pay, and one that would damage his credibility with Croatians.

★　★　★

Fate called Artuković out of exile, back to his homeland. It was time to start building the Croatia that he'd been fighting for his entire adult life. At the age of 41, Artuković was assigned an important post in Pavelić's new cabinet: Minister of the Interior, tasked with setting up concentration camps and assuming their overall command.

Also in the cabinet was another of Pavelić's and Artuković's fellow law school alumni, Mile Budak. He was given the crucial post of Minister

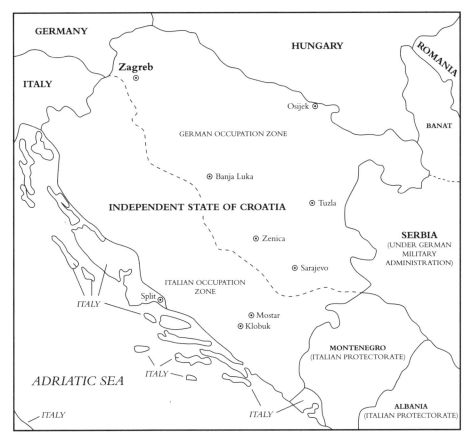

The Independent State of Croatia included modern-day Croatia, except for most of the Adriatic Coast, which was controlled by Italy until 1943. The NDH annexed what is today Bosnia and Herzegovina, as well as parts of Slovenia and Serbia.

of Education, Religion and Culture. A couple of months later, he gave a speech and publicly proclaimed his party's mission to wipe out all Serbs in Croatia. His vision was distilled into a formula that was easy to remember: kill one-third of Serbs, expel another third and force the remaining third to convert to Catholicism. 'The basis for the Ustasha movement is religion,' Budak declared. 'For minorities such as Serbs, Jews and Gypsies, we have three million bullets.'

The Ustasha's reign of terror was about to begin. Over the next four years, the campaign would involve Pope Pius XII, Adolf Hitler and his protégé, Poglavnik Ante Pavelić. The unrivalled brutality of the Ustasha would cause the Nazis to shudder.

At the centre was Andrija Artuković, the man whose Catholic community had nurtured him since childhood. The boy, named for the saint known as a messenger, whose Croatian name meant 'warrior', was about to embark upon a new destiny. The man who had failed to achieve his ambition of becoming a doctor because he couldn't stand the sight or smell of blood was about to earn a new name: 'Butcher of the Balkans'.

His reputation for bloodthirsty hatred would set him apart in a way that seems incongruous with his spiritual devotion and desire to become a healer: the war crimes Artuković was about to oversee were so repulsive that even the Nazis complained. Their concerns became part of historical records, advising Hitler that the Ustasha were making them, the Nazis in Croatia, look bad.

★ ★ ★

As the Minister of the Interior in Pavelić's cabinet in Zagreb, Andrija Artuković held a key post in establishing the new Croatia. The new government acted swiftly. On 21 April 1941, a Zagreb newspaper reported:

> The Minister of Public Safety, Dr. Artuković has stated [...] that the Croatian government wishes to solve the Jewish problem in the same way as the German government did. The Minister added that he will strictly monitor the application of racial laws, soon to be adopted.

A few days later, Artuković signed a decree prohibiting Jews from entering coffee houses, restaurants and hotels. Merchants picked up on the new rule and began to post their own signs in shop windows saying Jews were not allowed. Next, the word 'Jew' was stencilled in large yellow letters on the windows of Jewish businesses.

Artuković and the other members of Pavelić's cabinet set out to obliterate the signs of Serbian rule that had chafed for most of their adult lives. They ripped down every sign on streets named for Serbian kings or containing the words 'Yugoslav' or 'Royal'. Suddenly, streets all over Zagreb had been rendered nameless. They painted over the word 'Royal' on postal trucks, leaving delivery trucks to be identified simply as 'Post'. And, to drive home how much they hated how the victors of the First World War had usurped Croatia, Pavelić's government wiped out every sign that bore anything in English.

Artuković was finally in a position to realise the dream that he and other students had fought for back at the University of Zagreb. Their protests against the restrictions imposed on Croatians by Serbian rulers had taken twenty years to come to fruition. Thanks to Hitler, the promise of a new world order seemed feasible. Artuković had spent over half his life fighting for Croatians to have a homeland of their own, and now, after two decades of scrambling and scraping, he was at the top, playing a role in designing the new Croatia. His faith had kept him strong. And every day, Artuković prayed, thanking God for giving Croatians a Catholic homeland.

With Yugoslavia's King Peter in exile in England, Pavelić seized the opportunity to further ingratiate himself to Mussolini by appointing an Italian, the Duke of Spoleto, to the throne; on 19 May, wire services delivered news to the world that the new king would be known as King Aimone of Croatia.

The Associated Press reported to its American readers that 'the throne was offered by Ante Pavelić, Croatia's Poglavnik (Croat equivalent of Duce or Fuehrer) before a glittering audience at Quirinale Palace in Rome. Afterwards, Pavelić was given a private audience with Pope Pius XII.'

★ ★ ★

When news began appearing about the new Axis puppet state, Americans knew so little about Croatia that a syndicated Washington-based journalist dedicated his popular 'What Do You Want To know?' column to an encyclopaedic description of the region. Frederic J. Haskin wrote of its abundant resources and the sophistication of Zagreb, a city at least eighteen centuries old:

> This unique and interesting part of Yugoslavia stretches eastward from old Dalmatian coastal towns which were summer resorts for wealthy Romans under the ancient Caesars, where sardine fishing boats anchor in harbors that Venetian galleys visited, and where peasants dance the 'kola' in a ring immediately after Sunday mass. [...] In the forested parts of the highlands, the houses, furniture, and even forks and spoons are made of wood. [...] One of the ancient market scenes of the world is when the peasants of Croatia gather in Zagreb, the capital. Their clean willow baskets bring to the market a colorful array of melons and

peppers, and the old-fashioned scales weigh out family-sized dishes of beans. The women's bright kerchiefs and red-and-blue embroidered blouses show numerous small circles to ward off evil spirits.

Croatia, called the Peasant Province, is four-fifths agricultural and the life of the average farmer of the region is said to be the most content in the world. At least that was the state of affairs before Germany's invasion.

The last line of Haskin's report, with its suggestion that Croatia might no longer be peaceful or colourful, was prescient. It would not be long before the images coming out of Croatia were far less benign.

Pavelić assigned his Minister of the Interior the crucial task of building Croatia's concentration camps. Pavelić's regime was targeting Serbians and Jews, but also dissident Croats, Bosnian Muslims and Roma. When Hitler requested a meeting with Pavelić for 6 June 1941, Artuković was invited along. The Croatians were proud to report their tremendous progress to the Führer, and Artuković was able to showcase that his work on building twenty concentration camps was well underway. Special concentration camps for children were also under construction.

Artuković and Pavelić could cite examples that were lifted directly from Hitler's own policies, including the decrees on 'Racial Affiliation' and the 'Protection of Aryan Blood'. Passed on 30 April 1941, two weeks after the new Croatia was established, the laws forbade marriage between Jews and Aryans and laid out rules to determine who had sufficient Aryan blood to be considered Croatian. Among its provisions were that Jews were forbidden to employ women under the age of 45 and that all changes to Jewish surnames since 1918 were null and void. It fell to Artuković to implement the new laws. He was also the final arbiter in disputed cases.

On 25 June 1941, Jews and Serbs were ordered to turn over their radios to the Ustasha. A curfew was also enforced, with Jews and Serbs forbidden to be out from 7 p.m. to 7 a.m. Opposing the Ustasha was deemed against the law. Two months later, the concentration camps under Artuković's control were well established. Jasenovac, a series of five concentration camps along the Sava River about 75 miles south of Zagreb, quickly became the third largest concentration camp in Europe. Unlike at other concentration camps, children were separated into special camps, away from adults.

One of his deputies later claimed that Artuković boasted to him of the speed with which he got rid of Croatia's Jewish population. 'You see how I have resolved the Jewish question,' the deputy quoted Artuković as saying. 'I take everything from them, and then I kill them, and in a few months everything is over, not like the Germans who fuss around for years.'

Stories began to circulate about Artuković's boastfulness and his ruthlessness. The same deputy who claimed that Artuković bragged about his swiftness in killing off the Jews also told a story about getting caught in the middle of a plea from the wife of one of Artuković's enemies.

Franjo Truhar had been appointed chief of police in Sremska Mitrovica in April 1941, shortly after the Ustasha took over Croatia. He found himself in the position of being a gatekeeper to Artuković when a woman named Olga Vidić made her way to his office about 40 miles from her family's farm. She wanted to negotiate a heartbreaking bargain with Artuković: her husband's life in exchange for the family's farmland.

Truhar listened to her story. Her husband, Dr Ješa Vidić, was a lawyer who had been a Member of Parliament in the previous government. As such, he was Artuković's enemy. Artuković had ordered his arrest and Vidić had been shipped off to the camp at Danica.

Olga Vidić was terrified about what might become of her husband. She laid out the offer: a personal gift of 150 acres to Artuković. She thought Artuković would be delighted with the high price she was willing to pay for her husband's freedom. The farm was rich. The land represented one-half of the family's arable property. It was a stunningly lucrative offer to Artuković, one that was his for the asking. All that Olga wanted in return was for him to free her husband from prison and allow him to resettle in Serbia.

She placed her offer in writing and pleaded with the police chief to act as her messenger. Truhar agreed and promised to make a special trip to Zagreb to speak with Artuković on her behalf.

He made good on his word. 'I brought this request in person to Artuković in Zagreb, and handed it to him,' Truhar said. But even before Artuković replied to the request, Truhar could see from his manner that he was not moved. 'What did you bring this petition to me for?' he sneered. 'I will kill him and take, not 150, but 300 Jutros (acres) of land.'

Years later, Truhar recalled the vindictive outcome of the meeting: 'Later, Artuković himself sent the order for Dr Ješa Vidić to be killed, which was also carried out, and all of the land was taken and given to Ustasha Stjepan Vinek in Sremska Mitrovica.'

★ ★ ★

Less than a month after Pavelić and Artuković met with Hitler, the Germans became alarmed at the barbarous way the war was unfolding in Croatia. The Ustasha's thirst for blood horrified even the Nazis.

The German military attaché in Zagreb, Edmund Glaise von Horstenau, warned that 'Pavelić has been [*sic*] gone mad with hatred'. He sent a telegram to the German High Command on 28 June 1941, saying that 'according to reliable reports from countless German and civil observers during the last few weeks the Ustasha have gone raging mad'.

There were reports of Ustasha forcing entire Serbian villages into their Orthodox churches and burning them alive. Photographs circulated of a Ustasha soldier displaying the bloody head of an Orthodox priest. Reports came back to the Germans that the Ustasha were killing people for sport. Unlike the Nazis, with their systematic mass murders in gas chambers, the Ustasha engaged in killing by hand. They photographed each other killing people, showing off the bloodied small hand blade called the 'Serb-cutter'. It was an efficient tool: by holding the knife close to the wrist, a soldier could slit throats quickly and cleanly.

Pavelić himself was reported to have shown a journalist a pail filled with eyeballs that had been cut from murdered victims. Members of the Ustasha showed off their trophies by stringing eyeballs into necklaces and wearing them around their necks.

On 10 July, Glaise von Horstenau escalated the urgency of his message with a pragmatic telegram to the German High Command:

Our troops have to be mute witnesses of such events; it does not reflect well on their otherwise high reputation. [...] I am frequently told that German occupation troops would finally have to intervene against Ustasha crimes. [...] Ad hoc intervention in individual cases could make the German army look responsible for countless crimes which it could not prevent in the past.

Artuković paid attention to the words circulating about the Ustasha's reputation. In giving an order to Police Chief Truhar to carry out killings, he instructed him to 'slaughter Serbs and Jews, but do it cleverly, not like the ones at Slavonski Brod, where they threw corpses into the Sava River'.

Within months, the Nazis were appealing to Hitler to intervene because of the Ustasha's brutality. Lieutenant Arthur Hefner of the Wehrmacht transport corps was so shocked that he described the conditions in a letter to the German Foreign Ministry in Berlin as 'of the worst kind, equal to Dante's inferno'.

Witnesses described hundreds of men being beheaded and thrown into the Sava River. Hundreds of girls were gang-raped together. Photographs showed women with foetuses cut from the womb, others with their hearts cut out.

★　★　★

On 29 October 1941, The United Press carried a small news brief: 'A dispatch from Zagreb, in partitioned Yugoslavia, said today the Croatian government had decreed state acquisition of all Jewish fortunes for revival of the national economy.'

The decrees to expropriate their property were signed by the Minister of the Interior, Dr Andrija Artuković.

★　★　★

The chauffeur assigned to drive Artuković and Pavelić testified after the war that he witnessed Artuković personally order the slaughter of people. Bajro Avdić, who was barely 17 when he completed his Ustasha training in November 1941, was 'ordered into the motorized unit of the state escort service to escort leader Pavelić, Andrija Artuković, Minister of Interior Affairs and other ministers of the NDH, Independent State of Croatia'.

Barely a month after he started his new job, Avdić witnessed the killing of helpless prisoners. He claimed to hear Artuković giving a direct order to murder them because the camp was too overcrowded to handle them:

I was (present) at the end of 1941 at Kresimir's Trg when an autocade of trucks full of arrested partisans, Jews and others, in my estimate some seven hundred people, among them many women and small children was taken, as I overheard Artuković order Lahovski to Kerestinec, the collecting camp in the vicinity of Zagreb.

Artuković followed the autocade to Kerestinec and as I was his escort, I heard when Andrija Artuković told Lahovski that the back of the auto-cade of trucks must be disposed of because it would be too much for the camp.

So women, children, and men were taken out of the trucks, in my estimate some 400 to 500 persons and by machine-gun fire were killed by Ustashas at the order of Artuković, while the others were taken to the Kerestinec camp.

★ ★ ★

On 7 December 1941, there was a turning point: the Japanese attacked Pearl Harbor. The following day, the United States entered the war.

On 11 December, Hitler declared war on the United States and announced that Germany, Italy and Japan had pledged an alliance to fight together to the finish. On 15 December, Croatia declared war on the United States.

Suddenly, the atrocities occurring in Croatia took on a new meaning to Americans. Washington was now concerned about how the Yugoslavian conflict would affect the United States. Especially worrisome was the prospect of violence between Serbian and Croatian immigrants, many of whom worked in heavy industry. Their loyalty to the United States was needed to strengthen the domestic war effort.

The FBI had been keeping tabs on Croatians and Serbians for years before the war, and now began to speak with émigrés from both sides. One of the Croatians they spoke with was John M. Artukovich of Los Angeles. He told the FBI agent that he had not seen his brother, Andrija, since 1939. However, an FBI informant reported a conversation he had had with John Artukovich in which it was clear that the brothers remained in touch. The FBI informant said John had told him his brother was in charge of the 'Croatian Gestapo'.

The FBI began cracking down on minority newspapers and organisa-tions such as the Domobran, established by the Ustasha in the 1930s. One of those was the Los Angeles branch of which John had been president. The FBI also opened a file on John himself.

One informant advised that the fraternal organisation, the Domobran, first flourished in the early 1930s when, through Pavelić, it first became an organised party for the independence of Croatia. This source stated that the Artukovich family in the United States were among the most ardent supporters of the organisation due to their 'intense hatred for the Serbs'.

The source reported that John M. Artukovich and his uncle, John A. Artukovich, had visited Europe in the early 1930s, where Andrija 'inspired his uncle and brother to return to this country to foster the Domobran'.

★　★　★

Back in Croatia, Andrija Artuković spoke to the Croatian State Assembly, condemning 'world Jewry' as one of the 'most dangerous international organisations'. He blamed them for having 'prepared the world revolution, so that through it the Jews could have complete mastery over all the goods of the world and all the power in the world, the Jews whom the other people had to serve as a means of their filthy profits and of its greedy, materialistic and rapacious control of the world'. Artuković crowed that he 'would solve the Jewish question by exterminating the insatiable and poisonous parasites'.

By the end of 1941, most of the Jews in Croatia were on their way to death camps. By the end of 1942, most of Sarajevo's 10,000 Jews were confined in concentration camps or had been executed.

But the tide was turning; in the mountains of Yugoslavia and Croatia, partisan rebels were putting up a good fight against the Nazis.

Artuković's chauffeur witnessed firsthand how his superiors retaliated against people who supported the partisans. At the beginning of 1942, Bajro Avdić drove Artuković and others to the village of Vrginmost, where the Ustasha were carrying out a military offensive against the partisans. When Artuković learned that the Ustasha had locked the village's men, women and children into their houses, he ordered 'the tanks toward these houses, to penetrate and destroy them completely with all men, women and children inside'.

On their way back to Zagreb, Artuković and his entourage returned to the same village, where they learned that 200 Ustasha had been killed in fighting the partisans. According to Avdić:

When Artuković heard that, he ordered that all of the population of nearby villages be arrested and brought into the plain, which was done and many people, women and children were killed [...] by machine gun fire of German production. Machine guns were 'sharci' having 3,000 bullets in a belt.

I was also escorting Pavelić and Artuković when they are visiting the site of Kozara because they wanted to see the positions at which some 500 to 600 Ustashas had died in the battle with partisans [...] On that occasion, we drove to the monastery Moscenica [Mošćenička], a very nice monastery, and Artuković ordered Lahovski, the commander of escorts, to gather all the civilian population from the houses, old ones, sick ones, women, children, and men, to gather at least 5,000 of them and to kill them because all 500 Ustasha perished in the vicinity of the Moscenica [Mošćenička] monastery.

This was done and a large number of the civilian population from the nearby villages was gathered, mostly women and children, and shot, some of them then and there, close to the monastery and some of them were taken away and killed later on.

★ ★ ★

Many of the grisly crimes that so horrified the Nazis were carried out by Catholic priests. Stories circulated about Franciscan priests holding crucifixes as they led the Ustasha to massacre. One Franciscan, Petar 'Pero' Brzica, was known as the 'King of Cutting Throats'; another, Miroslav Filipović, was known as 'Friar Satan'.

Brzica and Filipović became notorious for killing thousands of prisoners at Jasenovac and nearby camps. Competitions were held to see who could kill the greatest number of prisoners in a single night.

One Ustasha member describes losing a bet to Brzica in a competition with three others:

The killings began and after one hour I killed many more people than them. I felt like I was in heaven. I had never felt such ecstasy in my life. After a couple of hours I had got to kill 1,100 [...] The Franciscan Pero Brzica won the bet; he had killed 1,350 prisoners. I paid it without saying a word.

Filipović became the chief guard at Stara Gradiška, a small camp near Jasenovac, after he was court-martialled by the Nazis for his involvement in a massacre in 1942. A schoolteacher would later testify that Filipović came into her school and asked her to separate the Catholic children from the Serbians: 'Filipović took a child, Vasilija Glamocanin, and slaughtered her with a knife in front of the class. He urged the Ustasha troops who accompanied him to deal similarly with the other children and assured them that he would take the sin upon himself.'

'Friar Satan', a large man described as having a soft, almost feminine, voice, terrified prisoners. Witnesses would later testify that his sadism, especially toward children, exceeded that of even the cruellest Ustasha.

★ ★ ★

In the midst of the war, at the age of 42, Andrija Artuković became a father for the first time when his wife gave birth to a daughter, Visnja, in August 1942.

Pavelić shuffled his cabinet. He moved Andrija Artuković into the Ministry of Justice and Religion, a crucial post suited to a man moulded by Roman Catholic priests from his first day of school. Now began the mass conversions that had always been part of the Ustasha formula: kill one-third of Serbs, banish one-third and convert one-third to Catholicism.

Artuković addressed the Sabor, or parliament, in February 1942 to lay out his plans. His department, which was made up mostly of Catholic priests, would create a new religion, the Croatian Orthodox Church. Serbs living in Croatia would become part of this new religion and the Orthodox churches that had been closed would now be re-opened as Croatian Orthodox.

Opposition came from a surprising source: the Roman Catholic Church. The international press reported that Archbishop Stepinac of Zagreb refused to go along with the plan, even though he had been a supporter of Pavelić from the beginning. One news item datelined New York reported that 'Catholic leaders in Croatia are perplexed over what, to them, is the inexplicable silence of the Pope on the atrocities being committed by occupying forces in Yugoslavia, especially Slovenia, which is preponderantly Catholic'.

The news report went on to say that Croatian clergy in the United States urged delegates to a Catholic convention to suggest 'that the Pope publish some pronouncement concerning what is happening in Yugoslavia'.

★ ★ ★

On 9 July 1943, the Jewish Telegraphic Agency published a brief item that would surely have distressed its readers:

> The liquidation of Jews in the Nazi puppet state of Croatia is reaching its final stage, according to information reaching here. Very few Jews are left in the city of Zagreb, the Croatian capital, and almost none in any other town. Those still permitted to live in Zagreb are physicians and Jews married to 'Aryans'.
>
> A Serbian officer who succeeding [*sic*] in reaching here after two years under Nazi rule stated that the Janice camp, near Belgrade, which was originally used for Jewish prisoners, does not have a single Jewish occupant now. 'All Jews in the camp have been killed by Nazis,' [the Serbian officer] declared.
>
> German newspapers reaching here this week report that the authorities in Croatia have leased the synagogues in the towns of Osijek and Zen to local Germans for a 'period of 99 years.' The synagogues are to be used for German labor clubs.

★ ★ ★

Artuković's chauffeur would later testify that in 1943, when he was 19, he witnessed killings that took place over a day and into the night.

'I was escorting Pavelić and Artuković when they went to Samobar,' Bajro Avdić said:

> We came to a castle where some several hundreds of partisans, men and women, were imprisoned. I know well that the commander of operative groups of Ustashas informed Artuković and Pavelić that partisans were captured at Zumberk ordered then, they both ordered, that all partisans imprisoned there be killed, which was done during that day and night and I have been present there.
>
> They were killed in such a way that they were taken into the field, tied and killed by machine-gun fire, while some of them were passed over by tanks.

Despite the mass killings, the Ustasha were losing the war. Partisan rebel soldiers were gaining traction. The Allies threw their support behind the charismatic rebel leader, Josip Broz, known as Tito.

The international press introduced the rebel leader to the world. Editors wrote glowing editorials, praising 'Marshal Tito' for his colourful and decisive leadership. The *St. Louis Star and Times* ran a feature, which began:

> A general without a uniform leads the National Liberation Army (Partisans) of Jugo-Slavia to new victories – victories that may open the Balkan door to Allied armies [...] Tito is a Croatian, born in the hilly region of northern Jugo-Slavia, near Zagreb. He is now 53 years old – a striking man – lean and sinewy and sharp-eyed as a mountain eagle. American veterans of the Spanish civil war knew him. They say he is of medium size, blond, with an attractive smile and a pleasant manner that inspires devotion among his men.
>
> A German poster, offering 100,000 marks for Tito – dead or alive – bears the Partisan leader's portrait. It pictures a handsome, half-smiling face, with strong, slightly-hooked nose, high cheekbones, and long, firm lips.
>
> Some observers believe that this general, who never went to war college, this general without a uniform, may prove himself to be one of the most valuable military leaders of the war.

Newspapers sometimes mentioned the fact that Tito was a communist. The reference was made in passing.

★ ★ ★

In the autumn of 1943, Pavelić's leadership was faltering. His credibility had already suffered the previous December when the Soviets nearly wiped out an entire Croatian regiment at the Battle of Stalingrad.

Then, in September 1943, Italy surrendered to the Allies. The Croatian public expected Pavelić to regain the Dalmatian coast, a loss that had always rankled. But Pavelić's attempt to annex Italy's territory made him look even worse. The Germans didn't trust the NDH and would not allow

Pavelić to run the strategic coast. In desperation, Pavelić tried to look like he was in control of Croatia. He shuffled his cabinet twice in a six-month period in 1943. In the first shuffle on 29 April, he sent Artuković back to the Ministry of the Interior. On 1 November, he assigned him Secretary of State, a portfolio Artuković held until the end of the war.

At home, Artuković's family life was flourishing. He and Ana were blessed with a second daughter, Zorica, in April 1944.

But Croatians had lost faith in the NDH and hurried to join Tito's Partisans. Croatian defeat appeared imminent, and during the winter of 1944/45, the Ustasha began to cover its tracks. Bodies were burned or buried in mass graves.

On 8 May 1945, the Germans withdrew from Croatia. The date went down in history as VE Day, Victory in Europe Day. Tito's Partisans moved into Croatia, seeking retaliation. The Ustasha, fearing for their lives after fighting a 'holy war', turned to the Catholic Church. Help came from Krunoslav Stjepan Draganović, the former military chaplin at the Jasenovac concentration camp. Draganović, who had spent time at the Vatican where he developed a tight network, set up a 'ratline' to move fellow Ustasha members and stolen loot out of the country. Ante Pavelić and Andrija Artuković, rumoured to have dressed as priests, travelled along this ratline, hiding in monasteries. Ana Artuković and her two daughters, Visnja and Zorica, were also given refuge by Catholic clergy.

By the time Artuković and Pavelić began their travels to safety along the ratlines, a new enemy, communism, had already emerged. And a new war with that enemy, the Cold War, was about to begin. This enemy, this war, would provide the same kind of protection that both Pavelić and Artuković had sought from Hitler and Mussolini when they were young lawyers fighting for an independent Croatia. Their new protectors would prove even more powerful and long-lasting.

Andrija Artuković, who had been at the height of his powers during the war, now began a new phase of his life. No longer a high-profile cabinet minister, he would rely upon the mercy of other, more powerful, leaders to keep him safe and secure. The man who had murdered in the name of religion was ready to call in a debt. And his familiarity with the new enemy, communism, was his trump card.

3

America, Land of the Free

Judith Schiftan smiled as she took in the view of the elegant cars that seemed to glide along Wilshire Boulevard. The palm trees reaching for the clear blue sky seemed to share the same sense of promise that filled the clean California air. The 27-year-old Judith wanted to pinch herself. She was here, in Los Angeles, independent and free. Free to do anything she wanted, become anything she wanted. She had been dreaming of living in the United States almost from the moment she set foot on the muddy streets of Guatemala City almost a decade earlier. As grateful as she was to the country for taking her family in and saving their lives, Guatemala had never grown on her. Her German sense of formality was not a good fit with Guatemala's Latin sensibility. Judith didn't want to be a snob, but the truth was that she found Guatemala City rather backwards.

As a refugee, she applied herself to learning Spanish, and it wasn't long before she fit in well enough with the locals to win the homecoming queen title for Guatemala's national baseball team. A chance encounter with the young wife of Mario Monteforte Toledo, a revolutionary leader, developed into a close friendship between the two women.

Nonetheless, Judith abhorred the country's politics. Having escaped Hitler's Germany, she longed for political stability. But politics aside, Judith had a more personal reason for wanting to flee her new home. Every moment she spent under her mother's roof felt like a vice was tightening around her soul. Her mother, Klara, was beyond angry. Her oppressive presence, her bitterness, her crippling austerity all combined to create a sense of being stuck in the past.

Klara had managed the family's finances well and had even fought to recover some of the family's losses in Germany, especially their five-storey apartment building at 5 Schillerstrausse in Breslau. But despite her fighting spirit, Klara had emerged a ferociously spiteful woman. In addition to the financial loss and humiliation, one irritating fact stuck in Klara's craw: among the tenants she had treated so well was the mother-in-law of Hitler's speechwriter.

Klara simply could not come to terms with the fact that one day she was fit to serve as a landlady to a Nazi and, the next, was deemed vermin. Her home, with its elegant high ceilings, was a desirable address. And Klara, by extension, was a woman of substance to be respected. Her children, Walter and Judith, held such promise. Judith, with her father's sparkling eyes, gazed upon the world with a full smile brimming on her cupid's bow of a mouth. The camera had loved her from the moment she was posed nude as an infant, as was the fashion for baby portraits in 1920. Even as a young child, Judith displayed the combination of spirit and beauty that would shape her life.

Klara and Sigmund were proud to show off their children, hiring photographers to capture their outings, dressed in lederhosen, to the German countryside. It was Klara and Sigmund who hosted family gatherings, Sigmund's impish humour drawing in the large family and creating an affectionate welcome that enhanced the ostentatious hospitality.

As much as it had hurt to lose Sigmund three years before Hitler declared war, Klara was relieved that he was spared the pain of seeing the military, in whose ranks he had ambitiously risen, rounding up Jews and stripping them of their rights as citizens. What happened next was so deeply traumatic that Klara knew she would carry the emotional scars to her grave.

As for Judith, she was full of conflicted feelings about Germany. Part of her still loved her native country. She yearned for the refined culture of Germany's concert halls, opera houses, art galleries and high fashion. Judith loved clothes, loved expressing herself through designing her own outfits. A creative streak ran through the Schiftan family, and drawing was in Judith's DNA. Her sketches of dresses and suits were a labour of love, their designs concocted in her head and painstakingly drawn into patterns. She thrilled at seeing the patterns come alive, stroking the lush fabrics, feeling their heft as they were sewn into garments that would catch the envious eyes of other women in Breslau's society. The warm memory was distinctly German, caught up in the culture, the language, the music, the sense of occasion, something that could never be recreated anywhere else. Breslau, her German hometown that reverted back to Poland after the war, was lost to her forever.

Oh, to be the belle of the ball once again and to join her cousins at dances and weddings. Judith could still see it in her mind's eye. She was thankful that her parents had splurged on professional photographs, their very existence proving that her family did gather to celebrate holidays and weddings, that it was not a figment of a cruel imagination.

How she wished that the other memories were, in fact, imaginary and that she would wake up one day and find that the Holocaust had been a bad dream, that her beloved Germany had not been responsible for the murder of her seventy-six aunts, uncles and cousins. Now that the war was over, the scale of the horror had sunk in. Six million Jews, a million of them children. For this, Judith brimmed with hatred for Germany.

Her own family, as well as relatives in Honduras and Guatemala, had helped rescue hundreds of Jews. But Judith, whose prized possessions included her father's Iron Cross and the helmet he wore in battle for Kaiser Wilhelm, felt a betrayal deeper than a physical war wound. As an Orthodox Jew, she could not reconcile her faith with a God who had abandoned the Jewish people.

Judith, like many distraught Europeans, was drawn to America. She wanted a fresh start in the land of the Allies who liberated Europe, who rescued the emaciated Jews still clinging to life in Hitler's concentration camps.

It took three years of studying English to pass her proficiency tests for her American visa. The moment she received her exit papers, Judith bought an airline ticket to Los Angeles.

Judith arrived in the city on 12 March 1947. She moved into an apartment on Citrus Street in Mid-Wilshire and set out to find work. With fluency in three languages and an indomitable work ethic, she was hired immediately as a saleswoman at the thriving new Army and Navy Surplus Store in Hollywood.

With her vivacious personality, Judith had no trouble making friends. Soon she was part of a group of attractive young women like herself who spent their weekends taking in the fabulous nightlife that Los Angeles had to offer. It was at a dance for Jewish singles at the Miramar Hotel in Santa Monica that she first laid eyes on Harry Whitelaw. He was trim and dapper, with his dark hair slicked back to expose his distinctive widow's peak. A little on the short side at 5ft 8in, but with an air of confidence that made him seem taller. When she held his gaze, she saw a vulnerability in his eyes that touched her heart.

As for Harry, the woman smiling at him from across the room seemed out of his league. She looked like she belonged in the movies, but Harry thought she was more beautiful than any Hollywood star. Judith, fashionably dressed to show off her slim waist and ample bust, was a showstopper with her rich dark hair and expressive eyes.

But there she was, without a doubt, smiling and looking right at him. Harry took a chance and asked her to dance. She slid into his arms, a perfect fit, almost as tall as Harry. For their first dance, her sensuous, lipstick-red lips grazed his cheek. They were smitten by love at first sight.

As they got to know each other, they discovered they were attracted to the other's sense of worldliness. They had both tasted adventure and had emerged with a sophisticated worldview. Both were independent, gutsy enough to make their own way in the world.

And neither was shy to admit that they were equally vain. They liked to look good, cutting a fine figure and maintaining an appearance that lasted after making a great first impression. But the two were drawn to each other by a deeper, more significant common bond: they had each lost the parent who had made them feel loved.

For Judith, it was the loss of her gentle, light-hearted father who died when she was 15, leaving her with Klara, an emotionally distant mother who grew even colder after the war. For Harry, it was the mother who showed him the only kindness he'd ever known as a child.

Harry had been only 5 years old when his mother, Lena Aronowitz, died a day after giving birth to her fourth child in 1921. His father, Joseph, a cobbler from Albany, New York, couldn't fathom how, as a widower, he could manage his young brood. His prospects of finding a new wife to raise four children under the age of 6 were bleak, especially since he was barely eking out a living. Who would consider taking him and the children on, except perhaps a widow desperate to feed a brood of her own?

Joseph persevered as best he could for a few months until he had the good fortune to meet a woman newly arrived from Poland. He married

Yetta Baumstein on 23 October 1922, and the family settled in Brooklyn. Yetta gave birth to twins, a boy and a girl, in 1924. However, when Yetta found herself pregnant with another child in the winter of 1925, family life became strained to a breaking point.

With three toddlers and an overburdened pregnant wife, Joseph made a heart-wrenching decision: he placed the children of his first marriage in an orphanage. On 13 May 1925, Harry and his three sisters were dropped off at the Hebrew Orphan Asylum in Brooklyn. Harry was 8 years old, Sarah 9, Yetta 6 and Lena, whose mother died after giving birth to her, was 4.

They lost touch with their father's new family growing up just a few blocks away. They didn't even know that five months after they moved to the orphanage, their stepmother gave birth to a new brother, Hyman.

The hurt of being abandoned was too much for Harry. He never forgave his father for spurning him and his sisters, for starting a new family when he couldn't afford to look after the one he had.

Nonetheless, Harry learned to follow the rules of the orphanage. He learned to look after himself. Wiry, with a fine mane of wavy black hair, Harry became a people-pleaser, learning a salesman's charm and its disappointing flip side, rejection. With a yawning emptiness inside his soul, Harry took to watching the sea, almost feeling the roll of the swells washing toward the Brooklyn Navy Yards. It wasn't hard to imagine the rhythm of the sea smoothing over the jagged shards of loneliness cutting a hole in his orphan's heart.

But as emotionally barren as life was at the Hebrew Orphan Asylum, the worst was yet to come. As Harry approached the tumultuous years of adolescence, his sense of betrayal exploded after the orphanage put him up for adoption. A boy already hardened by the pitiful life of an orphan may have seemed difficult to place, but a Jewish family stepped forward to take him in. The father was a cigar salesman, the mother a homemaker who looked after their two boys. With his adoption, Harry acquired a new name, Whitelaw.

However, the adoption didn't work out. Perhaps the Whitelaw family could no longer afford another mouth to feed during the Depression. Once again, Harry was rejected and shipped back to the orphanage. He remained there until six weeks after his seventeenth birthday, when he ran away and joined the Merchant Marine.

Later, when he passed the Whitelaw name on to his own three sons, Harry refused to tell them anything about the Whitelaw family, except to explain that he had legally changed his name to theirs. And although their surname did not sound it, the Whitelaw family was Jewish. In fact, Harry never wanted to hear his birth name, 'Aronowitz', ever again. As a new bride, Judith quickly learned that to ask any questions about Harry's biological family was to do so at her peril.

Only once did Harry allow the closed window of his past life to open a crack and allow two telling facts to escape. There was no missing his sadness as he described arranging and paying for his own bar mitzvah. When he added that he ran away in the middle of the night, it wasn't hard to imagine the deeply painful experiences that drove him to lie about his age and join the Merchant Marine.

At sea, Harry found his home. The Merchant Marine became family. When the United States joined the Second World War in 1941, Harry joined the US Naval Construction Battalions, fondly dubbed the 'Sea Bees', whose motto was 'We Build. We Fight.' The battalions were admired for their 'can-do' attitude and Harry volunteered for one of the least popular assignments: Alaska's Aleutian Islands campaign.

Harry trained as a refrigeration technician and wore the insulated khaki coveralls as proudly as he wore his navy blues. Later, he would hint that his skills were employed on a secret project: keeping the atomic bomb cool. He could, and did, speak more openly about his role as a member of the Sea Bees. Harry had helped build the airstrips and bases to protect the United States from Japanese invasion.

Alaska appealed to Harry's adventurous spirit; when the war ended, he stayed on to try his hand at his first business, a clothing store in Sitka. As the only Jew for hundreds of miles in remote Alaska, Harry was even more of an outsider. At the age of 31, he hankered to settle down. In 1948 he returned to Los Angeles, where he'd been posted with the Merchant Marine, and rented a room with a Jewish family, the Siegels, who lived on Stone Street.

Ex-servicemen like Harry Whitelaw were pouring into Los Angeles from all over the United States, especially the Midwest, lured by the booming economy. Harry, like Judith Schiftan, became part of a wave of immigrants that would triple the Jewish population of Los Angeles in the next three years. With 2,000 Jews arriving every month, they made up 13 per cent of all immigrants to the city. Already, 567 families who survived the Holocaust had arrived, along with another 10,000 Jewish refugees, supported by Jewish charities in Los Angeles. Soon enough, Los Angeles was trailing New York and Tel Aviv as having the third-largest Jewish population in the world.

Of the non-Jewish immigrants, there were also thousands of immigrants and refugees from Europe. Most had been traumatised by the war; many were victims of atrocities. But some were the perpetrators of those atrocities who downplayed their roles and hid their true identities, starting life over as aspiring Americans.

One of them was Andrija Artuković. He arrived in Los Angeles on 16 July 1948, along with his wife and their children. The Artuković family, when asked the purpose of their visit by US immigration officials, claimed to be tourists. That was just one of many lies they were to tell Americans. The fact that the names on their passports were also false would not catch up with them for a few years. By then, they would already have established a new life by the sea.

In the fifteen months since Judith herself had immigrated to Los Angeles, she had thrived as a new American. She could not have been more confident that starting over in the United States was the right decision.

Little did she know that one of her soon-to-be neighbours was Andrija Artuković, who settled with his family on a beach just a couple of miles away in Surfside. Judith, the Holocaust survivor, and Harry, the Second World War veteran, would not have believed for one moment that their beloved America had given refuge to a man whose brutality had horrified even the Nazis.

4

'I Am Stateless'

Andrija Artuković and his family started their journeys in Austria, where Ana had been born twenty-four years earlier. They made their way to Switzerland, where they applied to immigrate to Ireland. They were helped by the Vatican through the assistance of Krunoslav Stjepan Draganović, a Roman Catholic priest with a successful track record of spiriting Ustasha members out of Europe. He took their applications to the Delegate General of the Franciscans of Switzerland, who in turn presented them to the Irish immigration minister. The application made it clear that the family would not be a burden on the Irish government since they 'did not lack financial means'.

Artuković, now 45, was given a new identity. He would now be known as Alois Anich, passing himself off as a university professor hoping to engage in 'philological and historical studies' in Dublin. His immigration application said he was accompanied by a nephew, Reverend Father Anton Louis Ivandić, who would be looked after by the Franciscans of Merchants' Quay. Ana and the two girls also went by the name of Anich, with the children's names changed from Vishjna and Zorica to Katherina and Aurea. The Irish government accepted their applications, and on 15 July 1947, the family arrived in Dublin. They settled in the leafy suburb of Rathgar, one of the most desirable neighbourhoods in Dublin and the birthplace of James Joyce.

Rathgar, proud of its mix of 100-year-old Victorian, Georgian and Edwardian brick homes, must have felt extremely modern to the family after living amid the thirteenth-century and red-roof buildings of Zagreb.

But the religious animosity would certainly have been familiar. When the wealthy Protestants had refused to give their Roman Catholic servants enough time off on Sunday to comfortably walk to Mass in the next town, the Catholics had one-upped them by building a spectacular church in the style of Roman basilicas. With its magnificent dome ceiling, the Church of the Three Patrons was named for Ireland's patron saints: Patrick, Bridgid and Columba.

It was a convenient location for the Anich family to worship, a pleasant stroll from their home at 6 Zion Road. It is not known whether the family appreciated the irony of the name of their new street in a neighbourhood where Dublin's Jews settled in the late 1920s after fleeing the Russian pogroms.

The family was devout. Alois Anich became a familiar figure to the neighbours as he walked to and from Mass every morning. The two girls were registered for school at Sacred Heart Convent. Within a year of arriving, Ana gave birth to their third child, a son, at a private nursing home on Terenure Road, a short walk from their home, in June 1948. They named him Radoslav.

When the Anich family started over in Ireland, they were welcomed by a country that also gave refuge to between 100 and 200 Nazis after the war. Even before the war, Irish radio had broadcast Nazi propaganda. The nationalist spirit of the Nazi message resonated in Ireland, whose own nationalists felt an affinity with the German desire to reclaim a lost pride. To the Irish, it evoked their own anti-English rage.

Many of the Nazis accepted into Ireland by Éamon de Valera's government were considered freedom fighters for their country's nationalism or independence. Artuković, for example, had started fighting for an independent Croatia when he was in his teens, when the Irish nationalist movement was gaining strength. The fact that many of them were fleeing communism added to their appeal. The communist dogma, atheist and anti-religious, repelled Catholics.

The Anich family apparently didn't gain the social prominence of some of the other Nazis who flocked to Ireland. One of them, SS hero Otto Skorzeny, raised prize-winning lambs and flitted charmingly through high-society circles. Albert Folens, an alleged Gestapo officer, ran a publishing house that produced textbooks for Irish schoolchildren. Pieter Menten, a Dutch nationalist responsible for the deaths of hundreds of

Jews in Poland, lived comfortably collecting art on a large estate at Mahon Bridge in County Waterford. Célestin Lainé, a Breton nationalist, led a Waffen SS unit that committed atrocities in north-west France, and lived unmolested in Oranmore, County Galway.

But while other Nazis stayed in Ireland and built comfortable lives, the Artuković family expressed a desire to move to the United States. Perhaps the pull of family was too great. Or perhaps they saw opportunity in the Displaced Persons Act passed on 25 June 1948.

Whatever the reason, after a year of living in their house on Zion Road, the family received Irish travel documents. They booked flights with a stop in New York before travelling to Los Angeles. The journey, shorter than by ship, would nonetheless take two full days. And it was far from cheap: tickets for a family of five would cost more than $1,200, which, when adjusted for inflation, would be $11,000 today. It was quite a bit of money for a family who would claim refugee status with the added claim that they relied on relatives for support because they had no means of their own.

Their main benefactor was Andrija Artuković's brother, John. He had provided them with a little townhouse he had purchased a few years earlier as a weekend fishing retreat. It had a cosy wood-panelled living room and was situated on Seal Beach in Surfside, just 25 yards from the crashing waves of the Pacific Ocean.

John had immigrated in 1934 and joined several cousins who had fled Herezgovina in the early 1900s in search of the American dream. They had prospered in construction, building and repairing much of the city's sewer system. An Artukovich had built the aqueduct to the Mojave Desert. The family had achieved sufficient success that the name 'Artukovich' was embossed into the manhole plates covering sewers all over Los Angeles.

John set up his own construction business and married Lucille Papac, a Los Angeles native of Croatian descent. John anglicised his name from Ivan, changed the spelling of his surname to Artukovich and became a US citizen.

By the time the Artuković family arrived in 1948, John was wealthy. The beachside townhouse he gave his brother was one of several rental units he owned. In addition to the beach house, John gave the family a car. He hired Andrija as a bookkeeper for $100 a week, a decent salary at a time when the average family income was about $60.

Andrija and Ana were surrounded by a rich circle of extended family, including dozens of aunts, uncles and cousins, part of a diaspora who worshipped at St Anthony's Croatian Church. They relied on their support network to help them navigate the new world, especially as Ana had her hands full with an infant son and two daughters, soon to start school.

Artuković devoted his time to working at his brother's construction firm and improving his English, a language he learned to speak during his travels as a young man. When their six-month tourist visa expired, the family requested a six-month extension to remain in the United States. They each posted a bond of $500 to stay until 17 April 1949.

But the family had no intention of leaving California.

⋆ ⋆ ⋆

The Artuković family had arrived in California at a pivotal time in US history. The United States, and President Harry Truman especially, were newly cast in the role of world leader, thanks to their contribution to the Allied victory.

The newspaper stories and pictures from post-war Europe were bringing home the facts of the worst humanitarian crisis Americans had ever known. Photos showed lines of people walking with suitcases, sometimes following horse-drawn wagons with bags of grain and other food. But, as pitiful as the images were, they did not stir up a universal feeling that America should throw open its doors. When Truman announced his intention to ask Congress for special legislation to permit a fraction of the eight million European refugees, the reaction was swift. 'Isn't this supposed to be an Anglo-Saxon country, that is English speaking?' asked a Democrat from Texas.

Truman persisted. For the first time in American history, the United States changed its immigration laws to admit refugees. Truman intended the Displaced Persons Act of 1948 to welcome Jews who survived the Holocaust and other Europeans whose communities were bombed out and otherwise destroyed by the war. Many of them were in limbo, living in Displaced Persons camps in Germany, Italy and Austria which had been set up by the Allies after winning the war.

In calling for the Displaced Persons Act, Truman had imagined a law with humanitarian goals, rather than the usual immigration aim of bringing people who would contribute to the economy. The law allowed for a quota of European refugees over and above regular immigrants from those regions. The quota was set at 200,000 for the first two years and then increased to 415,000 in 1950.

In addition to the Displaced Persons Act, the United States also passed the Refugee Relief Act. In the period from 1948 to 1953, more than 600,000 immigrants from several European countries entered the United States under both the Refugee Relief Act and the Displaced Persons Act. Many of them were from countries now under Soviet control, claiming that they were anti-communist. Many of them were also Nazi accomplices.

★ ★ ★

In the spring of 1949, Andrija Artuković applied to have his family declared Displaced Persons. 'I am stateless,' he declared.

Many of the people admitted to the United States as Displaced Persons were from Balkan states and Artuković claimed that he and his family were stateless now that the communists had taken over their homeland. Andrija Artuković made a case that as a Catholic and vocal anti-communist, he should be granted permanent residency in the United States, along with his wife and three dependent children.

Artuković's first interview took place on 28 April 1949 with Franklin Davis, the officer in charge of the United States Immigration and Naturalization Service (INS) office in Santa Ana.

Artuković explained that he had entered the United States with a false name because he was a political refugee forced to use another name to get out of Europe. He said his travel documents were made in Switzerland because he couldn't get a passport from his native country.

If that part of the story contained omissions rather than actual lies, Artuković ramped up the fiction when he described his previous career. As he told it to Davis, he was able to retire from his law practice in 1932 'in order to study preparation for a Professorship'. He neglected to mention the Ustasha training camps that he ran in Italy.

To explain his years of bouncing around Great Britain and Europe, Artuković claimed to be travelling as part of preparing for his studies. He said he went to Berlin to study in 1936 but was arrested by the Gestapo at the request of the Yugoslavian government. He claimed to have been held in custody for fifteen days before being found not guilty and released. Artuković claimed this was his only arrest and vastly played down the amount of time he spent in prison, which was actually fifteen months rather than fifteen days. He didn't admit to his arrest in France on the suspicion that he was the mastermind behind King Alexander's assassination. And he certainly didn't tell the truth about where he lived and what he was up to in the years before the war, painting a benign picture with no resemblance to his role as a Ustasha leader in Berlin.

In his interview, Artuković made much of his strong Catholic faith and his opposition, as a Catholic, to communism. To bolster his case, he presented a letter to Davis written by Reverend Stephen Lackovic, pastor of Our Lady of the Sacred Heart of Jesus Roman Catholic Church in Lackawanna, New York State. Rev. Lackovic, the former secretary to Archbishop Aloysius Stepinac in Zagreb, said he knew Artuković personally. He was writing to attest that Artuković had been 'very active in carrying out the wishes of Archbishop Stepinac', who was now under arrest in a Zagreb prison.

The information that Artuković gave about himself in his interview with the INS became part of a narrative that he, and his supporters, would often repeat in the coming years. The narrative was built on the claim that Artuković would likely be executed by the anti-Catholic communist government of Yugoslavia. Tito, who now led the government, would certainly have a member of Pavelić's cabinet in his crosshairs. For proof of Tito's thirst for reprisal, Artuković could cite the Bleiburg massacre in May 1945, in which hundreds of thousands of Croatians were slaughtered as they attempted to surrender to the Partisans.

★ ★ ★

INS Officer Davis didn't buy Artuković's story.

Whether he doubted the details or not didn't matter. What mattered to Davis was Artuković's role in Pavelić's government. 'It would appear that the Croatian government was one of the Axis-dominated governments set up after the Germans overran the area. It was the government headed by Ante Pavelić, an Anti-Communist but Pro-Nazi dictator,' Davis wrote in his report. He rejected Artuković's application and turned over the information to the FBI. It was not until almost two years later that the FBI started its own investigation.

The FBI began probing Artuković's life in January 1951, with old-fashioned sleuthing: an agent watched his house and spoke with the caretaker, Stuart Briggs. Briggs told the FBI that 'Andrew' Artuković seemed to lead a quiet life, with few visitors outside of his brother John. Briggs had never observed any suspicious behaviour coming from the family living at 64B Surfside Colony.

'Stuart Briggs advised that the subject is studying English and is endeavoring to perfect his command of the language,' the FBI agent wrote in a confidential report:

> He advised additionally that the subject works every day except Sunday and that on Sunday he takes his children to Sunday School and spends the day otherwise with his family. John Artukovich, brother of the subject, just bought the subject and his family an automobile which Mrs. Artuković drives.

The information provided by Briggs was consistent with that given to INS Officer Davis by both Andrew and Ana Artuković, who claimed they had no means of support and relied on John to pay the family's expenses.

The FBI followed up on the observations made by Davis about Pavelić's government by reaching out to informants. One informant, identified as SD T-1, had first submitted information to US Intelligence in 1943, detailing Artuković's activities since his days as a lawyer in Croatia. The informant repeated the allegation that Artuković was 'deeply involved in the Marseilles assassination' of King Alexander. He also said that Artuković had been one of Pavelić's most 'active collaborators in the work of terrorism organized by Italy against Yugoslavia'.

In its first report on Artuković, the FBI sought to confirm his connection to Croatian groups operating in the United States before the war, connecting the dots on a web of personalities. They discovered that Andrija Artuković received regular payments from a committee known as the Croatian National Committee in Pittsburgh. The funds, which totalled $425 (about $7,500 in 2022 dollars), were sent to Andrija Artuković in Budapest in 1936 and Paris in 1937. One of the informants described Artuković as 'the keeper of the seal' in Pavelić's puppet state.

On 8 May 1951, US Marshals barged into the offices of John Artukovich's construction company. They placed his brother, Andrija, under arrest. He was accused of murdering a Serbian priest back in Croatia during the war.

After three years, the promising life that the family had established in California's ocean air could simply blow away. It wasn't just Andrija's fate that was at stake. The whole family could be deported back to Yugoslavia, where the communists would eat them alive.

★ ★ ★

Just 10 miles away, in Long Beach, the Whitelaw family had established themselves with similar hopes and dreams. The fate of the Artuković and Whitelaw families, both weighted down with the emotional baggage of the Holocaust, had become forever linked along the sunny California coast.

5

'The Holocaust Was Mother's Milk to Me'

Harry and Judith married in a Jewish ceremony in Las Vegas on 1 September 1949. They were eager to start a family, and Judith Whitelaw gave birth to her first son ten months later on 1 July 1950. They named him Stephen Leslie.

The joy of becoming a mother was mixed with severe loneliness for Judith. Never had she felt the sting of having no family in Los Angeles as sharply as when she found herself coping with a baby on her own. When she'd married Harry, she hadn't fully grasped that she was also marrying a US Merchant Marine. Harry was away at sea for weeks at a time, working mostly as a bellman on passenger ships. Her loneliness hurt all the more when she dwelt on how much she had given up for the man who seemed to promise everything she'd ever wanted: a family and a home. Now, thanks to her adventurous seafaring husband, Judith had even lost touch with the friends she'd made working as a saleswoman. Marrying Harry meant that she'd been forced to quit her job and sacrifice her familiar neighbourhood in bustling Mid-Wilshire for the convenience of being closer to Harry's work in the naval town of Long Beach.

And then there was life with Harry, stressful and exhausting most of the time. Working in the hospitality field, Harry had learned to be gracious and upbeat in public. But behind closed doors, he was a difficult man, prickly and impossible to please. The orphaned child who had felt unworthy and unloved had grown into a man who held his own loved ones to a standard so high that they, in turn, ended up feeling unworthy and unloved. Judith, traumatised by her own emotional youth, was no shrinking violet either. She returned Harry's barbs, tit for tat, with her own.

From the start, their marriage fell into a pattern of fighting, followed by remorse. In a letter to Judith from his ship in San Francisco just three months after Stephen was born, Harry apologised for his bad behaviour the night before. Expressing his frustration at being away so much of the time, he hoped that their family life would improve when the three of them were together without the pressure of him sailing away.

His craving for a better family life coincided with his dream to start his own business. Travelling the world, Harry could see opportunities in the post-war boom. After all the dark years of the Depression and the war, middle-class Americans had well-paying jobs and money to spend.

Without the wherewithal to start his own business, Harry found a business partner with a solid track record in retail. They called their company Royal Hawaiian Imports and capitalised on a knack for importing the kind of trinkets and souvenirs that were in demand from gift shops around the country.

Harry approached Walter Knott, whose boysenberry farm had grown into the major tourist attraction in Orange County, to ask if he could set up a booth at Knott's Berry Farm. Walter and his wife Cordelia had grown fond of Harry and Judith through the Whitelaw family's regular visits. Baby Stephen, with his big brown eyes and black hair, was also a big hit, exhibiting a charismatic charm that he'd clearly inherited from Harry.

The Knotts agreed to rent space to Harry and also invited Judith to join their sales staff, selling pies on the farm in Buena Park. The friendship thrived, as did the sales of Harry's trinkets. Americans may have jokingly dismissed 'Made in Japan' as junk, but the tourists and local visitors alike snapped up Harry's tchotchkes. His wares may have been cheap, but the sales volume was high enough to pay the bills and sustain the family.

Even though their marriage was tumultuous, Harry and Judith grew confident in the business and they decided to buy their first house. It wasn't much of a stretch for them to settle on Buena Park, since they were already spending so much time in the quaint little city. They bought a house at 8049 Cyclamen Way, in an almost all-white neighbourhood with streets named for flowers.

On 23 July 1955, Judith gave birth to their second son, David. Big brother Stephen, just a few weeks past his fifth birthday, was less than thrilled to have a new baby stealing the limelight. A new dynamic developed: Harry fawned over Stephen, Judith over baby David. The family dynamic had solidified destiny: Stephen was Daddy's boy and David, Mommy's.

Five years later, on 1 August 1960, Judith gave birth to a third son, Billy. He was born into a family already in turmoil. Judith and Harry were constantly bickering; 10-year-old Stephen had become a miniature Harry, oozing charm or snarkiness to his mother and David; 5-year-old David felt as if he were walking on eggshells, waiting for Stephen's 'mommy's boy' putdowns and the angry explosions between his parents. Billy's birth tipped the family over the edge.

It was clear from the outset that something was wrong with Billy. He wouldn't sleep. He wailed. Judith walked the floor with him, rocked him in his pram, took him for drives, but to no avail. Nothing could calm him down enough for any of them to get rest. As Billy grew into a toddler, he would climb out of his crib, the first signs that his behaviour would become uncontrollable. The doctor reassured her that her son was merely hyperactive, a condition that he would probably outgrow. Judith braced herself for the 'terrible twos', growing ever more resentful at Harry for ignoring Billy's needs, not to mention her own.

It seemed to Judith that every other family was perfectly happy. Outside their window, everyone else's life looked as sunny and optimistic as the era itself. To David, the images of his life in the late 1950s and early 1960s tell a story, mostly in black and white, of an idyllic existence.

There is a photograph of David, taken in 1957 by a photographer who hustled business door-to-door, walking with a pony through the sub-division. The photographer's portable studio included a cowboy hat, a set of suede chaps, cowboy boots with spurs and a holster with a toy gun. For a couple of dollars, he would dress the little boys in the cowboy outfit, lift them onto the pony and snap the black-and-white photo.

The year 1959 saw family outings to Disneyland, the amusement park that had opened in nearby Anaheim on 18 July 1955, just five days before David was born. Checking out the rides, David developed an aversion to the adrenaline rush. Stephen laughed, mocking David for being 'chicken', and demanded the thrill of another turn on the wildest ride.

In 1960, David saw his first fish aquarium at his preschool. He was transfixed by the guppies swimming around inside the tank in its metal frame. The aquarium was a new invention, thanks to the ingenuity of a fellow Los Angeles Jew, Martin Horowitz, who figured out a way to make a sealant to prevent the aquarium from corroding.

When Wingo preschool held its open house, David excitedly dragged his parents by their hands away from the sandbox to show them the aquarium. From that moment on, David pestered his parents to buy him a fish tank. Unable to afford a hobbyist's aquarium with its expensive tank, pumps and filters, Harry and Judith compromised and bought a fish bowl instead. David might not have inherited the charm and wit that his father passed on to Stephen, but his love of the ocean was definitely in David's DNA. Staring at his two goldfish in wide-eyed wonder, David would try to imagine all the different kinds of fish that lived in the sea.

The year 1961 was one of non-stop construction and development. David, now 6, was fascinated by the bulldozers and dump trucks, roaring around, building freeways. From the backseat of his father's station wagon, he marvelled at how quickly the view was changing. Farmland and mountains suddenly gone. New buildings. New houses. New neighbourhoods.

Even to a child's eyes, the construction of buildings and roads was a soaring symbol of optimism. The future held promise. David, the son of a German refugee, took to heart his mother's message that his country, the United States, was the place where everyone's dreams could come true. The fact that his parents were forever bickering did not seem disconnected from that optimism. To David, it seemed as normal for adults to shout at each other as it was for them to smile and chat with strangers. The way adults behaved at home was simply different from the way they acted outside.

Nonetheless, the noise inside the Whitelaw home was sometimes too much: Billy's relentless screaming as he jumped up and down in his crib, Judith's yelling at Stephen, Stephen answering back, Harry shouting at Judith to leave Stephen alone. David would try to quiet Billy, singing to him, trying to distract him with his goldfish. If nothing worked to calm Billy down, David would retreat into his imagination, drowning out the noise around him by drawing pictures of the trees and flowers outside his window. Once his parents stopped shouting, David would go into the kitchen and sit quietly with his mom, watching Judith cook dinner, telling her how good it smelled.

If Harry stormed out of the house, David would follow him, asking him if he could come along for a car ride, but being careful not to demand anything that might set Harry off again. In the car, Harry might remain silent. Or he might talk to his 5-year-old son about how impossible it was to please Judith.

By the time he started kindergarten, David had learned that the expectations of adults were fraught with unfathomable rules. What a relief it was, then, to discover a whole new world at Dysinger Elementary School, the calm, welcoming world of his kindergarten teacher, Mrs Oveson. She smiled at David's every comment and praised him lavishly for every picture he drew. She seemed to dote on him as much as he did on her, making him feel safe for the first time in his young life: 'She was one of my earliest role models and she made me feel wonderful. In my mind's eye, I can still see Mrs Oveson standing over me, admiring the colour of crayons I chose. She'd tell me how creative I was and to keep practising my art. Sometimes she'd suggest what colours would go well together. I adored her. What kid wouldn't adore that kind of nurturing from a role model?'

At the end of the year, Mrs Oveson submitted a picture that David had drawn to an art contest. The picture of a man wearing a red hat was simple, but it stood out among the kindergarten art for its strong drawing and colour. David won the contest, reinforcing all of his positive feelings about school and Mrs Oveson.

As impressed as David was with the award, he was overjoyed to receive a letter in the mail from the art director of the Central School District. It was addressed to Mr David Whitelaw, advising him that his picture would be displayed for the following two months at the Bank of America.

'They called me Mr Whitelaw!' David exclaimed to his mother. He beamed with the pleasure of feeling grown up. It was his first memory of being admired by anyone besides his mother. David liked the feeling. A lot.

★ ★ ★

At home, the colour TV brought two very conflicting worlds into the family's living room.

David's world of TV revolved around Engineer Bill, a local Channel 9 TV role model who encouraged children to drink their milk with a play-along-at-home game called 'Red Light, Green Light'. The choo-choo trains that huffed up a hill, panting 'I hope I can, I hope I can', inspired David to do his very best. When the host read the letters of the children who would be invited on the show, David was consumed with a longing that one day his turn would come. What he wouldn't give to win those prizes!

His mother was equally absorbed by TV news and current affairs programmes. Judith worried about the Cold War, shaking her head in 1960 at reports of Soviet leader Nikita Khrushchev banging his shoe on the podium of the UN and declaring, 'We shall destroy you from within.' When Adolf Eichmann was captured in Argentina in 1960, David felt Judith's excitement, and that of the entire congregation, as they discussed the upcoming trial in Jerusalem. When the Berlin Wall went up in 1961, Judith was saddened by news of East Germans being shot and killed as they tried to flee the communists.

In October 1962, the world seemed especially ominous. David lay in his bed, too frightened to sleep, with a terrible feeling that something was wrong with the world. 'Are we going to die, Mommy?'

His mother stroked his head, assuring him that the world was safe. 'No, no, *mein Puppele*, we are not going to die.'

David wasn't convinced. He didn't understand the event that held the world on the brink of nuclear war. He only knew that his parents were distracted every day for two weeks by news of the Cuban Missile Crisis. All of the adults in his world tried their best to put on a brave face, but their fear was palpable.

When President John F. Kennedy was assassinated in 1963, David had a sense that 'something really horrible had happened to the world'.

The feeling of safety that his kindergarten teacher had provided proved fleeting; the world outside his home, as well as inside, had made David feel helpless.

★ ★ ★

There was only one other Jewish family, the Watermans, who lived nearby. Their house was a few streets away on Columbine Circle.

When their neighbours went all out to decorate their homes with Christmas trees, Santa Claus and exterior lights, the Whitelaws placed a menorah in the window for Chanukah. One of David's earliest photos shows him as a toddler holding a menorah, looking pleased with himself as only a toddler can.

One year, David was invited to a Christmas party and came home loaded down with candy. 'I was so happy. But my dad got madder than hell. He spanked me. He said, "We're Jews. We don't do that. Don't ever do that again."'

The lesson that their family was different was driven home again in 1963 when David answered the door to find a man asking for signatures on a petition. It was directed at the Whitelaw and Waterman families with the demand: 'We want them out.' David, tasting antisemitism for the first time, couldn't figure out if the man had stumbled unknowingly onto a Jewish home, or was just being provocative. Either way, he simply closed the door. It seems most of the neighbours did the same. Few of them signed the petition, and it never went anywhere.

But the petition's message that Jews could be forced out was seared indelibly into David's memory. He was 8 years old.

With no synagogue in Buena Park, the Whitelaw family drove their 1957 Ford Fairlane station wagon to nearby Anaheim to worship at Beth Emet Temple. Housed in a Craftsman bungalow, it was the first synagogue in Orange County. But with the influx of Jews from all over the country, the congregation was growing. The small building was cramped, and the congregation welcomed a fund-raising campaign to buy land and build a larger temple. Harry and Judith, active members of both the sister- and brotherhood, contributed to the efforts. Hearing their names given credit at the services, young David beamed with pride.

But Judith was conflicted about her faith. And along with instilling Jewish values and pride, Judith taught her children that Jewish identity carried a price. Her faith had cost her dearly. She could not reconcile faith with a God who had allowed six million Jews to perish, including a million children.

Sometimes, Judith's children would find their mother lost in her own world, watching news footage or documentaries about Hitler's concentration camps. Jews referred to the genocide as the Shoah, and the word 'Holocaust' was just becoming part of the lexicon in the early 1960s. As Judith struggled to come to terms with her own fate, her own survival, she became obsessed with the Holocaust. She scoured the TV listings to make sure she never missed an item. David slid onto the sofa to join her, curious about the images that consumed his mother. The pictures showed starving people using their fingers to scrape the last flecks of porridge from the bowl. Children devouring soup made of potato skins. Tears streaming down his face, David vowed never to waste food. The images of starving, cold and lonely children formed an inchoate sense of injustice in David's soul.

Judith's sadness and anger were palpable. Living freely in the United States, a world that she defined as a sanctuary, safe and sane, Judith saw the Holocaust as part of the legacy she must pass on to her children. Never could she allow them to forget. She told him about watching the flames shoot into the heavens during Kristallnacht, how her grandfather fought back when the Nazis came to shut down the private shul in which he invited lonely Jews to worship from his home. She told him how she was kicked out of her Protestant school because she was a Jew. And of the friends who would no longer speak to her when their fathers moved up the Nazi ranks. Of the friend of her sister killed as she tried to flee, her suitcase arriving months later in Guatemala as an eerie, ghostly reminder.

At night, David would toss and turn, remembering the images, remembering the stories. 'I've never slept well in my entire life,' David says now, in his sixties. 'The Holocaust was mother's milk to me.'

David doesn't remember when he started to feel the terrible void left by the seventy-six missing relatives. But he does remember hearing from other kids about all of the cousins, aunts and uncles and grandparents who would be visiting for the holidays. He asked his mother why no one ever came to their Passover Seders. 'Why is it just us, Mommy?'

Judith would explain that they once had a large family. Her father had nine siblings, and her mother twelve. Their holiday celebrations had been huge, joyful. But when she was a young girl, a bad man named Adolf Hitler came along. He had destroyed their family. Dozens of her cousins never had a chance to grow up and have children of their own. A few cousins survived by fleeing to Guatemala and Honduras, as Judith did. One cousin now lived in the United States, too, but thousands of miles away in New York. Her name was Herty, and she was married. She had children. David did have cousins. Maybe someday, they would come to visit.

David, in his envy of friends and other Jewish boys, developed an idealised and romantic view of life with cousins and grandparents. He hungered for *mishpokhe*, the Yiddish word for family, a word that conveys everything about the unconditional love of belonging to a clan.

Meeting his grandmother for the first time was disillusioning. In her photographs, Klara Schiftan was pretty, just like David's mom. But in person, she looked mean. David couldn't imagine anyone further from the image of a sweet and kindly grandmother. Yes, Klara did bring gifts to her grandchildren. But a hug or a kiss? A smile and an affectionate word? Never. On the contrary, she would come from Guatemala City every couple of years, creating tension as soon as her flight touched down. Judith would pick up her mother at LAX, Harry having declined to drive to the airport to delay greeting his mother-in-law.

If Klara's treatment of her grandchildren was cold and distant, her disdain for Harry was even more so. Her air of general disapproval was mostly directed at Harry, whose lackadaisical approach to the clock irritated his German mother-in-law no end.

David was puzzled by his grandmother, a confusion not helped by the fact that she and his mother spoke to each other in German. David could pick up the tone, and even though he wasn't fluent in German, he understood enough to deduce that Klara and Judith were not enjoying pleasant mother and daughter chats. From what he could tell, his grandmother really didn't want to be around them. It wasn't just what she said. It was how she acted. Klara made it clear that she couldn't wait to get back to Guatemala City, away from California, away from her family.

Waving goodbye without so much as a kiss, David sighed with relief.

It was only later that David learned how cruel and vindictive Klara could be. When her only son Walter died in 1952, leaving two children behind, Klara offered little support to his widow, Ruth. Three years after Walter's death, Ruth met and married a kind-hearted Jewish man who took on her children as his own. Klara reacted by disowning them. A woman who had lost her husband, seventy-six relatives, her home, her business, and who lived thousands of miles away from her only living child, might be expected to embrace every blood relative in the vicinity. But not Klara. Instead, she banished Walter's widow, Ruth, and his daughter and infant son.

'My grandmother called Aunt Ruth a slut and said she betrayed the sacred memory of Walter. But Aunt Ruth had kids to raise. She was a young woman. She got on with her life. My grandmother had Uncle

Walter's tombstone altered to remove the word "husband". There was still "father", there was still "brother", there was still "son", but she had "husband" etched out. Never in my lifetime have I seen anyone hate someone enough to do that.'

For David, whose sense of loyalty was ingrained through family battles and Jewish identity, Klara's actions demonstrated an incomprehensible lack of loyalty. How could she abandon her own grandchildren?

David still clings to the only positive memory he has of Klara, a gift of a handmade leather briefcase she brought to him from Guatemala soon after he started elementary school.

As an adult, he's philosophical about his grandmother. 'Imagine my grandmother losing her husband, her five-storey apartment building, her business, losing everything in the world that she knew and loved. A person would be shattered on multiple levels. What would even the nicest human being be like after going through all that crap? Anyone would be filled with all kinds of hate. And my grandmother really showed it. She hurt a lot of people, even when she didn't mean to. She shut us out and didn't give us our birthright of a grandmother's love. But, that cold, steely-eyed pragmatism got them out of Germany. She probably saved their lives.'

His grandmother's visit to sunny California had reinforced the beliefs that already had shaped David's destiny: anger and hatred can be intermingled with love. And sometimes, it can be hard to understand the difference.

For the boy who drank in the Holocaust as 'mother's milk', hatred and anger, commingled with love and faith, would soon come to define him.

A few miles away, those values also defined another man, the man who would become David's Goliath.

6

'Like Trying to Put Together the Pieces of a Shattered Chandelier'

Yugoslavia wanted Andrija Artuković back. For five years, Tito's government had been tracking its wartime enemy. In 1946, just one year after the war ended, Tito's intelligence branch acted on a rumour that Artuković was living in the United States and sent a request to have him deported. The rumour turned out to be false since Artuković did not actually arrive in California until 1948. But Yugoslavia's Tito, the guerrilla leader who had gone head to head with the Ustasha, was bound to show the world that his communist country was serious about bringing Hitler's puppets to justice.

The stakes were high for Artuković and his family as Yugoslavia began making its formal request for the United States to extradite him. Yugoslavia wanted Artuković to stand trial for war crimes, a term that was so new to the language that newspaper reporters placed quotation marks around the term.

Yugoslavia had built its case around affidavits of Jews and Serbs who described the atrocities they were subjected to under the Ustasha. They told of witnessing bloodthirsty acts that had appalled the Nazis. They detailed the horrors of the Ustasha's camps for children. And they gave names of the women, children and men burned alive, ploughed down or shot by machine guns. Among the documents cited by Yugoslavia were decrees created by Artuković that mirrored the Nazis' own laws to strip Jews of many rights.

Yugoslavia, in requesting that Artuković be tried as a 'war criminal', claimed that he signed the death orders for hundreds of thousands of people, a number that was difficult to calculate but whose estimates ranged as high as 770,000. But despite the accusation that he signed the orders for the deaths of nearly three-quarters of a million people, Artuković felt confident that he would not be sent back to Yugoslavia.

There were two major factors in his favour: Americans' fear of communism and the support of the Catholic Church. Catholic clergy and Croatian émigrés all over the United States considered Artuković a hero for having fought the communists in his fervour to maintain an independent Croatia. In the dying days of the war, when the Allies sided with Marshal Tito and his band of patriots, Artuković and the Nazis were on the losing side. But many Americans viewed the communists as the greater threat to the free world. The atheist philosophy of communists, and their high-profile persecution of many religions, inflamed the fear that fuelled the Red Scare.

Artuković had already begun his narrative as an anti-communist who would be persecuted if returned to Yugoslavia. When he asked to be considered a displaced person, he planted the seed of the narrative with the US government. Even though the United States denied his application, Artuković remained in the country. He continued to live freely in the country, joining the Knights of Columbus, growing his network of support and promoting his message that the godless communists would kill him if the United States sent him back.

Andrija and Ana Artuković had become pillars of their church and developed a close relationship with their parish priest, Reverend Robert Ross. He frequently joined them for lunch, one of the many friends and supporters who welcomed the family as new Americans, calling Andrija 'Andy' as he now preferred. In May 1951, their first American child was born, a daughter they named Ruzica, or Roseann.

For the rest of the summer, the family of six relaxed on the beach. The three older children played in the sun while Ana and Andrija watched over their new baby, looking the picture of a happy and relaxed American family. If the Artuković parents were as relaxed as they seemed, it was for a good reason. They felt secure in the knowledge that their lawyers would successfully fight both deportation and extradition.

But as the summer of 1951 came to an end, Artuković was arrested again. Yugoslavia had been successful in its application to persuade the

United States to issue an extradition warrant. Yugoslavia, perhaps mindful that the United States had yet to extradite a single war criminal, kept its application modest. Far from accusing him of mass murder, the warrant claimed that he was responsible for the deaths of twenty-three people.

'Before God and high heaven, I am not guilty of taking any human lives,' Artuković testified to Judge Pierson Hall. He had been arrested on 29 August and, for the three weeks leading up to the hearing, had languished in Los Angeles County Jail. During that time, his supporters in the Catholic and Croatian communities raised $50,000 for bail, the equivalent of more than half a million dollars today. On the day of the bail hearing, 20 September 1951, 200 supporters packed the courtroom, cheering as the defence team took the unusual step of recommending the amount of bail. The judge accepted the offer.

If the bail ruling offered a hint as to where Judge Hall's sympathies lay, his comments later in the hearing left no doubt. He made it clear that he would consider the extradition request only after determining whether the treaty made between the United States and the Kingdom of Serbia in 1901 was still in effect. This would prove to be a crucial point because the country that was now Yugoslavia didn't exist at the time of the treaty.

Most encouraging of all for Artuković was another comment from Hall that showed he considered the Ustasha not puppets of Hitler, but perhaps even victims:

> I'm impressed by the special circumstances such as the dates of the alleged offenses, 1941 and 1942, at a time when Artuković's country was invaded by the Nazis.
>
> If the terms of this treaty, regardless of whether it is found to be valid, were strictly enforced many countries could demand the extradition of any member of the armed forces of World War II on the grounds that they had committed murders.

Artuković was released on bail the following morning.

The supporters who had fundraised on his behalf were waiting for him at the elevator of the Los Angeles County Jail. When the elevator doors opened, they greeted Artuković with a loud cheer as four men stepped forward to hoist him on their shoulders. The *Los Angeles Times* ran a four-column picture at the top of page two, showing the happy, smiling group that carried Artuković through the Temple Street entrance of the Halls of Justice.

In the meantime, the deportation hearing for the Artuković family began with Hearing Officer George Scallorn presiding. Both Andrija and Ana were dressed neatly and formally, he in a suit and she in a hat. Andrija, 5ft 8in tall with silver hair and a California tan, leaned toward stockiness despite a fitness regime that included weekly handball and daily walks on the beach. Ana, 31, wore little make-up, her hat setting off the dark, wavy hair tucked neatly behind her ears and grazing the nape of her neck. Except for the twenty-one-year age difference between them, they presented as an unremarkable formal-looking European couple.

Most of the day was taken up with Ana's testimony. She spent four hours on the stand, defending her family's right to remain in the United States after entering illegally three years earlier under false names.

The New York Times reported that an aide to Deputy Attorney Gerald Peyton Ford instructed immigration that Artuković 'should not be sent to apparently certain death at the hands of the Yugoslav communists', adding that 'in fact if his only crime was against communists, I think he should be given asylum in the US'.

At the end of the day's proceedings, on 25 October 1951, the deportation hearing was postponed indefinitely. Hearing Officer Scallorn decided he could not deport the family until the extradition hearing was settled.

Support continued to come from people in high places, both directly and indirectly. The anti-communist sensibility of the Cold War, reflected and reinforced on every newsstand, often screamed outrage at Artuković's arrest. Others were more subtle, such as the *Independent*, Pasadena, California, which ran two front-page pictures of the Artuković family, with the caption:

Fears Red Death: Andreja [*sic*] Artukovic, Former cabinet minister of Croatia, terms war criminal charges brought against him here by Tito's governments as a political trick to return him to Yugoslavia for certain death. Artukovic, a resident of South Los Angeles for the past three years, has been hailed as a Croat patriot and ardent foe of communism by the former private secretary of imprisoned Archbishop Stepinac. Artukovic is held without bail in L.A. pending extradition hearing next Monday. He's shown here with daughter Visnja in picture taken in '42 when he was Croat's Secretary of the Interior.

The newspaper didn't point out that the photo, 'taken in '42 when he was Croat's Secretary of the Interior', was also taken at a time when Artuković was a senior member of a government at war with the United States.

If the media turned a blind eye to Artuković's war record, some law-makers actively advocated to protect him. As Judge Hall deliberated over the extradition treaty, the Artuković family took new hope from legislation before the Senate and the House of Representatives.

The record of proceedings for 11 June 1952 illustrates some of the most pressing issues facing the United States. Among the bills discussed were those dealing with federal funding for highways, the emergency powers of the president pertaining to the Korean War and a civil rights bill that would make lynching a federal offence.

One of the key pieces of legislation before the Senate was a new immigration bill that had polarised debate even among the Democrats who presented it. The Immigration and Nationality Act of 1952 was partly intended to keep communists out of the United States. Led by Senator Pat McCarran, a Democrat from Nevada, and Congressman Francis Walter, a Democrat from Pennsylvania, it was based on a fear of communist infiltration. The two Democrats won the day by citing national security concerns that communists and unassimilated immigrants would destroy the American way of life.

Before the vote, Senator McCarran entered an editorial published in the *New York World-Telegram* of 26 May 1952, an excerpt of which reads:

America can still be a haven for aliens capable of becoming first-class citizens, but it no longer can afford to be a dumping ground for those whose main qualifications merely are the desire to escape from where they are. There are too many of those for us to absorb.

If the anti-communist immigration bill gave hope to the Artuković family, they had cause to celebrate another piece of federal legislation introduced the same day.

HR8186 was a private member's bill submitted by Democrat Harry Sheppard, entered into the record as 'A bill for the relief of Andrija Artuković and family; to the Committee on the Judiciary'.

For the Artuković family, the bill could not have brought better tidings. As long as it was before the House, the family could not be deported.

Whether or not it was passed was of no importance. The fact that it existed as part of the record meant that the family was safe in America.

★ ★ ★

Just over a month later, on 14 July 1952, Judge Hall ruled that Andrija Artuković could not be extradited to Yugoslavia. He had accepted the argument put forth by Artuković's lawyer, Edward J. O'Connor, that the 1901 treaty between the United States and Serbia was not valid because Serbia no longer existed. Furthermore, a later treaty made after the First World War between the new Kingdom of Serbs, Croats and Slovenes had never been ratified by the Senate. In Judge Hall's opinion, it was also invalid.

The front page of the *Los Angeles Times* carried a picture of Andrija and Ana smiling into each other's eyes, her loose-fitting coat modestly disguising her pregnancy of seven months.

'I was absolutely confident that I would get real justice in an American court,' Andrija Artuković told reporters. 'I'm sure that all free people in the world will be happy with me. I am innocent of all the charges.'

Yugoslavia's lawyer, Ronald Walker, reacted by saying that Yugoslavia would file an immediate appeal.

The deportation order was also delayed pending the appeal.

Once again, Artuković was safe for several months.

★ ★ ★

And so it went on.

The repeated delays and appeals became a pattern that would last for another seven years.

Artuković's legal team argued each time that their client was innocent. Every time a hearing was scheduled to deport him, another private member's bill was introduced in the House to prevent it, but the Yugoslav government continued its quest, waging a public relations battle in the media and promoting its message in Serbian and Jewish communities.

The FBI followed the action. Dozens of informants and several FBI agents in New York, San Francisco and Los Angeles exchanged information and wrote reports, always carefully referring to Artuković as an 'alleged' war criminal.

In October 1952, Artuković was invited to speak in Chicago. The Yugoslav government appealed to its lawyer, Ronald Walker, demanding that he do something to prevent the speech. Alas, Walker told them, in America Artuković enjoys the right to freedom of speech.

★　★　★

In September 1952, Ana Artuković gave birth to the couple's fifth child, and the second to be born in the United States, a daughter. They named her Nada, signifying hope. But another blow was yet to come. Artuković faced deportation once again on 14 October 1954, when the Supreme Court struck down Judge Hall's extradition decision.

At home in Surfside, Ana was interviewed by the sympathetic local newspaper, the *Long Beach Independent*. 'I just don't know what we'll do now,' Mrs Artuković told the reporter. 'We haven't heard from our attorney in Washington yet. Until his report comes, we can't make any plans.'

The Washington lawyer, Robert Reynolds, was one of three lawyers whose fees were covered by Artuković's rich and powerful supporters. Another was Edward J. O'Connor, who later became a Superior Court judge in Los Angeles, and Vincent Arnerich, a Croatian American.

The legal team played a skilful strategy over the years, keeping the focus away from questions about Artuković's guilt or innocence. They kept testimony revolving around questions of international law and the communist menace. They stressed repeatedly that Yugoslavia's charges were 'politically motivated' and that their client would be killed immediately upon setting foot in Yugoslavia. They maintained that Artuković didn't murder anyone and that the Ustasha were controlled by the Nazis, going so far as to present an argument that Artuković had actually run afoul of the Nazis by helping Jews.

During the extradition hearing, Artuković told reporters outside the courtroom that the German ambassador refused to speak to him after he rescued Jews in the spring of 1942. 'I learned at the last minute that a whole trainload of Jews was to be transported to Germany. On my own responsibility, and at my own risk, I ordered the train stopped. All were sent back.' This claim, that he helped Jews in Croatia, would be repeated over the course of his long legal battle, both by Artuković himself and his supporters.

One of those supporters was Representative James Utt, a conservative Republican from Orange County, who introduced several private members' bills to help keep the Artuković family in the United States. In a long speech to defend his bill in July 1955, Utt started his argument by comparing Artuković with American rebels who overthrew the British.

Criticising the allegations entered into evidence at the latest deportation hearing, Utt objected to the very notion that Artuković was guilty of crimes:

Here, repeatedly stated, is the government's theory in a nutshell. The Croatian administration in the period 1941–45 was bad and wicked; Artuković was an official of the administration; therefore Artuković was bad and wicked. It makes no difference whether he acted properly individually, whether he advocated a course in opposition to the alleged and bad and wicked course of the administration; he was in a barrel with rotten apples, so he too must be a rotten apple.

Utt submitted several letters of support which then became part of the Congressional record.

One of them was from Reverend Robert Ross, Artuković's parish priest and friend who had known him since he first arrived in California. Ross spoke of Artuković's fine character and offered to help secure the testimony of 160 Croatian priests now living in America, who had submitted a memorandum of support:

The majority of these are refugees from Tito's communist Utopia and they are alive because they were able to escape from Yugoslavia. Here are men who knew Artuković and who know the truth. They are willing to testify for Artuković. I hope that the Congress of the United States will give them a chance.

Ross slammed the evidence provided by witnesses from Yugoslavia. 'Can the sworn testimony of communists be believed?' he asked:

I think not, since they profess no belief in God, have no moral code and time after time in their writings have stated that the end justifies the means. Their end is the destruction of our country and the other free countries of the world. Any American is certainly naive if he believes that the brand of Communism that Tito professes is different from Moscow's communism. It is time that we began to protect those, such as Artuković, who have from the beginning fought communism.

★   ★   ★

Despite the Supreme Court's decision, 1954 passed with no deportation. Likewise 1955 and 1956, as the legal wrangling over Artuković's fate continued. In 1957, the case ended up once again before the Supreme Court.

Artuković was making legal history: he was the first person ever accused in an extradition hearing of being both a common criminal and a war criminal. The single criminal charge against Artuković was that of murdering a Serbian priest. But Yugoslavia was also accusing Artuković of being a war criminal: its case included the names of 1,293 people murdered in Croatia's concentration camps.

Yugoslavia's lawyers were mindful of the fact that no war criminal had ever been deported from the United States and that extradition was a rare and last resort, one that presented questions of 'the gravest importance'.

The United States 'has traditionally and invariably shown profound humanitarian concern for the fate of racial and national minorities subjected to exterminatory practices by their oppressors,' wrote the Yugoslavian legal team. 'Never before has an alleged perpetrator of such crimes sought refuge here and become the object of extradition proceedings.'

When the nine Supreme Court justices convened on 6 October 1957 they were facing a mountain of cases. The extradition of Andrija Artuković, now before them for the second time, was only one of 800 cases being appealed. Three of the justices were new to the case, having been appointed since Yugoslavia's first appeal in 1954.

Three months later, on 20 January 1958, the Supreme Court justices voted 7–2 in favour of Yugoslavia. But that vote against Artuković did not seal his fate. The court also ordered that another extradition hearing be held after the State Department argued that 'not all of the acts alleged by the Yugoslav government to have been committed by Artuković are necessarily of a political character'.

The new hearing was set for Los Angeles. Artuković told his local paper that he didn't know what to expect, but he reiterated his belief that extradition would mean certain death. 'After the tremendous effort (Yugoslavia) made in seven years to get me, the idea of a fair trial in a communist country is impossible,' he told Bud Lembke of the *Long Beach Independent Press-Telegram*. 'If they did get me, I would expect the worst. They would have cut me to pieces, as they have done to a few hundred priests.'

The journalist, seemingly conflicted about the images presented by Yugoslavia versus the man who frequently opened his home for an interview with him, wrote: 'Bringing the true picture of the man's innocence or guilt is like trying to put together the pieces of a shattered chandelier.'

Lembke described Artuković as 'ageing, with gray-hair but still vigorous and apparently as sturdy as a block of granite', and a devout Catholic 'firmly convinced that God is on his side'.

The reporter described their three-bedroom bungalow as crowded, with threadbare furniture, noting that the legal bills had run into the thousands, paid for by friends and well-wishers. Neighbours 'ring out with cheery greetings', and a friend had just bought a television set for the family.

Artuković told the reporter that he could no longer expect the kind of life they had enjoyed when he was a lawyer. 'It is impossible for me and my wife to arrange our life the way we want. That is destroyed. But we are grateful our children have their daily bread.'

As for the five children, Lembke wrote this: 'The children, puzzled but nevertheless accustomed by now to the hubbub which is periodically generated around their daddy, are bright-eyed and as Americanized as the kids playing hopscotch in the next block.' The 15-year-old Zorica, the Artukovićs' second daughter, 'won a country-wide essay contest sponsored by the American Legion last year. Her topic: The Four Freedoms.'

Artuković took advantage of the interview to state his innocence once again, claiming that the crimes against him were of a political, rather than criminal, nature: 'My conscience is absolutely clear. I wait. This is a case for every anti-communist in front and behind the Iron Curtain. This persecution could happen to you.'

★ ★ ★

On 15 January 1959, US Commissioner Theodore Hocke ruled there was insufficient evidence of criminality and the charges against Artuković were 'of a political nature'. Artuković had won. He would not be extradited to Yugoslavia.

'I'm very happy at this moment,' he told reporters. 'I feel better and am happier than at any other time in my life. This is not just my case but the case of the Croatian nation and all the Croatian patriots around the world.'

Ana, wearing her trademark hat, rushed to embrace and kiss her husband. 'Our prayers have been answered,' she told reporters. 'We thank God for his blessings.'

The Yugoslavian government said it would not appeal the decision. The battle that had started eight years earlier with his arrest in May 1951 was almost over.

All that remained was the deportation hearing, but Representative James Utt promised to introduce another private member's bill. As long as it was before the House, Artuković could not be deported.

Over the course of Artuković's life in California, his congressmen in both Washington DC and Sacramento introduced eight private members' bills to keep him in the country.

It would take another fifteen years before Artuković would reappear on the public radar. And, like the turbulent 1970s themselves, this time change was in the air.

7

'Things Were Ugly and They Were About to Get a Lot Uglier'

Nine-year-old David Whitelaw was trying his best to keep his family together. Sometimes he thought his heart would break as he felt the pain of both his mother and his father. His parents leaned on him, opening their hearts to him, sharing their pain of the past and fear for the future. But when it came to communicating with each other, both Harry and Judith shut their hearts tight and pulled out the emotional knives.

It was obvious to David that his parents were exhausted, Harry from trying to keep the business afloat, Judith from running the household, coping with Billy's hyperactivity and working alongside Harry in the family business. The couple tried hard to capitalise on the soaring economy. In the free-spending atmosphere of the late 1950s and early 1960s, a favourite luxury was a cruise from California to Hawaii. Harry's company won the contract to supply the garlands of Hawaiian leis presented to travellers as they set sail. Judith took on the tedious but lucrative work of stringing together thousands of artificial flowers, preparing leis to greet the 700 passengers on each voyage.

David was eager to help and was surprised when his father chose him over Stephen to join him at the warehouse east of downtown on Sunset Boulevard. His happiness at being given the grown-up job of unloading inventory was tainted by the reaction of his brothers. The 14-year-old Stephen sneered, making his usual implication that David was a brown-noser, and 4-year-old Billy wailed uncontrollably as David and Harry got ready to leave. The family dynamic revolved around frustration with Billy, adding to the tension between Harry and Judith and casting David even more firmly into the role of mediator.

Billy seemed obsessed with Harry, pestering his father with questions, demanding repeatedly: 'Where are you going? Can I come? Let me come.' Harry, ignored as a child and taught to 'be seen and not heard', could not fathom that his youngest child would not obey when ordered to settle down. The more Billy clung to his leg, begging for attention, the more Harry shut down. David would try to tire Billy out by running around, playing hide and seek, but his efforts were often futile. Billy would race manically around the house, inevitably leading Harry to yell at Judith, accusing her of not being strict enough with Billy. This suggestion rankled Judith to the bone since, in her opinion, Harry's own lack of strictness was at the heart of their family's trouble.

Harry, who refused to engage with Billy and indulged Stephen's every whim, placed her in the position of the 'bad cop'. And when Stephen got lippy with his mother, Harry was more likely to laugh at their eldest son's quick wit as he was to admonish him for not respecting Judith.

David shook his head at almost everything Stephen said or did. First of all, David couldn't imagine talking back to his parents. And secondly, David was disgusted at what Stephen could get away with, especially as he observed Harry ignoring sad little Billy. David secretly, resentfully, thought of Stephen as the 'crown prince'.

Harry and Judith spent lavishly on Stephen's bar mitzvah, one of the first held at Temple Beth Emet's stunning new building. It wasn't long after Stephen's bar mitzvah that the young man, seeming to grow taller and more handsome by the minute, began to show an even darker side of his personality. The witty sarcasm, tempered with charm, that had characterised Stephen's personality gradually disappeared. The funny and easygoing boy became moody and volatile. He had always been an indifferent student, but now he showed no interest in school. He expressed his anger and lack of respect for Judith by staying out late or not coming home at all. Harry and Judith, feeling defeated at their inability to motivate their son, made a decision that strained their finances: they shipped their 15-year-old son to a military academy. Harry thought it would straighten him out. Judith hoped that the imposed structure would teach him discipline. Deep down, though, Judith feared it would make no difference. Stephen seemed to have inherited one of the traits of his father that grated on Judith most of all: a lack of ambition.

Judith feared that her husband's business was staying afloat not *because* of Harry, but *in spite* of him. She constantly nagged him to get up and go to work, admonishing him that while he was relaxing over his morning coffee, his partner was already on the job.

Harry resented her interference and retaliated by going for Judith's emotional jugular: sniping about her cooking. Too much salt. Too sweet. The soup is too thick. Too many vegetables. Not enough vegetables.

David, who loved coming home from school to the smell of his mother's cooking, tried to compensate by demanding seconds of everything. 'Save the carrots for me,' he would say when his mother made chicken soup from scratch. 'Those carrots at the bottom of your soup are the sweetest.'

Her matzoh balls were the fluffiest, floating to the top of the pot.

David's appreciation pleased Judith. 'Thank you, *mein Puppele*,' Judith would say, using the Yiddish words of endearment that translate into 'My sweetie pie'.

David would watch with anticipation when his mother prepared German pastries: 'She would make a filling with dried fruit, currants, ginger and spices, kind of like Christmas fruit cake and she would roll it up like sushi. She would baste it with eggs, using a horsehair brush. And the smell. The smell of that ginger wafting from the oven. It was absolutely intoxicating. She cooked with so much love and all she wanted in return was a smile.'

Smiles, though, were hard to come by. The atmosphere in the Whitelaw home was thick with tension. When his parents fought, David would step in, trying to reason with them to diffuse their anger. His parents developed the habit of complaining about each other to David, an emotionally draining experience that left David feeling like the only adult in the family. David became hyper-sensitive to their moods and focused his energy on placating them. 'I became a counsellor to the adults in my life. Trying to explain my mother to my father and him to her. In that respect, I never had a childhood.'

Over the next year, family life became increasingly fraught. David, caught between bad boy Stephen and hyperactive Billy, retreated into his own world. He began collecting stamps, foreign money and coins, fantasising about sailing the ocean for adventures in a faraway world.

'The ocean was a window into learning about other countries. I learned about the economies of countries around the world by studying stamps. Agriculture, manufacturing, all the icons of a country's economy are illustrated on its stamps. Its heroes and monuments teach you about its politics, sports and culture. The animals and wildlife, about the natural environment. My lifelong desire for learning started with the world I found in stamp collecting. And for a kid whose parents were too preoccupied with their own problems, it was my way of escaping. Of not causing any trouble.'

In 1965, the Whitelaws' family life in Buena Park imploded. Harry's business partner cheated him, and their business failed. It was the final straw for Judith, who had worked so hard to help Harry succeed. She sued Harry for divorce, citing irreconcilable differences.

David, at the age of 10, had a hard time grasping the meaning of divorce. He knew of no one else whose parents did not live together. But with his sense of responsibility to keep the peace, he felt like a failure. David blamed himself.

His parents did not sit the children down and hold a family meeting to explain how family life was changing. One day, Judith simply told the boys that their father wouldn't be living with them any longer.

Five-year-old Billy, who adored his father's company, was devastated. The hyperactivity that had kept Judith chasing after him from the minute he could walk turned into angry outbursts. He was already a misfit at kindergarten, creating so much disruption that his teacher sent him home.

At 15, Stephen was feeling alienated from the family. Judith's obsession with the Holocaust had always irritated him, and he couldn't forgive his mother for the insults she hurled at Harry, especially in the last days of their marriage.

David, who sensed that his father considered him 'Judith's protégé', felt a burden of responsibility toward his mother and Billy. 'I felt dirty, unclean and soiled,' he says now. 'I know all of those words mean the same thing, but it's the only way I can describe the stigma and sense of isolation. Why did everyone have a daddy to play with? Why was everyone else's mommy comfortable when mine was so upset and struggling?'

David might have felt that his family was alone, but in fact, the divorce rate was rising steadily across the country, part of a changing social landscape. The contraceptive pill, the rise of feminism, civil rights and the Vietnam War were transforming attitudes about nuclear family life and America itself. Too young himself to participate in the counterculture even if he wanted to, he watched his brother Stephen gravitate to drugs and rebel against authority.

David knew that 'things at home were ugly. And they were about to get a lot uglier.'

Harry filed for bankruptcy. The court ordered him to pay $12.50 a week in child support for each of their three children. He was not required to pay alimony to Judith. With no means of supporting his family, it was with considerable bitterness that Harry found himself signing up again for the Merchant Marine. He was almost 50 years old.

But yet, the sea had always served him well. Calm or raging, the sea matched Harry's own personality, unpredictable in both its force and volatility. At sea, Harry was in his element, certain of the rules of conduct. Harry understood what was expected of him and what he could expect of others. The sea provided a security that was a far cry from the bewildering pressures of home life with Judith and their three boys.

David imagined his father travelling to far-off places. Was his father trying to escape from them? Seared into his memory was a fight between his parents when Judith had begged Harry to take the boys on an outing. Harry had refused, and the yelling escalated. The last words David remembered were his father's, thrown at Judith with such bitterness. 'Why should I do anything with them?' Harry had spat. 'My father never did anything with me.'

Even then, before his tenth birthday, David intuited that his father was still hurting from the emotional wounds of his own childhood.

David clung to a gift Harry had spontaneously given him a couple of years earlier. It was a toy replica of the *Santa Maria*, the largest of the three ships sailed by Christopher Columbus. 'We were in my dad's shop and, as usual, he had a big stogie hanging out of his mouth. I was perched on a stool, watching him unpack a shipment of trinkets from Japan. The boat was one of the items in the box. It was beautiful. It had three sails, the biggest one with a cross on it. And a couple of cannons. My dad saw me looking at it. He just picked it up and handed it to me. "This is for you," he said.'

The prized possession of his childhood still warms David's heart sixty years later. 'It's my Rosebud,' he says earnestly. 'You know the symbol of innocence and childhood that Orson Welles mentions on his deathbed in the movie *Citizen Kane*? In the movie, Rosebud refers to the sled that brought Kane so much joy before his life was torn asunder by being taken from his mother. The boat represents a time of innocence, of childhood hopes and dreams. It connected me to my dad. And it still does. And the other thing about the boat is that it represents the sea. I loved that my mom and her family escaped Germany on a boat. To me, the boat was their saviour. The ocean was their saviour. It was nice to know that a boat saved them.'

The *Santa Maria* was an apt metaphor for the forces that would shape David's destiny. Just as Columbus believed that God had directly brought about his journey, David's fate was being shaped by his faith, his identity as a Jew.

The voyage that led Columbus's ships to forever alter the destiny of people in the New World was rooted in its captain's spiritual quest. David, fed on the Holocaust as 'mother's milk', was led on a spiritual quest pre-determined by the religious hatred that forced his mother's family to sail from Europe.

The replica of the toy boat on the bookshelf in his bedroom would come to represent the tides of change washing over his family. And like the seas that had sunk the *Santa Maria* itself nearly 500 years earlier, the waters awaiting the Whitelaw family would prove rough.

★ ★ ★

The court gave Harry visiting rights, but Harry didn't establish a new home nearby. Bankrupt, he was able to avoid paying rent by living and working on a ship. In Buena Park, Judith tried valiantly to keep the family intact and functioning.

David took solace in listening to the music on his pocket transistor radio. The Beatles were a sensation with a string of hits, as were The Beach Boys, Herman's Hermits and The Byrds. They all sang about love, which seemed to be the topic on everyone's minds in 1965, including David's.

But despite the comforting messages coming through his radio, David's premonition that his home life would get uglier came true. As a single mom with no income of her own, Judith couldn't make the mortgage payments on the house, and eventually, the sheriff came knocking on the door with an eviction notice. Judith was forced to move her family into a cramped two-bedroom apartment in the Mid-Wilshire neighbourhood of Los Angeles.

Desperate, and worried that the family's toxic environment would damage David, Judith called on the only family she had in the United States. Her cousin, Hazel Miller, was the product of divorce herself. Hazel (known by her nickname, 'Herty') had been 10 years old when her parents divorced, the same age as David. She knew what he was going through and it seemed obvious that David would be better off in a stable family like her own. 'Send David to me,' she insisted. 'We'll look after him.'

Judith was reluctant. For one thing, she relied on David as her own ballast. And for another, she couldn't imagine being separated from her adorable son, the boy who seemed forged from her own heart and soul.

Herty loved Judith like a sister and considered her one, even though they were first cousins. Judith's mother, Klara, helped raise her after her parents' divorce. She reminded Judith of how they had thrown her a lifeline when she was drowning in sorrow all those years ago. Hearing Judith's anguish over the phone, Herty threw the lifeline back.

Judith took it, her heart breaking at the idea of not seeing David's sunny smile every day.

Herty lived in Brooklyn. And so it was that in the winter of 1966, David found himself in a new outfit of plaid trousers, a bow tie and a heavy winter coat, boarding a flight to JFK airport in New York to live with relatives he had never met.

David had always dreamed of becoming an astronaut, and as he sat in the window seat of the Trans World Airlines Boeing 707, watching the clouds below, he felt like he was already on his way. The glamorous stewardesses in their smart blue skirts and jackets and peaked hats fussed over David, their unaccompanied minor on the eight-hour flight.

As the flight descended into JFK airport, David stared out the window, watching in awe as Manhattan's skyscrapers came into view. For a kid from Los Angeles, with its cluster of tall buildings hemmed in by mountains and sprawling for endless miles, the tight density of Manhattan was a sight to behold, and David's trepidation about leaving his family behind was momentarily alleviated.

Family. *Mishpokhe* in Yiddish. Family was the word that sprang to his mind as the TWA airport employee escorted David to the baggage carousel.

He could almost feel cradled by the warm welcome as he approached the three people waiting for him. They were easy to spot, holding up a 'Welcome Cousin David' sign and jumping with excitement.

Herty was pretty like his mother, with the same dancing brown eyes, but she did not possess his mother's Germanic reserve. She grabbed him in a tight hug, smothered him in hugs and kisses, and urged her two children to do the same. Debbie, age 9, and Gary, 8, were ready to embrace David as an older brother. It was all a bit overwhelming to a boy who was used to being left to his own devices.

His nose pressed to the glass on the drive from JFK airport along the Belt Parkway through Queens and across the whole of Coney Island, David's face grew longer with the sight of each block passing by from the car window. The magnificent New York skyline that had enthralled him on the plane did not mesh with the freezing temperatures and grey slush on the ground. His eyes, accustomed to the placid, lush yards of Buena Park and Los Angeles, took in the blocks of high-rise apartments of bleak housing projects. Whereas Buena Park's tree-lined streets were quiet and peaceful, Brooklyn was teeming with people. Some of them were huddled around fires lit in rubbish bins, trying to keep warm. There were women dressed in tawdry clothes standing on the street corners. David asked what they were doing and Debbie's reply, 'They're hookers,' was not helpful since he had no idea what that word meant.

Unlike Buena Park, where almost everyone was white, Coney Island seemed to be full of African Americans. David assumed he was in Harlem, a place he'd seen on TV news for its crime and civil unrest.

As they crept along Surf Avenue, David's eyes were riveted upon the chickens hanging by their necks in the butcher shop windows and by the signage in Yiddish, which he could read, thanks to his weekend studies at Hebrew school.

Arriving at the Miller home, David was surprised to see houses so close together with small yards and steps to climb to the front door. His bedroom was not a bedroom at all, but a curtained-off niche in an alcove barely large enough to accommodate his single bed.

Culture shock didn't even begin to describe it.

★ ★ ★

Herty Miller was defined by two characteristics: talking non-stop and wildly expressing affection for her family. David had never heard the term 'unconditional love', but when he did, he recognised Herty as the embodiment of it. Unconditional love. Love, period. That was Herty.

She doted on her two children and now, David. But Herty's most effusive adoration was for her husband, Clarence. Clarence was disabled, having been stricken with polio on his fourth birthday, forcing him into hospital for much of his childhood. He had learned to read with the help of nurses who held books up to his eyes. Now he held a PhD from New York University and was on his way to earning a second.

It was this image of Clarence, his head bent over his books, that first greeted David when he arrived at the Miller home in Brooklyn. So struck was David by this reverence for books that he barely took notice of his disability. David gravitated immediately to Clarence's library, with piles of books covering every surface. The books threatened to topple over if David made a wrong move. He would navigate carefully, sliding sideways between the stacks of books on the floor.

David was inspired by both Clarence's genius and determination to reach his goal of becoming an academic philosopher and teacher. Clarence's main source of income was writing *True Detective* novels, which he would research by interviewing detectives involved in often grisly cases. Clarence wrote his popular paperbacks hunched over a desk strewn with papers describing case materials and crime scene photographs that had been furnished by cops eager to share stories that would pique public interest.

The children, especially Debbie, were embarrassed by their mother's extravagant worship of their father. Herty, whether in the privacy of the family home or in public, thought nothing of covering her husband's face with kisses, declaring that he had the most beautiful eyes.

David, whose favourite song was 'I Can't Stop Loving You', had never seen, or felt, anything like the devotion between Clarence and Herty. All those love songs on his transistor radio came to life as he watched Herty and Clarence touch, kiss and smile lovingly at each other. Debbie and Gary might be embarrassed, but David was secretly envious. What he wouldn't give to watch his parents fawn over each other.

Herty's expression of love was the opposite of Judith's implied, dutiful love. 'My mother showed love by cooking for us, buying us nice clothes and dedicating herself to our home life and being involved with our schooling. She would also tell us she loved us. But she was very proper, very Germanic,' recalled David. 'Herty was reckless with her love, and I mean that affectionately. She had a loving and giving heart. She gave completely of herself with absolute selflessness. Herty didn't have much, but what little she had, she gave from the heart. She loved taking care of me. We were *mishpokhe*, family.'

Debbie and Gary could see that David was down in the mouth, and, unable to grasp the depth of his culture shock, assumed he was missing his family. Nonetheless, they were impressed at how David immediately switched his focus to figuring how to navigate his new circumstances. 'He adapted incredibly quickly,' Debbie says. 'It seems like he adjusted and made new friends in just a couple of days.'

Herty made sure that David stayed connected with Judith with frequent phone calls, back at a time when long-distance calls were a rare luxury. 'She'd call up my mother and say, "Judy, do you want me to put David on?" And my mother would say, "No, no, Herty, that'll cost too much money." And Herty would go, "Nah, don't worry about it." After a couple of minutes, my mom wanted to get off the phone. She was concerned about how much it would cost.'

The Millers strove to make ends meet. To supplement Clarence's income, Herty and Clarence also took in boarders and the cluster of strange people was another discombobulating feature of the Miller household that made 10-year-old David feel like he'd landed in an alien universe.

The Millers' boarders were patients who had been released from Brooklyn State Mental Hospital in Staten Island. They had ended up with the Millers at the suggestion of the hospital's doctors who felt that Clarence and Herty, with their empathy for disabled people and their challenges, would help the patients adjust after years of institutionalisation. At the time, laws were changing to make it harder to involuntarily commit people with mental illness. The patients referred to Herty and Clarence could not be sent home and several of them stayed with the Millers for years, becoming part of their family.

David was fascinated by a middle-aged, heavyset woman named Theresa and a young man named Saul, affectionately nicknamed 'Shloimele' by Herty. Another boarder, Lenny, was in his thirties and adjusting to life outside Brooklyn State Mental Hospital where he had been placed at the age of 17. Although their presence in the house seemed weird to David at first, he quickly picked up the family's attitude of acceptance and would join the group every evening in the living room.

Everyone crowded into chairs arranged in a circle, set up by the ebullient Herty to encourage dancing. Her selection of record albums reflected her taste in big band music, and she would kick off the evening by grabbing one of the boarders by the hand and doing the swing.

The whole family loved rock and roll, and David remembers 'Mack the Knife' as one of Herty's favourites. David's own choice of music simultaneously made him homesick and soothed him. He would tune his little Japanese Crown Electronics transistor radio and wait for the disc jockey to play his three favourites that contrasted the easy life of sunny California with gritty New York. 'California Dreamin'', the new hit by the Mamas and the Papas, with the poignant image of 'all the leaves are brown and the sky is gray', spoke to his soul. Likewise, the lack of sunlight and cold summer that Brian Hyland sang about in 'Sealed with a Kiss' to describe a boy's loneliness during a temporary separation from his true love. David, yearning for the Pacific Ocean, felt the writers of 'New York's a Lonely Town' could see into his soul when they sang about 'the only surfer boy around' who 'feels so out of it walking down Broadway'.

Yes, David was homesick. But part of him was relieved to be away from the emotional chaos. He had entered a whole new world. It seemed he had stumbled into the 1960s aspirations of equality, empathy, peace and love simply by being in the Miller household. Herty and Clarence were teaching him, by living example, how to empathise with people who were different, how to communicate with them, and how to navigate a world far more diverse than Buena Park. David absorbed their lessons, not knowing that their teaching would one day give him the tools to set his own course in life.

David didn't quite understand the full story behind Herty's and Judith's closeness or their fluency in Spanish and German. He knew that Herty had lived with Klara and Judith during her teens when Judith, who was seven years older, was a young woman. But what he didn't fully understand was that Judith and Herty had formed a deep bond that went beyond blood, a bond of their shared loss. The loss that was the legacy of the Holocaust.

Through a cruel quirk of fate, Guatemalan-born Herty had become a Holocaust survivor. A couple of years before the war broke out, Herty's father had divorced her mother. The break-up was sufficiently acrimonious that Herty's mother fled Guatemala for her native Berlin at a time when many Jews were thinking about leaving Germany. Herty's mother wanted to be with her parents, wanted Herty to know her grandparents and to feel their love. To know *mishpokhe*.

One day in 1939, the Nazis came to their home. Herty's grandparents were taken and never seen again. A few days later, the Nazis came for Herty and her mother. Herty's mother agreed to go with them but refused to let them take Herty because she was a Guatemalan citizen. The Nazis paid attention; the Guatemalan consulate got involved and rescued Herty. She spent the rest of the war at a boarding school in Switzerland, wondering if she'd ever see her mother again.

When David arrived at her home in 1966, Herty was still asking that question. In the twenty-one years since the Holocaust ended, Herty had searched countless records looking for her mother. The Nazis had kept excellent records detailing their atrocities, including times and places of interrogation, deportation, property confiscation and death camp reports. And while many Jews had pieced together the last days of their lost relatives, Herty had not. She could find no trace of her mother. Yet she had not given up hope.

Herty talked incessantly about the Holocaust, always clinging to the belief that her mother was alive. Sometimes, she would fantasise that a kind and handsome Nazi soldier had fallen helplessly in love with her mother. In this fantasy, he risked his life to rescue his beautiful Jewish lover and was so devoted that he was willing to spend the rest of his life in hiding with her. Herty imagined that her mother was alive somewhere in Europe, pining for her.

But one story that Herty would not discuss was her memories of Kristallnacht, the pogrom imprinted on Judith's mind as the night her mother decided to flee Germany. Herty's own experience might have been too painful to discuss, or perhaps she had wiped it from her memory. But the story that her family told was that Herty had been burned by the flames when the Nazis set fire to her grandparents' restaurant, Cafe Tranon. Herty's legs, now prone to swelling, remained scarred from the burns. Her grandparents had been beaten that night in 1938 and Herty carried the emotional scars of witnessing their humiliation. She was 11 at the time, close to the age David was.

David, feeling the love that Herty poured into him and the rest of her family, felt her pain. She was another living example, like his mother and grandmother, of the trauma wrought by the Holocaust.

It was beginning to dawn on David that the emotional damage wasn't just shared by the survivors. The wound had spread to the next generation, to Stephen and Billy, lashing out even as they were looking for love. And to himself, too, always accepting and adapting, keeping his head down, avoiding trouble. Even Debbie and Gary, bathed in a constant shower of unconditional love, were on the receiving end of Herty's need to protect them, to inoculate them against hatred.

For David, the images of those starving children licking the empty bowls in the concentration camps came into sharp focus. It seemed to him that the children of those children were destined to suffer, too. He began to grasp what his family had suffered. Their survival was impressive, to say the least. He marvelled at their spirit, their determination to raise their families, carrying on the old traditions.

Herty's cooking, using the same recipes as Judith, reinforced the sense of history. Her oxtail soup rivalled Judith's own, and David was simultaneously homesick and comforted by the luxurious aroma that filled the house. Herty, like Judith, simmered the meat on the bone for hours in a big pot until it thickened into a dark, buttery broth. And, as at home in Buena Park, David demanded the carrots that cooked in the stock, absorbing its intense flavour. Food was *mishpokhe*, too.

David ate it all up, the food, the harrowing story of survival, the injustice of what had been stolen from them. What little was left of their family grew more precious to him because so much had been lost. It had a profound impact on adolescent David, one that would take hold in his psyche and shape his actions in just a few short years to come.

Around the table, social justice was served up as a topic of discussion. New York City had become one of the most influential in the civil rights movement, and Clarence and Herty were activists on the front lines.

The civil rights movement had been building momentum in the decade since Rosa Parks refused to give up her seat to a white man on a bus in Montgomery, Alabama. The term 'Black Power' entered the lexicon, and in Chicago, Martin Luther King Jr led demonstrations demanding better housing. When walking through white neighbourhoods, demonstrators were attacked by bricks as white people shouted 'White Power'. Feminism escalated with the founding of the National Organization for Women, modelled after the Black civil rights movement. And, as Clarence struggled to find an employer who would look beyond his disability, affirmative action was always on the table. Clarence was at the forefront of fighting for the rights of disabled people. The family was also heavily involved in human rights for all minorities, including African Americans and Latinos.

David, with his homogenous, suburban perspective, was expected to contribute to the conversation. The ideas percolating in his head about the injustice of the Holocaust gelled into a firm belief: people could fight for change. Ordinary people could make a difference. It was a heady experience, and David quickly came to enjoy life in the Miller home.

Stepping outside the house, however, tested him in new and different ways.

Debbie and Gary attended Yeshiva school, receiving daily religious instruction. Judith couldn't afford the fees, so David was sent to PS 288, the public school a block from the Miller house at 2919 W 36 St.

Coney Island was changing. The neighbourhood was still mostly Jewish, with Jews owning all but a handful of the shops and businesses. But Mayor John Lindsay had targeted Coney Island as one of the key neighbourhoods for his urban renewal policies. Jewish families were starting to move out, making way for the housing projects and creating resentment among their Latino and African American neighbours. David remembers it this way: 'The Blacks hated the Puerto Ricans. And the Puerto Ricans hated the Blacks. But everyone hated the Jews.'

Debbie and Gary were accustomed to the taunts, punches and occasional muggings that had become part of life in Coney Island. Readily identified as Jews by the school they attended, they were the target of bullies. Debbie and Gary kept their heads down and hoped for the best as they made their way to and from school.

Not David. He was incensed that these bullies picked on them because they were Jews. Here were Clarence and Herty fighting for the rights of African Americans, Puerto Ricans and all other minorities, only to have their family targeted for their religion. David had never met a Black person or a Puerto Rican until now, but no matter what injustices they felt, David felt injustices of his own. Attack his cousins? Fuggedaboutit.

David learned to fight back. Turns out, he could throw a pretty good punch himself. Before long, he was wearing his bloody nose and blackened eyes like badges of honour. When it came to protecting Debbie and Gary, David was willing to take whatever kicks and punches came his way. Welcomed it, in fact. They were his family. *Mishpokhe*.

Under his protection, Debbie and Gary grew more confident. He had taught them to stand up for themselves. David glowed with pride. He no longer saw himself as a kid who tried to make everyone get along.

He was a fighter. Injustice demanded that he fight.

His destiny had been forged.

★　★　★

Every Friday night, as Herty and Debbie lit the Shabbat candles, David felt a deeper connection with his Jewish identity. Attending the synagogue with the Miller family immersed him in a Jewish milieu far richer than Buena Park with its two Jewish families.

Besides the signs in Yiddish and all of the Jewish books and shops, the streets were full of Jews. There were many Holocaust survivors, and David grew accustomed to the numbers tattooed on their arms. The images of the tattoos stayed with him as he made his way home from school, fending off his attackers by throwing punches of his own.

Back inside the safety of Herty and Clarence's home, David lapped up the love they dished out. Herty, so fun-loving and vivacious, was the perfect foil for Clarence with his thoughtful and quiet intellect. David became a sponge for Clarence's genius. Clarence, with his head bowed over a book and his papery white hands crossed, became a role model for David. Clarence was a fighter, too, relentlessly leading the charge for the right to become a full-fledged teacher. His activism led to New York's recognition of human rights for the disabled.

David was in awe of Clarence's mind and his dedication. David, already a favourite of his teachers for his natural curiosity and intelligence, now learned the discipline of applying himself. Clarence taught him how to be studious. 'Clarence was such a gentle man, a beautiful man. He was very patient, which he had to be to be married to Herty because Herty could drive you nuts.'

★ ★ ★

'There's ocean, and then there's ocean,' David thought to himself the first time he visited the Coney Island Pier, in the summer of 1966. Like the rest of New York, the ocean seemed dirty and industrial. David would stick his toe in the water and feel a wash of homesickness for the Pacific surf, for fishing with his dad off Wilmington Pier. But his first summer in Brooklyn was more than trips to the beach and the rides of Coney Island.

It was here that David earned his first dollar. He had stood on the wharf across from Coney Island's amusement park, with the view of the roller coaster directly in front of him, looking at men dropping wire-mesh traps into the water, waiting and pulling out crabs. 'That looks like fun,' David thought. When he learned that the men sold the crabs to local restaurants, David saw an opportunity to make some money for 15-cent comic books like *Sad Sack*, a hilarious depiction of a bumbling soldier in the Second World War.

All he had to do was get the traps and learn the technique. It turned out to be pretty simple: stick a stinky piece of squid in a wire-mesh cage and toss it over the side until it hit the bottom. The sides would drop down, and when a crab entered to eat the bait, David would close the sides and pull it up. It didn't take long before his harvest was large enough to sell to local restaurants. David was elated to be earning his own money and motivated to work longer to boost his pay. In Brooklyn, his work ethic had taken root.

His cousins urged him to join them in having fun at Coney Island. Debbie and Gary gushed over Mary's sandwiches, Nathan's hot dogs and the rides, especially the Cyclone. Never one for the dizzy-making rides at the best of times, David took one look at the Cyclone and thought it a relic whose time had passed, much like litter-ridden Coney Island itself.

He longed for Disneyland with its scrupulously clean grounds, modern, colourful rides and family-friendly atmosphere. And then, there was the Boardwalk. David knew that each time he stepped onto the Boardwalk, he was likely in for a fight. 'There you are with a bloody nose and a black eye, walking along the Boardwalk. You're 11 years old, and you can hear people having sex. Panting. I didn't even know what a condom was, but there they were lying used on the ground. Heroin addicts are shooting up and discarding the needles.'

Later that summer, David had his own first sexual experience. A girl of his own age had been hanging around all summer, mooning over him. Debbie, Gary and the other kids teased her about her crush on David, while David himself tried to ignore her. One day, David was sitting in the kitchen watching the 6-inch black-and-white TV when he saw the screen reflecting the 'shadow of something undulating behind me'. It was the prepubescent 11-year-old girl, stark naked, who now rushed toward him and jumped on his lap, trying to kiss him.

David was mortified. 'I was at the "girls have cooties" stage. I just froze up like a clam. What the heck is going on here?' He pushed her away, reeling from the experience, as she ran crying from the room.

It took David a while to process what had happened. 'It was a loss of innocence. Like Dorothy said in *The Wizard of Oz*, "I've a feeling we're not in Kansas anymore."'

Later, as an adult, David speculated that the girl must have suffered some sexual trauma in her childhood. As a boy, all he understood was that something was wrong. And he was grateful that nothing more happened. Both he and the girl were upset, but they remained friends, never mentioning the incident.

After more than a year in Brooklyn, David had grown and changed in ways that would shape his attitudes for the rest of his life. He had grown confident, even and cocky. His newfound sense of family history had grounded him, cementing a foundational belief that wrongs not only *could* be righted, but *must* be righted. That civil rights were worth fighting for and that standing up for yourself, protecting those you love, sometimes meant fighting back.

In December, Judith called to say she wanted David to come home. By now, dirty old Coney Island and the Miller family had found a place in his heart, and David hated to leave.

Herty's family hated to see him go. 'He was like a brother to us,' says his cousin, Debbie Weiss. 'We wanted to keep him forever.'

Dressing for the trip, David put on the trousers he wore for his first flight. He had grown so much that the hems reached halfway to his knees.

Herty smothered him in kisses and waited until he was out of sight before she stopped waving goodbye at JFK airport.

He felt the transformative intensity of Herty's love. The unconditional love tied up in family bonds. *Mishpokhe* love.

David boarded the TWA flight to Los Angeles.

The route, and the airline, were the same taken by Andrija Artuković eighteen years earlier.

Little did David know that their journeys would be forever intertwined.

8

'I Will Build a Better Tomorrow'

Judith wept at the sight of David disembarking from the TWA flight from New York in trousers that were 5 inches too short. Her boy, still a year away from his bar mitzvah, was becoming a man. David, who had started to feel like the man of the house even before he left for New York, immediately felt the weight of his new responsibility.

He was coming back to a home nothing like the one he had left behind more than a year earlier. The cramped, two-bedroom apartment on 3rd Street in the Mid-Wilshire district was on the top floor of a low-rise apartment building. And as if to drive home the point that the family had come down in the world, their humble lodgings were just a couple of blocks from some of the most spectacular mansions in Los Angeles.

Unlike Buena Park, where almost all the kids were from middle-class, single-family homes, or Coney Island, with its ethnic diversity, Mid-Wilshire skewed rich, with a high percentage of its population composed of Hollywood entertainment industry executives. David would quickly learn that his new schoolmates were much wealthier than he was.

Family life was unrecognisable, especially now that David's perspective had been changed by the purposeful life with Herty and her family.

Judith had a new boyfriend who made her smile, but he proved to be a cheat who would eventually break her heart. Stephen had moved out and was surviving by picking up odd jobs and shacking up with whatever girlfriend would support him. He had big dreams of growing rich that seemed at odds with his fondness for drinking and hanging out at the head shops on Sunset Boulevard.

David, leaning toward pudginess, envied his handsome brother and wondered if he'd ever attract the kind of girls Stephen did. Stephen had grown to 6ft 5in, and it seemed that every girl had a crush on him.

Harry, away at sea with only sporadic visits with David and Billy, began hanging out with Stephen. It seemed to David that they acted like buddies rather than father and son. For his eighteenth birthday, his parents bought Stephen a fancy sports car, a limited edition Dodge Challenger RT. 'The crown prince', thought David, jealous and shocked at the expense. When Stephen wrapped the car around a telephone pole a few months later, David was not surprised. Nor was he surprised at their parents' reaction of forgiveness and grateful prayers that he had not been hurt.

Visits with Harry were rare and painful. Judith would drive her 1960 Buick Invicta to the Wilmington Pier, where Harry waited at the union hall when his ship was in port. Judith, David, and occasionally Billy, would meet Harry for lunch. Inevitably, Harry would bring an exotic present for Judith, such as a piece of cheese or some other delicacy that he'd picked up in Europe. Also, inevitably Judith would 'hit him up for money' to help cover household expenses.

David, with a gift for seeing into the hearts of others, could see his parents' pain. Looking at them, it seemed to David that they still loved each other. He remembered Herty's description of them after she tried to play matchmaker and get Judith and Harry back together after the divorce. 'Those two,' declared Herty. 'They can't live with each other. And can't live without each other.'

At the end of their visit, Harry would return to his ship. Judith and David would return to their small apartment on 3rd Street, each with their own complicated and conflicted feelings about the direction of their family life.

Not for the first time in his life, the phrase 'the sins of the father' crossed David's mind. He wondered if he were to have children of his own, would he be destined to run away as his father and grandfather had done?

★ ★ ★

It was around this time that David learned that Harry's own father had died just a few years earlier. Joseph Aronowitz, who had placed four of his children in a Jewish orphanage in Brooklyn, had lived to age 75. David was incensed that his father had kept secret that they had a grandfather who was still alive while they were growing up, especially considering their loneliness for the family killed in the Holocaust. David couldn't begin to comprehend how Harry could be so selfish and cruel as to deprive his children of a relationship with their grandfather.

Equally painful for David was Billy's heartbreaking reaction to the news that his grandfather had died. 'Do you think he would have loved me?' Billy asked repeatedly. 'Would my grandfather have loved me? Do you think I look like him?'

Since his return from New York, David despaired that Billy's emotional needs seemed impossible to meet. Billy had always been hungry for Harry's attention, but after the divorce he seemed obsessed with his father. 'Billy would write "Harry Whitelaw, Harry Whitelaw, Harry Whitelaw" over and over, trying to copy Dad's signature. I'm sure that he could have forged the signature if he wanted to.'

The hyperactivity that Billy had exhibited as a toddler had led to a diagnosis now known as Attention Deficit Hyperactivity Disorder or ADHD. A doctor prescribed Ritalin, a stimulant to control his impulses.

Looking after Billy became an exhausting full-time job for Judith. With her son's shattered emotional state and constant challenges, Judith felt a need to hover over him. She no longer trusted the school system to handle Billy and started to go to school with him, volunteering and making her presence known, just in case her boy needed her. David was on his own, relying more than ever on the survival tips he picked up in Coney Island.

Their faith became a beacon for Judith and David. Neither Stephen nor Billy expressed any interest in Judaism, but as David approached his bar mitzvah, his identity as a Jew had grown spiritual as well as cultural.

He and his mother worshipped at Temple Israel of Hollywood, a Reform Jewish Synagogue started forty years earlier by entertainment moguls. The synagogue attracted people in the entertainment industry, and its membership included television and film stars, as well as directors, producers and writers. Among its stars was Elizabeth Taylor, who had converted to Judaism at the temple in 1959 following the death of her Jewish husband.

Judith's own connection to Temple Israel of Hollywood was deep and personal. The rabbi, Max Nussbaum, had been a tenant of her mother's apartment building back in Breslau when he was a rabbinical student. Rabbi Nussbaum was famous for having saved the Torah from the flames of Kristallnacht. This Torah was housed at Temple Israel of Hollywood, protected by an embroidered cover which Judith helped create.

Judith seemed to have come to terms with the crisis of faith she suffered in Buena Park, perhaps as a result of her respect for Rabbi Nussbaum, who had introduced more Hebrew and Jewish traditions into the temple's services.

The temple, with its long tradition of bringing in Hollywood entertainers and speakers, provided a stimulating and welcoming atmosphere for Judith and David as their lives evolved in the new neighbourhood. Over the years, the shows they hosted included such entertainers as Lucille Ball, Judy Garland, Sammy Davis Jr and Frank Sinatra. A young Bob Dylan performed at the end of the Vietnam War.

The temple was also a national leader in political and civic discussions and in 1965 hosted Martin Luther King Jr, who preached from its pulpit shortly after he delivered his speech 'How Long, Not Long' on the third Selma to Montgomery march in Alabama.

Rabbi Nussbaum was a fervent Zionist, and under his leadership the temple raised both money and support for Israel. During the social disruption of the 1960s, when Judith's and David's own lives were in upheaval, Rabbi Nussbaum's guidance provided stability and enhanced their conviction to take a political stand.

As David moved into his teens, the transistor radio that helped him cope with the alienation of Brooklyn became his new constant companion. The moment classes ended at John Burroughs Middle School, David would race home, change into his sneakers, grab his radio and go for a walk. He would lose himself in long walks through the neighbourhood, gazing upon the mansions and dreaming that he, too, would someday live in one. 'Walking and listening to my radio was my way of escaping from all of the problems at home. I would listen to talk shows or music and forget about my tortured family life. Stephen's problems, the conflict between my parents, and poor little Billy, so starved for love. I would walk for hours.'

Despite his solitary walks, David was an outgoing boy who quickly made new friends. One was Dave Blocker, the son of Dan Blocker, the actor who played Hoss Cartwright on the hit show *Bonanza*. David and another friend, Michael Tanner, would walk over to Dave Blocker's house after school and hang out, seeing little of their friend's famous father, who worked long hours on the set. Michael Tanner was also part of the Hollywood entertainment scene, having started acting when he was 4 years old. David and Michael had bonded immediately, partly because their mothers were both European and Holocaust survivors. Michael's mother also became friends with Judith, cementing the budding friendship between their sons.

However, the boys and their mothers differed in their approach to how the Holocaust shaped their lives. Michael's mother had told her two sons only that she lost her father and grandparents in Auschwitz's death camp. She and her mother had survived and made it to the United States. In her new life, she wanted to put the experience behind her. She felt that by talking about the Holocaust, she would traumatise her own children.

But Judith was determined to tell David, with his endless curiosity, every detail. David's sense of injustice and zeal for Judaism was paired with idealism and patriotism, a faith in the goodness of the United States.

Passionate about history, especially American history, David devoured written material about George Washington. The distinctive way Washington signed his name inspired David to style his own signature with a flourish. With growing artistic flair, he practised adding loops to the 'W' until he was satisfied that the Whitelaw he signed paid homage to his political hero.

As protests against the Vietnam War escalated, David vowed to serve if ever called upon. He admired the soldiers who were willing to risk their lives to fight communism, just as he admired the Warsaw Ghetto fighters who had put their own lives on the line to fight the Nazis.

David also felt an affinity with the military, a respect for people who defended their country, as his father and maternal grandfather had done.

Part of his grandfather's legacy, now tucked safely away, was the helmet he wore in battle, the leather Pickelhaube with its distinctive spike, and original photographs of him on the battlefield. Kaiser Wilhelm himself had travelled to the battlefield to commend Judith's father, Sigmund Schiftan, and his regiment. Sigmund's Iron Cross was displayed in a glass globe beside framed family photos in the living room.

David would stare at the photograph, full of conflicted emotions. 'Some thanks,' he would think, calculating that just a little more than twenty years after his grandfather was honoured for risking his life for Germany, the same country murdered six million Jews, including seventy-six of his grandfather's own relatives.

But at the same time, he admired his grandfather, posing in his uniform, ramrod straight, tall, slim and handsome with his waxed moustache. What was he like? David wondered. What would it be like to have a grandfather?

★   ★   ★

On 10 August 1968, David stood in front of his Jewish community at Temple Israel of Hollywood for his bar mitzvah, the Hebrew term which means 'son of commandment'. The coming-of-age ritual marked his new rights and obligations as a man.

His bar mitzvah was much more low-key than Stephen's five years earlier in Anaheim. David, with his resentment of his older brother as the 'crown prince', noted that his donations totalled $600, only one-fifth of the $3,000 given to Stephen.

Judith must have had a sense of having come full circle as David addressed Rabbi Max Nussbaum, whom she had met more than thirty years earlier when they were both barely out of their own teens in Germany.

Addressing the assembly of 'Parents, Rabbi Nussbaum, Cantor Silverman, Relatives and Friends', David spoke of *nachamu*, or comfort. Just three weeks after his thirteenth birthday, David declared to the congregation that 'the world of today yearns for comfort'. Sharing his ambition to become a scientist, he expressed a desire to 'promote peace to all corners of the globe and to bring comfort to all mankind'.

David credited the faith with ensuring centuries of Jewish survival, saying, the 'Holocaust, century after century, evil, bloodthirsty leaders and cruel demons have tried to annihilate the existence of the Jew'. He promised that when he became a scientist, 'I will build a better tomorrow.'

'And only by fulfilment of true brotherhood,' he continued, 'can we erase the obstacles that men have imposed upon men. Only if men would cast aside all hatred towards one another will we see the day of peace and contentment.'

Peace and contentment were elusive in 1968, a year noted for American triumph and turmoil, polarised by the Vietnam War. The new year had barely started when North Vietnam broke a tradition of truce during the

Vietnamese Lunar New Year and launched the massive Tet Offensive, catching the US-led forces off guard. After bombing thirty-six villages, the Viet Cong attacked the US Embassy in Saigon.

On 2 February, newspapers around the world carried an Associated Press photo of a South Vietnamese police chief executing a Viet Cong prisoner of war on a street in Saigon. The photo became iconic and, along with the defeat of American troops during the Tet Offensive, led to a turning point in the Vietnam War. Public support began to waver, and protests against the war gained momentum.

On 4 April, Martin Luther King Jr was assassinated, prompting violence and riots across the United States.

In May, more US servicemen were killed in Vietnam than any other month during the war.

Two months later, on 5 June, Senator Robert Kennedy was shot in Los Angeles after giving a victory speech following his win in the California presidential primary. He died the next day.

As 1968 came to a close, David's own dreams for peace were reflected poignantly by the three American astronauts circling the moon in Apollo 8. David watched, along with millions of people around the world, to drink in the words of the first human beings to orbit another world.

The astronauts read from Genesis, explaining later that they chose to read this passage of the Bible because it expressed the aspirations of all faiths.

'The first ten verses of Genesis is the foundation of many of the world's religions, not just the Christian faith,' astronaut Jim Lovell later explained in a NASA interview celebrating the mission's fiftieth anniversary. 'There are more people in other religions than the Christian religion around the world, and so this would be appropriate to that, and so that's how it came to pass.'

William Anders led the astronauts as they took turns reading the passage of scripture:

In the beginning God created the heaven and the earth.

And the earth was without form, and void; and darkness was upon the face of the deep. And the Spirit of God moved upon the face of the waters.

And God said, Let there be light: and there was light.

And God saw the light, that it was good: and God divided the light from the darkness.

Jim Lovell picked it up:

> And God called the light Day, and the darkness he called Night. And the evening and the morning were the first day.
>
> And God said, Let there be a firmament in the midst of the waters, and let it divide the waters from the waters.
>
> And God made the firmament, and divided the waters which were under the firmament from the waters which were above the firmament: and it was so.
>
> And God called the firmament Heaven. And the evening and the morning were the second day.

Frank Borman continued:

> And God said, Let the waters under the heaven be gathered together unto one place, and let the dry land appear: and it was so.
>
> And God called the dry land Earth; and the gathering together of the waters called the Seas: and God saw that it was good.

It was the most-watched television broadcast in history. The astronauts were mindful of the millions of people whose memories would always carry the words, images and feelings associated with seeing humans orbit the moon for the first time. Borman ended their broadcast with the words: 'And from the crew of Apollo 8, we close with good night, good luck, a Merry Christmas, and God bless all of you, all of you on the good earth.'

David, glued to the TV in the living room of their apartment, was moved by the words. 'I was already in religious school, so I related to it. I always wanted to be an astronaut as a child and hearing those words made me feel like I was part of something bigger. It reinforced my idealism about finding what unites us, not divides us.' The 13-year-old David closed his eyes and said a silent prayer. The boy who dreamed of building a better tomorrow asked God to lead him on a path to help heal the people he loved.

As 1968 came to a close, David reflected upon the dramatic changes that he'd already experienced in his own life. It was as if all of his own turbulence mirrored the 1960s, part of a destiny guiding him. He would be part of something bigger.

★ ★ ★

Judith resolved to give David a strong religious education and enrolled him in Hebrew school, where he was taught by Miss Ethel May Ewans. When David was a teenager, he picked up some extra money by running errands for Miss Ewans, helping carry her shopping and unloading her parcels. After the work was done, he would sit with her and discuss Jewish issues, in effect receiving free tutoring to supplement his Hebrew education. David was an eager student. After one of their sessions, Miss Ewans presented him with a gift: her personal copy of Adolf Hitler's *Mein Kampf*. David consumed, and was consumed by, the book Hitler wrote in 1924 while in prison for leading the Nazi Party in a failed coup to overthrow the German government. Hitler had been convicted of high treason, although the judge was lenient in sentencing and the five-year minimum security term of imprisonment ended up only lasting eight months. During that time, Hitler was treated so well that in addition to wearing civilian clothes, he was also allowed to confer with his personal secretary, Rudolf Hess. Hess, who was also serving time for high treason, took dictation from Hitler for the first volume of *Mein Kampf*. The political treatise laying out his plans for Nazism was published the next year. Between 1925 and the end of the war in 1945, the book sold more than twelve million copies. It made Hitler a multi-millionaire, with sales escalating after Hitler became German chancellor in 1933.

David, reading *Mein Kampf* almost fifty years later, felt sick as he read about Hitler's hatred of Jews. The antisemitic, racist ideas presented in the book led to the near destruction of his people. And to the loss of his seventy-six relatives.

It was incomprehensible to him that educated people could follow the rantings of a madman who proclaimed that 'Jews are our bad luck'. The book had a profound impact on the teenage David.

Judith Whitelaw remained a proud German, a pride that baffled David. She listened to German radio programmes, loved German music and subscribed to German newspapers. Judith's dishes, from recipes written in German, were the heart of her kitchen. The songs played on the piano were German songs.

Yet her anger about the Holocaust never abated. Judith began to write newspaper articles sharing her own experience about fleeing Hitler, describing the awful three days of Kristallnacht.

Having absorbed the hateful messages of *Mein Kampf*, David's own desire to fight for Jews had grown even stronger. He shared his mother's militancy. Never forget. Never again.

★ ★ ★

In September 1970, David enrolled at Fairfax High School to begin tenth grade. The iconic school on the border of West Hollywood had won a reputation for holding one of the top academic records in the entire country, with 90 per cent of its graduates progressing to college. Since its opening in 1924, Fairfax had also become famous for turning out graduates who made their mark in Hollywood. Its list of alumni reads like a Who's Who in the entertainment industry and includes Mickey Rooney, Herb Alpert, Timothy Hutton, Larry Gelbart, Warren Zevon and Ted Sobel. Famous authors included James Elroy and Janet Fitch, while one of David's classmates and friends was Kitty Bruce, the daughter of the late comedian Lenny Bruce.

Fairfax was considered a Jewish high school and was located in the heart of the Jewish district of Los Angeles, just three blocks from Canter's Deli and a short walk to Pink's Hot Dogs. At the corner of Fairfax and Melrose was the Fairfax Senior Citizens Center, where many elderly Jewish men and women could be seen walking together or sitting on benches enjoying the sun and and watching the world go by. A good number of them were Holocaust survivors, their stories woven into the fabric of Fairfax in the twenty-five years since the war ended.

David had gotten to know several Holocaust survivors, middle-aged people who had suffered as children in the camps. There was the elderly Mr Pearce, who wandered the neighbourhood looking lost and sad. His wife, who also survived the camps, always appeared cheerful, despite living through the torture that continued to haunt her husband. Another was Mel Mermelstein, who inspired David with his trips back to concentration camps to collect artefacts for his personal museum.

Several of David's classmates and other students at Fairfax were the children of Holocaust survivors. Besides his friend Michael, David became friends with Suzie Berliner, whose Hungarian mother had been in Auschwitz. Suzie and David were both close with a girl named Gayle Freiburg, whose father had fled Europe before the Holocaust. 'We seemed to gravitate toward each other, even though it wasn't something all of them wanted to talk about,' David recalled.

But whether they talked about it or not, David was keenly aware that, as the children of Holocaust survivors, they all shared a common trauma.

For his part, Michael appreciated David's warm, outgoing personality and his generosity. On the downside, David was a bit too political, but Michael was willing to overlook his friend's focus on Jewish causes because he enjoyed his company so much.

David and Michael bonded over their love of music and eventually formed a garage band with two other boys. David used his bar mitzvah money to buy an amplifier. With two guitars, a bass and drums, the aspiring rock stars dubbed their band Central Nervous System and set their sights on performing at the Battle of the Bands at the Teen-age Fair. The fair, held in the car park of the venerable Hollywood Palladium, was a week-long spring break event that was part-carnival, part-marketing and part-education. Mixed in with the ear-splitting rock music blasting from the speakers were games, avant-garde films and sex education. Booths to teach teenagers about sexually transmitted diseases shared the aisles with display tables of the head shops on Sunset Boulevard. A must-purchase item was a black-light poster.

David's band spent hours practising its title song, 'Central Nervous System', with its anti-establishment lyrics. 'It went something like this,' says David, chuckling at the time warp of the words. 'Police brutality! We hate war! All you do is ask for more! Ho Chi Minh hanging on the wall! All you do is let us fall!'

Most days, David rode his bicycle the twenty-five blocks to Fairfax High, although sometimes he would hitchhike, knowing that his mother would freak if she found out.

David loved Fairfax for its Jewish flavour and variety of classes, including driver's education, woodworking and printing. He learned that in addition to his scholastic ability, he had an aptitude for working with his hands.

One of David's favourite classes was history, especially American history. David's teacher, Dr Odell, made an indelible impression upon him with his lesson on the story behind America's Great Seal. David was riveted by the story of Benjamin Franklin in 1776, suggesting the imagery of the dramatic historical scene described in Exodus.

Franklin wanted a seal illustrated with a scene showing Jews confronting a tyrant to gain their freedom. Franklin's seal was never adopted but he described his vision for it:

Moses, standing on the shore and extending his Hand over the Sea, thereby causing the same to overwhelm Pharoah who is sitting in an open Chariot, a Crown on his Head and a Sword in his Hand. Rays from a Pillar of Fire in the Clouds reaching to Moses to express that he acts by Command of the Deity.

But it was the words Benjamin Franklin suggested as the motto that seared into David's memory: 'Rebellion to Tyrants is Obedience to God.'

David stared at the illustration, images of the Holocaust flashing before him. The Warsaw fighters who rebelled against tyranny. The highly educated Germans who did not. The children yanked from their mothers, only to watch them marched off to the gas chambers. The children licking their fingers to wipe up the last bit of gruel from the bowl.

Benjamin Franklin's words would never leave him. Later, they would become as important to him as the motto 'Never Forget. Never Again.'

★ ★ ★

David Whitelaw had just finished his junior year of high school and was approaching his seventeenth birthday when a mundane encounter of his mother's forever changed his destiny.

Judith was dropping off some dry cleaning when she saw a small group of young men sitting and standing around a table they had set up on Fairfax. She was even more intrigued by their sign: 'Jewish Defense League'. She stopped to chat with the group's leader, Irv Rubin, and was drawn in by his quick wit and fierce passion. Rubin, who stood an imposing 6ft 5in, had just finished a four-year stint in the US Air Force, and at the age of 26 had taken over as the West Coast co-ordinator of the Jewish Defense League. The group was militant, and Rubin more so. Their motto, 'Never Again', implored Jews to defend themselves to prevent another Holocaust.

Rubin believed that Jews should arm themselves. He was fond of urging Jews to buy .45 calibre guns. 'Stay alive with a .45', he would deadpan.

Judith had never heard of the Jewish Defense League, but she instantly liked Rubin for his gregarious personality and forthright militancy. And she liked the message of 'Never Again' even more. When she learned that Rubin was recruiting 'soldiers' to fight in the Jewish Defense League, she seized the opportunity for David to sign up.

When Judith gushed to David about the man and the organisation, David was enthusiastic. The idea of emulating the Warsaw Ghetto fighters, to stand up for Jews not just as a big-brother protector as he had been for his cousins in Brooklyn, but as an actual warrior in a group whose sole purpose was to defend Jews. It felt as if the role were tailor-made for him, a destiny he'd been following since he first saw those images of starving children in the concentration camps. Fed on the Holocaust as 'mother's milk', David was primed to serve as the perfect warrior. He wasted no time in heading over to Fairfax to check out the Jewish Defense League.

The office of the Jewish Defense League, or JDL, at 581 S. Fairfax Avenue, wasn't much to look at. The walls were shabby and the furniture sparse, cobbled together as a collection that originated as a few chairs and tables donated from the basements of sympathetic Jews. The posters on the wall showed the clenched fist over a Star of David with the slogan 'Never Again'.

'Never Again' resonated with David. It was the essence of the message that his mother had been reinforcing his entire life.

'Never Again' was the conclusion David himself had reached as he got to know his friends' parents who survived the concentration camps, as he read *Mein Kampf*, as he contemplated the destruction wreaked on his family. Even before he saw the logo with its Star of David and the clenched fist, David had intuited that he was a soldier, fighting a battle instilled by his mother to prevent another Holocaust.

For a battleground, the offices of the JDL were pretty high-spirited. Young men, most of them a little older than David, drifted in and out. Their energy was electric. The JDL leader, Irv Rubin, his brown wavy hair already starting to thin and his moustache scraggly, commanded an audience the moment he opened his mouth. He was one of the most articulate men David had ever met. 'He knew how to frame an issue and define an issue. He knew how to work a room. He was charming. And fearless. I learned that he could take on any opponent with vigour.'

Rubin quickly became a mentor, fleshing out the narrative of injustices against Jews that David picked up from everyone who had influenced his young life. Rubin was not religious. And even though David would have preferred a leader who followed the rules of the Jewish faith, he didn't judge Rubin for his lack of religious fervour. 'If I had to choose between a militant Jew who fought for Jewish rights and one who said all the prayers and let people go to the gas chambers, I'd choose the militant Jew any day.'

The JDL's national leader, Rabbi Meir Kahane, was in the habit of saying, 'Every Jew, a .22', meaning that Jews should pick up a .22 calibre gun, or generally take up arms against those who would hurt them. With Rubin's own twist of 'Stay alive with a .45', he reinforced the JDL message that had Jews fought with armed resistance, there would have been no Holocaust. And if Jews didn't start fighting back, they'd be killed again.

For David, who had grown up idolising the 7,000 Warsaw Ghetto fighters who died resisting the German Army, the message reverberated into his soul. He rushed to fill out an application form.

The questions were standard, no different from the job applications that David was familiar with as he looked for summer jobs. He began to fill it out. One question gave him pause. 'It asked, "Do you know how to use a gun?" I didn't. But I liked the question.'

David, with his straight As and dreams of becoming a doctor, signed up to join an organisation already under surveillance by the FBI as a terrorist organisation.

David's friend Michael Tanner was turned off by David's militant enthusiasm for the JDL. To David, Michael's lack of interest was beyond puzzling, considering that Michael's own mother had survived Hitler's concentration camps, and the two friends grew apart.

David's new circle of JDL friends included a young man he first met at Temple Israel of Hollywood even before his bar mitzvah. Like David, this young man was a student of Ethel May Ewans, who helped their former Hebrew school teacher when she was sick.

His friend, who used a JDL *nom de guerre*, had grown more militant since he moved out of Fairfax and into Chatsworth in the San Fernando Valley. The friend explained that he had been reluctant initially to get involved with the JDL because the group advocated violence, which he abhorred as a law-abiding citizen. His negative feelings had been reinforced by a *Time* magazine article depicting Rubin as a womanising thug.

However, his opinion changed after notorious Los Angeles gangs like the Crips and the Bloods began to prey upon elderly Jews, many of whom were Holocaust survivors. 'These elderly people would walk everywhere, and the gangs would do things like grab their canes and beat them with it,' the JDL member, who asked to remain anonymous, said in an interview. 'Sometimes the gangs would rob them, too. The police wouldn't come, or if they did come, it was forty minutes later, and it was too late to do anything.'

The JDL stepped in, its young men patrolling with baseball bats. 'On Fridays when the shops would close early, these old people would try to get there to buy whatever they needed for the weekend. They'd be walking with their shopping bags, and we'd be there with our baseball bats, protecting them. They'd be so grateful, they'd want to pay us. We wouldn't take anything from them, so they'd reach into their shopping carts and hand us an orange. We wouldn't take their oranges either. We just wanted to protect them.'

The FBI had begun keeping tabs on Meir Kahane and the JDL, concerned that Kahane was building up an arsenal and that the National Rifle Association was training JDL members to shoot.

The FBI was paying close attention to the JDL for two reasons. First of all, the JDL's high-profile protests against the Soviets had reached the highest levels of international diplomacy. Secondly, Meir Kahane was suspected of defrauding the US government by channelling money intended for charity to the JDL.

In a confidential message sent by teletype on 21 January 1971, the FBI ordered its Los Angeles office to interview people who attended the meeting where Kahane offered tax receipts in return for membership fees.

At this point, Kahane had been arrested several times, along with other JDL members, for rioting and resisting arrest. JDL protesters had been harassing Soviet diplomats and their families attached to the United Nations in New York. The JDL threatened to shut down Strategic Arms Limitation Talks (SALT) between the United States and the Soviet Union. President Richard Nixon and his national security adviser, Henry Kissinger, were seeking to reduce the number of strategic offensive missiles each side could deploy. The SALT treaties were a key initiative of the Nixon administration, especially as Nixon opened relations with China, another communist superpower.

By the time David joined the JDL in 1972, the group claimed to have about 15,000 members in the United States and Canada, although the FBI estimated the figure was closer to 8,000. David immediately joined JDL demonstrations to draw attention to the oppression of Jews living in the Soviet Union.

Sometimes David's mother would join the protests, standing shoulder to shoulder with her son in his fight. Discussing the JDL's protests with David and walking side by side with him, Judith could not have been more proud of her son. David had grown into a fine young man, handsome and outgoing with a disarming personality and sense of humour. She loved that he was militant, but his militancy was reserved for Jewish causes – deservedly so – and especially for the plight of Soviet Jews. No one needed fighters standing up for them in the free world more than they did.

One of the JDL's tactics was to disrupt Soviet cultural events and harass people as they tried to enter art galleries or concert halls. When the Russian ballet came to Los Angeles, David was among the dozen protesters chanting in front of the Shrine Auditorium.

He was arrested for disturbing the peace in September 1974, a shocking development for the honours college student. However, the charges were dismissed thanks to Mitchell Egers, a sympathetic lawyer who defended the JDL pro bono.

It was the first, but not the last, time that David would meet Mitch Egers.

★ ★ ★

David's life was forever changed one day when he casually dropped by the JDL office. He heard of a piece of news that turned out to be fateful, one that would alter the course of his own life: 'I heard the name Andrija Artuković for the first time.'

The name was not delivered with any drama, or any hoopla to indicate that this was big news. 'Irv Rubin was talking about the priorities of the JDL, the Russian Jews and Andrija Artuković. I didn't know who that was, so I asked him. He was surprised I'd never heard of him, and said something like, "What? David, you don't know about the Nazi war criminal living in Surfside?" I was reeling at this and Irv went on to explain that this monster, a mass murderer, was living happily and openly with his American-born children in Surfside. I couldn't believe that this guy is practically my neighbour.'

And then, Rubin delivered an even more shocking piece of news. He told David that the US government was fully aware of this man, known as the 'Himmler of Croatia' and the 'Butcher of the Balkans' for signing the death warrants for 770,000 people. Furthermore, the State Department was protecting him.

David, with his 'my country 'tis of thee' ethos of patriotism, couldn't wrap his head around the idea that his government would not exert the full force of the law to bring this war criminal to justice.

Judith, a proud American who flew a gigantic flag in front of her house, was horrified to hear of Artuković. The fact that he had sneaked into America under a false passport fifteen months after Judith herself had immigrated through proper channels incensed her further. That this mass murderer lived 10 miles away, raising his family just as she began to raise hers, was an affront that Judith could not countenance.

Talking with his mother about Artuković, David struggled to process the fact that this war criminal was free. Determination solidified in his gut. He would fight to get this monster out of the United States.

Never again.

★ ★ ★

Even though the JDL had set its sights on Andrija Artuković, it was impossible to actually get near him. Artuković lived in a gated community, protected by a security guard at a gatehouse and dozens of friendly neighbours. The best the JDL's young band of demonstrators could do was make a nuisance of themselves by crowding around the public area near the guardhouse.

At first, David was gung-ho. He summoned all of his Brooklyn in-your-face aggression and yelled, 'How do you like living beside a war criminal?' to neighbours entering or leaving the community.

Carrying signs that said 'Himmler of Croatia' and 'Butcher of the Balkans', they would shout slogans and yell at the neighbours. Inevitably, the gatehouse guards threatened to call the police if the protesters stepped onto private property. David and the others paid attention, careful not to cross the line. Their goal was to draw attention to Artuković's presence. If the neighbours couldn't find it in themselves to turn against the man who had lived among them for almost thirty years, perhaps the media would sit up and take notice.

The problem was that no one seemed to care. A known war criminal was living in their midst; David couldn't understand how no one was disturbed. Was it because the Vietnam War consumed the public's attention? Had they forgotten the Holocaust? The Second World War? It was barely thirty years ago. Or was it that there were so many causes, so many protests, so much hatred, that people tried to tune it out?

Whatever the reasons, David concluded that the demonstrations were nothing more than an exercise in frustration. Never once had they caught a glimpse of either Artuković or any of his family.

With his scientific bent, David began collecting his own data. He needed more information. If what Irv Rubin said was true, Artuković was more sadistic than the Nazis.

He sat down at the table in his mother's breakfast room and composed a handwritten letter to the Yugoslav consulate in San Francisco, asking for information about Yugoslavia's case to have Artuković extradited.

The reply was quick. It was explosive. The thick brown envelope that arrived in the mail contained documents that detailed Artuković's role as a mastermind of the genocide. It included 526 pages that listed the names of people who were killed, their ages, their villages and the circumstances of their murder.

As he read about their deaths, their lives rose from the page like photographic images emerging in the red light of a darkroom. Innocent people, infants, children, parents, grandparents.

Sickened, David read their stories:

Carrying out the order given by the accused, Artuković, in June, 1941, Kresco Togonal and his group killed in the Golubnjaea ditch: Rade Kosovic, Gligo, Kosutic and Rade Govedarica, peasants from the Miholjaea village, they killed 19 persons, I.E. members of three families in such a way that they were all locked up in a house which they have set on fire so that the following persons were incinerated alive: Mitar Govedarica, his wife Petra, their son Into, 12 years of age, their daughters Boba, 18, and Andja, 16 years of age and two more small children, as well as Petar Govedarica's mother, Vule Bijelogrlie, his wife and their seven children: Nada, 20, Petra, 17, Zarko, 14 years of age and four more small children, Jovo Govedarica and his 18-year-old daughter.

David's torment about his seventy-six relatives who died in the Holocaust took on a new dimension of sorrow. In choked desolation, he read about the children. New images of starving children piled on top of those already haunting him:

> Further, about 2,000 children whose identity could not be established and who were killed in August 1942, with poisoned gas (Zyclon B) in the concentration camp at Stara Grndiska and more than 13,600 children whose identity could not be established and who were detained in the concentration camps [...] These children were killed by starvation, mixing caustic soda in their food and by various infectious diseases.

David put the file down, tears brimming in his eyes. 'They poured caustic soda into children's mouths? What kind of monster was this guy?' And the next question: 'How can my country allow him to live here? To live anywhere? How can he be allowed to live?'

He thought of himself as a lightning rod. 'When you're literally breast-fed the Holocaust as part of your diet, there's a festering wound that doesn't heal. I saw both the macro, the injustice against my people, and the micro, the vacuum in my own family and how the Holocaust had damaged us. The way I was starting to see it was that seeking vengeance would be doing God's work.'

On a personal level, David needed to look no further than the photo of relatives in Germany, posing happily at a family celebration. Cousins, aunts and uncles, and their future offspring, wiped out, never given a chance to celebrate holidays with Judith and her family.

'For the holidays, the best we could hope for was the four of us sitting at the dinner table. If Stephen was drunk and didn't show up, it would just be my mom, Billy and me. And if Billy was in a bad mood, it would just be my mom and me. The Nazis robbed us of the family that was our birthright.'

David surmised that the sincere demonstrations of the JDL were too sporadic and haphazard to deliver Artuković to justice. A more strategic approach was called for, a concerted effort to target the right people.

David devised his own campaign. Undaunted by the David-and-Goliath proportions of the battle, he was confident that a nice Jewish boy could persuade the US government to do what no one else could: kick Artuković back to Yugoslavia to stand trial. David had no choice. He just had to make it happen. Regardless of the consequences, David was compelled to shine a light on the fact that the worst war criminal in America, the worst mass murderer in America, was not only living in his country but was being sheltered by his country.

David felt compelled by destiny, and by God, to force America to extradite Artuković. This monster must be forced to stand trial for the murder of 770,000 people. For the babies, mothers, fathers, and grandparents whose lives now lived as images in David's mind.

★ ★ ★

By the time David graduated from Fairfax High in 1973, his fierce resolve to attain justice had evolved into a mission. By day, he commuted two hours to a factory that manufactured brass door knockers, knobs and handles. The job was hard, but he took comfort in the fact that it had a connection to the Holocaust. He was working for Herbert and Mary Wilzig, a kind couple who had survived Hitler's concentration camps.

After arriving home at night, David's passion delivered the energy to toil on the endeavour that had turned into a second full-time job: a letter-writing campaign to spark action on Artuković by his government.

Every night, he would set up his mother's portable electric Smith Corona typewriter and apply himself to the undertaking. It never occurred to him to photocopy and send a form letter. He personalised each one, looking for the angle that would most resonate with the reader. Always, he included information about himself. 'I'm 18 years old. My mother is German. She is Jewish. She escaped Hitler's camps. Seventy-six of her people were murdered.'

The body of the letter always included the pertinent details to make his case for bringing Andrija Artuković to justice, the same case that Yugoslavia had been presenting for almost thirty years.

'Dear Secretary Kissinger,' he began, confident that his plea would be heard by the Secretary of State who fled Nazi Germany in 1938 as a Jewish refugee, exactly at the same time his own mother did.

'Dear President Nixon ...'

'Dear Governor Brown ...'

'Dear State of Israel ...'

'Dear *Jerusalem Post* ...'

'Dear Jewish Federation of Rabbis ...'

'Dear Director of the FBI ...'

'Dear Director of the CIA ...'

'Dear Director of Immigration and Naturalization Service ...'

David knew that some of the people reading his letters would already be familiar with the case. To them, he wanted to prove himself enough of a pain in the neck that they'd finally take some action. And even though many journalists had devoted a lot of ink to Artuković, it seemed to David that John Q. Public was not aware of the mass murderer living within California, just as he himself had been oblivious.

It was the masses that David wanted to reach, to wake up ordinary Americans who would see beyond the Red Scare. He hoped to reach them through civil activists' organisations.

Sometimes, his mother would join him in writing letters. Judith was a much better typist, and the two of them would sit at her table, typing and writing, knowing that time was running out.

One of the politicians did send a reply, thanking him in a note that sounded sincere. Her name was Elizabeth Holtzman, who, at 31, was the youngest woman ever elected to the House of Representatives. Holtzman, the daughter of Russian Jews, had grown up in Brooklyn. When she ran for the Democratic nomination in 1972, she was a long shot, short on campaign money but long on grassroots support. Her highly energetic campaign contrasted sharply with that of her opponent, 84-year-old Emanuel Celler, who was confident of re-election after representing Brooklyn for fifty years. As a young lawyer, Representative Holtzman was assigned to the powerful Judiciary Committee. She learned from a

Justice Department bureaucrat that the United States was harbouring Nazi war criminals. She was surprised and curious.

Her letter to David lifted his spirits. Perhaps, finally, something would be done.

9

'The Uncrowned Leader of the Croatian Movement'

For the first time since he slipped illegally into the United States twenty-six years earlier, Andrija Artuković was beginning to feel like a prisoner in his own home. The family had integrated well into American society and, despite the years of legal battles, they had always felt safe in their little house on the beach.

Long gone were the days when Ana fretted that her children would be harassed at school. The worst that ever happened, Ana told a friendly reporter, was that 'they would hear things'.

Their children had been safely launched into adulthood; the youngest was now 23. The children had thrived in spite of living under the threat of deportation themselves or the danger of losing their father. At one point, when deportation seemed imminent, the family's lawyers made a plea that their American-born children would be left in economic hardship.

The Artuković children had achieved some distinction. Daughter Visnja was a promising actress and producer, receiving positive reviews for directing a theatrical production of *Beauty and the Beast* in Long Beach.

While raising his children, Artuković had maintained a high profile. In fact, his cause had won him considerable support as a fighter against communism, and in some circles, he was considered a celebrity. He was highly sought after as a speaker and travelled within the United States to address like-minded audiences. In a speech to 300 members of the Catholic Maritime Club of Long Beach, Artuković railed against Tito's communists. 'This is the regime which dares to accuse others of war crimes,' he passionately declared.

His speaking engagements, perhaps suggested by lawyers as a legal strategy to bolster his profile and credibility, attracted the ire of some newspaper columnists. Among them was Milton Friedman, the economist who would go on to earn a Nobel prize.

As far back as 1953, Friedman had used his syndicated column in the Jewish press to detail Artuković's crimes, beginning with his order that Jews should wear a yellow badge with a 'Z' for Zidov, a label that was also an ethnic slur. 'Later he bragged that he outstripped Hitler with the speed which his police squads "solved the Jewish problem",' Friedman wrote. 'He supervised the deportation of Jewish children. One supervisor testified that things of such enormity took place at one of Artuković's concentration camps that orders were issued for a temporary "clean-up" so that visiting Nazi commissioners would not be shocked.'

Friedman quoted California Republican committeeman John J. Knezevich, who served as commander of the Balkan section of the US Army and Navy Joint Intelligence Collection Agency during the Second World War. Knezevich, who said he had personal knowledge of Artuković's atrocities, had heard from several people that Artuković should be left alone because he was an enemy of communism. 'Well, dammit, Hitler, Goering, Himmler, Mussolini and the rest of the Nazi league were enemies of communism, too,' said Knezevich. 'But they were also enemies of our country.'

With the headline: 'Will US protect Nazi Croatian leader?' Friedman derided American politicians and community leaders for protecting Artuković simply because he was anti-communist: 'As an expert in the menace of communism, he has addressed the Optimist, Kiwanis and Knights of Columbus clubs of Los Angeles. At the Kiwanis appearance, he was applauded by the mayor of Los Angeles.'

Artuković was the highest-ranking Nazi collaborator living in the United States. And even though the US government had been aware of his role in an Axis government since 1949, there was no appetite for exporting or extraditing him.

During the Cold War, most Americans shared Artuković's view that communists were dangerous. The Red Scare was based on the fear that the Soviet Union would take over the world and remove the freedoms that

Americans cherished, among them freedom of speech and religion. The Catholic Church, especially, was a ferocious opponent of communism, a stance that has been explored by several prominent historians. They argue that the Catholic Church, and Pope Pius XII, fostered Cold War tensions for both spiritual and economic reasons. Atheism was a key tenant of communism. And if religion was banned, churches would be closed, shutting down a source of revenue. Furthermore, the assets of the church would likely be nationalised or confiscated.

In the United States, Artuković's supporters cited his opposition to communism, hailing him heroic as well as a victim. The Brooklyn Catholic newspaper *The Tablet*, with the banner headline 'Titoism Marches on Dr. Artucovic,' ran a story in which Reverend M.D. Forrest urged readers to write to their elected representatives to demand support for Artuković.

Rev. Forrest railed against the Supreme Court for rulings that allowed Yugoslavia's extradition request to remain open after eight years. Describing Artuković as 'innocent of the accusations made against him as is an unborn child', Rev. Forrest condemned his communist accusers as people who 'cannot spell the words truth, justice and freedom'.

He questioned whether any 'reasonable [American] judge or commissioner [would] be prepared to accept the testimony of vicious Communists who defy God and think nothing of perjury?'

The Red Scare, born after the Second World War, grew in the 1950s, escalated with Soviet–US tensions of the 1960s, and continued into the 1970s when the idea of a communist domino effect in Asia crystallised into the Vietnam War.

Artuković's prominence as an opponent of communism had kept him on the FBI's radar, both as a threat by Yugoslavia and as a source of information. The FBI tracked his movements, with agents filing reports on his speaking engagements. They took note when Artuković was the keynote speaker in Chicago at a Croatian event.

In a report on 28 January 1974, the FBI noted that both Andrija Artuković and his brother John had supplied information about the communists. The FBI informant considered the intelligence from John Artukovich to be 'of the utmost importance'. The source reported that John told him that 10,000 to 15,000 Soviet military personnel had taken over several hotels in three Yugoslavian ports. The soldiers had operated in secret and were wearing plain clothes. This information had come to John from his brother Andrija and was considered important because, at the time, there was a great fear that the Soviets would move into Yugoslavia after Tito died. The FBI took the informant's report seriously enough that it immediately sent agents to Andrija Artuković's home to interview him.

Artuković, whom the source described as the 'uncrowned leader of the Croatian movement in the United States', said he had 'maintained contact with various knowledgeable contacts from within Yugoslavia and is generally aware of activities in that country'.

In his interview with the special agents, Artuković offered to help in any way that he could, but at the same time, he declined to identify his sources. Artuković, who had risen from his peasant life to enter university at the age of 16, wasn't about to be underestimated by the FBI. He was a lawyer, after all, and a former Minister of Justice in Croatia.

Asked by the FBI to present the letters so that they could see for themselves what the communists were up to, Artuković demurred. He shrewdly replied that it was his usual practice to destroy letters containing this kind of information immediately after reading them.

Artuković was bolstered again in the spring of 1974 when the US Immigration Service ruled that it would not act upon the outstanding deportation order against him, meaning that he could remain in the country indefinitely. The *Los Angeles Times* interviewed Jewish leaders and found the reaction to be muted. Some said Artuković was not a priority and that there were 'more pressing issues to contend with at this time'. Charles Posner, executive director of the influential Jewish Federation Council of Los Angeles, was succinct: 'We have no brief for Artuković. But the man is 75, and maybe it's time to forget.' Irv Rubin was incensed by both Posner's comment and the ruling. He told the newspaper the decision was 'a travesty of justice and a copout' and warned that the JDL would be stepping up its protests.

With the threat of renewed JDL protests, the pressure was mounting again. Artuković no longer accepted speaking engagements. He rarely left their gated community, limiting his outings to walks on the beach. Ana was the breadwinner, holding down a job as a supervisor at the data control centre at St Mary's Hospital in Long Beach.

Ana was becoming afraid. Several times she called the police to report seeing strangers loitering near their property. The FBI noted that her calls were frequent.

The FBI wasn't just watching the Artuković family. It was also watching the JDL, having identified it years earlier as a domestic terrorist organisation. The FBI had infiltrated the JDL with a mole operating inside its Fairfax Avenue office.

The FBI's informant reported that the JDL was planning to kidnap Andrija Artuković. Two different sources confirmed that leader Irv Rubin and his right-hand man had discussed the idea of acquiring a 'motor boat or a beach landing craft'. One source said Rubin 'may get to Artuković by use of a motor boat which will allow them to take him by surprise as he walks along the beach'.

Both sources expressed doubt about whether the JDL could pull off a kidnapping. The first informant said that even though Rubin appeared very serious about attempting the kidnapping in the next two to three weeks, this might be 'another of his wild schemes that are all talk and little, if any action'. The other source scoffed at the JDL as amateurs. 'Source Two indicated that the idea of the JDL's kidnapping of Artuković appears far-fetched in view of the ineptness of the JDL and its leaders, but their actions in connection with this matter will be followed very closely.'

When David Whitelaw would visit the office, he heeded Irv Rubin's warning to be careful about what he said and did. Rubin always suspected that the phones were wiretapped and that police had the office under surveillance. Despite this, Rubin and his lieutenant, Earl Krugel, talked openly about JDL's plans and strategies, never suspecting that an informant might be in their midst. Irv Rubin trusted his people. When he decided to shift the strategy for going after Artuković, the JDL leader outlined the new plan to his key members. The JDL would stop protesting at the Artukovićs' gated community because the neighbours were becoming increasingly fed up with the protests and exponentially more protective of the Artuković family. Instead, the JDL's new plan was to shift the demonstrations away from Artuković's gated community and onto the public street in front of his brother's house. John Artukovich's home in upscale Sherman Oaks had no gate, and it seemed less likely that the neighbours, with houses on large, leafy lots, would care as much about what was happening on their street.

On 14 March 1974, the mole inside the JDL told the FBI that member Cliff Schwartz was planning protests in front of John and Lucille Artukovich's home at 16011 Meadowcrest Road in Sherman Oaks. The vigil, planned for 23 March at 7.30 p.m., was expected to last all night. Cliff Schwartz told Irv Rubin, in the presence of the informant, that it would be a good idea to do something newsworthy to draw media attention to the purpose of the demonstration.

David Whitelaw was working that night and could not attend the rally. But he liked the idea of putting pressure on Andrija Artuković's brother and his family. 'If we can't get to the "Butcher of the Balkans" himself, his brother is a reasonable facsimile,' David declared drily. 'John was his benefactor, after all.'

The JDL wasn't the only group that had attracted the FBI's attention for its desire to catch Artuković and bring him to justice; informants also advised that the Yugoslav secret police might attempt an assassination. The FBI passed on the information to the LAPD so that they could watch over Artuković.

★ ★ ★

As Christmas 1974 approached, the families of Andrija Artuković and his brother John were being threatened as never before. The FBI and LAPD kept active files as the danger escalated.

On 11 December 1974, the family of John Artukovich experienced the terror firsthand when a car drove past, a passenger firing shots at the windows of their house. A bullet sailed past John and Lucille's daughter, barely missing her.

No one was ever arrested, no charges laid. But from then on, LAPD kept watch on the house on the quiet street in Sherman Oaks.

10

'We Can't Let this Guy Get Biological Amnesty'

With the goal of becoming a doctor, David enrolled in college and volunteered at a hospital in 1974. He took a part-time job as a nurse's aide to
add a competitive edge to his application for medical school. 'I wanted to
become a doctor because I thought it was a noble thing to do. I'd realised
in junior high that I wasn't strong enough in math, or fit enough, or smart
enough to become an astronaut. I was analytical and strong in science,
though, so medical school was appealing.'

He was also compassionate. And although he prided himself on his 'in-
your-face' Brooklyn toughness, David often found himself playing the
sensitive role of listener, even adviser, to the adults in his life.

At home, David felt like he was the head of the household. His mother
needed help, emotionally and financially. 'All my life I felt like the adult,
talking with my dad about my mom, talking with my mom about my
dad. As much as I loved my parents, I couldn't help but feel resentful.
Sometimes I felt like I was playing the role of husband instead of son.'

His mother had suffered another setback that further cemented her
anger and sense of family abandonment. This latest betrayal came about
when she was swindled out of an inheritance by a cousin in Guatemala.
Judith had been counting on the money, which she had been promised,
and when it did not materialise, she found herself financially strapped.

Part of the reason for her money problems was that Billy was now
attending private school. It was an expensive last resort that Judith could

ill afford, but at the same time, she could think of nothing else to help Billy. He had been kicked out of every public school because he acted up in class and screamed profanity at his teachers. Sometimes, in frustration, he would rip at his own face with his fingers, in self-mutilation. Increasing doses of medication and therapy had not helped.

'Billy was a really smart little kid,' David says. 'He could tell you the names of the wives of American presidents, for example. And ships. He knew every shipping line, every ship, its capacity, its size. He was obsessed with the ocean and dreamed of joining the Merchant Marine. I'd take Billy down to the Wilmington Pier, and he'd sit and stare at the ocean, dreaming of the day when he'd ship out,' David says, emotion clouding his throat. 'The poor kid never had a chance. In his heart of hearts, Billy knew he would never be able to join the Merchant Marine. But I always went along with him. What else could I do?'

Judith was determined to get Billy an education even though his dream of a seafaring career seemed unlikely. She chose a military academy in San Diego, banking on its rigid structure, smaller classes and individual attention to give Billy a chance at making his own way in life.

When the money that she expected from her inheritance didn't materialise, an uncle in Guatemala took pity on Judith. He sent her $10,000 as a down payment on a house. Judith found a house on South Crescent Heights in Pico-Robertson, a neighbourhood without many Jewish families. She also started dating a man with whom she was utterly enthralled. But the handsome new boyfriend proved to be emotionally unavailable, causing Judith more emotional distress.

Adding to her troubles was her concern about her eldest son, Stephen. Stephen had joined the Merchant Marine, thanks to Harry, who had pulled in favours from his bosses and union contacts and persuaded them to take Stephen on. But far from turning his life around, the carefree life of a merchant mariner seemed to fuel Stephen's excesses.

Tall, lean and handsome, Stephen resembled the actor Vince Edwards who played Dr Ben Casey on the TV series of the same name. In a weird twist of coincidence, Stephen also had a gambling addiction in common with the actor. In port in Los Angeles, he would take his latest girlfriend to a restaurant, where he was often mistaken for the actor, usually because Stephen had booked a reservation in the name of Vince Edwards.

To David, stuck in the dutiful role of family mediator and caretaker, it seemed that Stephen's fate had cast him in the adventurous life with a girl in every port. 'Stephen was living the high life. He stole money from my mom, and from me, to pay his gambling debts. He was starting to get into trouble with the maritime authorities.'

One night, in a drunken rage, Stephen pulled a knife on David and threatened to kill him because David refused to give him money. It was a turning point in the brothers' relationship. After that, David never trusted Stephen. Whenever his older brother was around, David's guard was up.

David also found it bewildering that their father didn't show any despair. Harry continued to stick up for Stephen, expressing pride in the smallest accomplishment. Yet Harry, capable of kindness and compassion for Stephen, could also fly off the handle about the inconsequential failings of others.

'He had high standards, especially for service in restaurants,' said David. 'This was partly based on his professionalism because by now he was training other merchant mariners in catering and service. But every time we'd get together in a restaurant, my stomach would be in knots because I knew something about the service wouldn't measure up. If the waiter brought a plate of sugar with no doily underneath, my father would cause a scene. I'd just cringe and try to overcompensate with politeness. I'd say, "You know, Dad, I don't think you can expect your Splenda to be delivered in style. We're at Denny's." To him, it didn't matter. Service was service.'

It seemed to David that both his father and brother would never grow up. Both of them were always looking for a way to get rich quick. Yet both of them blew any chance of doing so. Harry had invested in several promising businesses, only to bail when it turned out to be more work than he'd bargained for. As for Stephen, he gambled everything away.

David, with his gift of reading people's hearts, chalked it up to 'the sins of the father'. Harry's own father had abandoned him, leaving a hole in his soul that nothing could fill. And Harry passed on this void to his own children. Why, after all, was Stephen gambling and drinking, if not to fill a gaping hole in his soul?

★ ★ ★

1975 arrived in Southern California with a storm. Winds gusting up to 70mph made the 57°F temperature seem all the colder. The 1.5 million people lining up for the Rose Parade in Pasadena lit fires and bundled up in parkas against the cold, even though the high winds threatened to shut down the parade for the first time in its eighty-six-year history.

By the afternoon of 1 January, the winds had settled to 25mph, and the parade went ahead. At home, David watched the Rose Bowl on TV, nursing a hangover from too many Bloody Marys consumed the night before at a New Year's Eve party with friends in Westwood.

The Rose Bowl was one of the most exciting games David had ever watched. The University of Southern California Trojans, the team David supported in the hope that he would soon be attending their school, won the game with a touchdown pass in the last two minutes. What a great start to the new year!

He was in his second year at Los Angeles Valley College. He was in the best shape of his life from riding his bicycle across the canyon every day to attend school in the San Fernando Valley. He was involved with Hillel, the Jewish student campus organisation, and was striving to set up a branch of the JDL on campus.

His social life had never been better. He'd developed two close friendships at college, one with Mitzi Mogul and the other with Gary Levin. Mitzi, a talented singer and songwriter, and Gary, a fun-loving party animal, became constants in David's life. The trio could always find a party to attend. From time to time, David dated nice girls, cute girls who might be interested in a relationship. So far, a steady relationship had not materialised, a fact which Gary attributed to David's being 'too picky' and overly cautious.

Gary thought that David's good looks ought to be serving him better with the ladies. He teased David about his vanity, accusing him perpetually of 'being too busy checking his hair in the mirror' to saunter over and introduce himself to an attractive woman.

David shot back that a little vanity might not hurt Gary, whom he had nicknamed 'Swamp Man' after Gary, dishevelled, unshaven and having a very bad hair day, had the chutzpah to ask a girl who was clearly out of his league for a date.

'Gary, you gotta be kidding,' David had said. 'You look like you climbed out of a swamp. She is not going to go for Swamp Man.'

From then on, Gary was known as Swamp Man. The nickname became entrenched after Mitzi wrote a song about Gary emerging from the swamp. Gary took it all with good humour, reminding David that it would likely be Swamp Man who found him a woman since David was too stuck on combing his hair to find one himself.

David was in a buoyant mood, especially after the USC Trojans won the Rose Bowl. He was grateful for his good fortune and for his rich circle of support. His involvement with the JDL gave him a strong sense of purpose. He had grown fond of Irv Rubin, who, in turn, treated David with respect. David felt a sense of belonging, a feeling that he knew eluded his brothers. 'Billy had no real friends, so you know what? He made up friends. I used to see him and hear him talking with his imaginary friends. And Stephen, for all of his popularity with the girls and despite being such a fun guy, really had no close friends either. You know how they say, "It takes a village"? Well, Billy had no village. Stephen had no village. But I had a village because I was forced to go out and find my own village.'

David's village, starting with his kindergarten teacher in Buena Park, to the Millers in Brooklyn, had provided a circle of mentors that assured his destiny, shaping the convictions that would prepare him for the most important moment in his life.

★ ★ ★

It was shortly after the day Christians mark as Epiphany that David himself had an 'epiphany of sorts'. He and another JDL member, Mike Schwartz, were sitting in the office on Fairfax with their feet up, 'being the cocky young punks that we were'. Irv Rubin was talking with his young band of radicals about the JDL's priorities.

'By then, the deportation of Andrija Artuković was a cause célèbre for us, and we were planning another demo. We'd already done this, and we'd done that, because we didn't want to give this monster any peace of mind. And Irv leaned into me, and he said, "David, we can't let this guy get biological amnesty." For a minute, I had to think about what he meant. And then I realised biological amnesty meant that Artuković would die without ever having been brought to justice.'

It was a tipping point for David. 'The idea of biological amnesty for this guy, this monster who was the mastermind behind the murders of 770,000 people, there was no way to overstate the urgency of bringing this guy to justice. This guy was not some garden variety guard in a concentration camp. He was Number Two after Josef Mengele.'

David listened as Irv Rubin talked about the JDL's plans for another demonstration to draw attention to Artuković's cosy life in Surfside. 'Three ideas converged in my mind at that moment. I'd been writing letters and protesting, following the law, for two years. No one is cooperating. Maybe they're even collaborating. The civil route is not working. And Artuković is old. I realised this monster could die. And if he did, I'd be part of the problem. I analysed all of this. And I realised even a good boy sometimes has to make a rough decision. The idea started percolating inside my head that if this guy dies and I've done nothing at all, what does that say about me?'

David thought about the reactions he had received when he spoke to groups about Artuković, as well as the indifferent comments from those who bothered to reply to his letters. '"It happened a long time ago." I heard that one a lot. Also, "We've already tried. There's nothing we can do." Or "We feel for your plight." Most of the time, I was patronised like that. I was starting to feel like David and Goliath. And I was asking myself, who do I think I am? Who's David Whitelaw? A nobody. This guy had powerful friends. He was being protected.'

Irv Rubin preached the necessity of resorting to violence when peaceful means failed. In David's opinion, that moment had arrived. Or, to put it more bluntly: 'I want this bloodthirsty bastard to stand before a judge and answer for what he did.'

David made a decision that would change his life. He decided to take on his Goliath.

Artuković welcomes the Nazis in 1941 after they invaded Yugoslavia and created the independent state of Croatia. (Jasenovac Memorial Site)

Artuković is carried on the shoulders of supporters in 1951 after being released on bail, leading to his first legal victory. (University of Southern California)

Artuković with his wife and children at their home in Seal Beach, California, 1958.
(University of Southern California)

The Ustasha employed a tool designed to slit the throats of enemies. (United States Holocaust Memorial Museum, courtesy of Muzej Revolucije Narodnosti Jugoslavije)

Above and below: Ustasha guards competed to see who could kill the most prisoners and celebrated their victories, causing the Nazis to shudder at the brutality. (Jasenovac Memorial Site)

A Croatian soldier stands amid bodies of civilians killed by the Ustasha and thrown in a mass grave. (Jasenovac Memorial Site)

The Ustasha was the only Nazi/Axis organisation that had separate concentration camps for children. (Jasenovac Memorial Site)

Judith Whitelaw's parents, Klara and Sigmund, on their engagement day while Sigmund was on furlough from the Germany Army in 1917. (David Whitelaw/Myth Merchant Films)

Herty Miller, Judith's first cousin, who insisted that David come to live with her family in Brooklyn after the Whitelaws divorced. (Debbie Weiss/Miller Family/ Myth Merchant Films)

Judith Whitelaw won a beauty contest in Guatemala before emigrating to the United States. (David Whitelaw/Myth Merchant Films)

Judith and Harry were married in Las Vegas on 1 September 1949. (David Whitelaw/Myth Merchant Films)

David Whitelaw, right, with mother Judith and brothers Billy, left, and Stephen, behind. (David Whitelaw/Myth Merchant Films)

David Whitelaw realised at an early age that the optimism of 1950s California contrasted starkly with his own family's tragic past. (David Whitelaw/Myth Merchant Films)

The Whitelaw boys in 1961, a few years before their family life imploded. (David Whitelaw/ Myth Merchant Films)

David Whitelaw as a teenager, shortly before he joined the Jewish Defense League. (David Whitelaw/Myth Merchant Films)

October 2, 1975

Dear Mom,

This letter was written shortly after your visit today. I know your intentions are good but I hope in your efforts you are not overlooking over a number of important factors. Do you realize that the more notariety you give yourself and myself the more difficult it will become to lead a normal life? It will become much more difficult for me to assimilate back to the normal mainstream of life. The more you get attention on my future plans regarding Artukovic the more complicated it will become for me to pursue my career. You must realize realistically Mom, there is no one else risking themselves the way you are! Where are all the hoards of people supporting you?!? Why is there no one else outspoken as much as you? Do you realize the very serious risks you take everytime you gain more publicity on yourself?

Mother, the Ustashi are known to be "cut-throats" here in the U.S. too! I do not think you really realize how seriously you may be jeopardizing us!
(over)

David wrote frequent letters from prison to express his feelings. (David Whitelaw/ Myth Merchant Films)

You are every noble. We are both very noble. But the real test is if there are people willing to sacrifice as much as you? I'm sorry Mom, but I regret I even gave that interview! Not because I scared, because if they want trouble I'm ready! I do not cower to people like that so easy. But I do know that you have done more than your part. I have done more than my part. Now let someone else! – Do you understand?

I am not interested in gaining notoriety for Artukovic. I want to go into Medicine. The more I get into the "limelight" the difficult you will make it for me to lead a normal life, and to pursue my career.

Do you understand, it isn't because what your doing is wrong, it is just unfair to you and I to carry the entire burden of the issue. You – let someone else! Or isn't there anyone who cares as much as you? If not, then this issue is an entire waste.

I really do not want anymore publicity given on me, for an ungrateful, unappreciative world. I want to look forward to a beautiful future in Medicine. I sacrificed too much already for too many ungrateful people. Now I want to think of myself and my loved ones. Everytime you give more publicity on me you hinder me from accomplishing that goal.

Think this over. I'm not sure you are carefully considering the future implications that will follow. Remember sometimes Heroism can border Foolishness. Good Luck. Love always

your Son,
David

To BE READ:

Written By: DAVID WHITELAW SEPTEMBER 7, 1975
(1) written for the people listed below: as a tribute
to their sincerity, loyalty and love — David Whitelaw

"If anything should happen to me..."

To my dearest, sweetest Mother:
I love you with all my heart and soul.
You are the most wonderful Mother
any son could possibly ever have. I love
you very deeply and cherish you.

To my dearest, wonderful Father:
My love for you is only comparable to
that of Mother's. I know I was not
always such a great son, but I tried.
I love you very much and could not
get a more wonderful Father. Please
do not forget I love you very deeply.

To my dearest, wonderful, loving, Mitzi:
In all my life, I never met a girl as
wonderful as you! Your dedication,
loyalty and love will always have
a special place in my heart. You
were always there when I needed you.
You're a rare and wonderful person.
I'll always love you. Thank you Mitzi.

To my dear, loyal, friend Mary:
I want to thank you for everything
you have done for me! You were
loyal and consistently proved your
dedication. You are a rare friend who
I will not ever forget. Thank you, Mary

To my loyal friends Cherie, Suzi,
and Richard: In the short time

With neo-Nazis imprisoned in the same cell block, David wrote a 'last will and testament'. (David Whitelaw/Myth Merchant Films)

COULD NOT WRITE ENOUGH ABOUT EACH OF YOU YOU ALL MEAN
SO MUCH TO ME. I ONLY HAD ONE SHEET OF PAPER LEFT (THIS ONE)
AND I TRIED TO SAY WHAT I COULD IN THIS LITTLE AMOUNT OF
SPACE. I'M SORRY IT WAS SO RUSHED, BUT THIS HAD TO BE DONE
IMMEDIATELY. I MAY HAVE NOT LATER HAVE A CHANCE TO WRITE EVEN
THIS LITTLE. PLEASE REMEMBER I LOVE YOU ALL. —

(2.)   David Whitclew

continued

I knew you, you were just fantastic
and loyal friends. Please donate the
money to my Mother to help her out.
You all are tremendous individuals.
I will never forget just how kind, good-
hearted and genuine you were to me in the
short time I knew you. Thank you for
being my friends. I'll never forget any of you.

to all my friends: Please do me a favor that I would be
eternally grateful to you for. Please, please
console my grieving Parents during this crisis
in their lives. My Parents have suffered
so terribly much. Please try and ease their
suffering. It hurts me so bad that they may have to
go through this. I don't want them to suffer —
please. Thank You very, very much.

some personal notes: This entire situation has caused much untold
grief. Not just for myself but the wonderful
friends and my dear Parents. It tears me apart
to think of the misery this may finally bestow.
But please, everyone must understand, I did
not want to injure anyone. I only meant to bring
this issue to public light. I did not want to hurt
anyone, please believe me. But now the most
innocent people are going to be hurt, the people
who concerned themselves with me because they
cared. I've cried many tears for that reason. I
love all of you, my Parents & friends. Thank you
all. God Bless You. — I'll always love you all. David

Attorney Vincent Bugliosi, who successfully prosecuted the Manson family in the Tate-LaBianca murders, won David's freedom from prison. (Los Angeles Public Library)

Phil Blazer, founder of Jewish Life Television and publisher of *Israel Today*, advocated tirelessly for David. (Blazer Family)

Vincent Bugliosi became one of David's key mentors. (David Whitelaw/Myth Merchant Films)

David, during his successful campaign for student council vice-president at University of Southern California in 1977. (David Whitelaw/Myth Merchant Films)

David graduated from University of Southern California in 1980 and later attained a teaching degree. (David Whitelaw/Myth Merchant Films)

David met the love of his life at the age of 45. He and Edith Galvez married in 2003. (David Whitelaw/Myth Merchant Films)

David with his first class of students in 1985. (David Whitelaw/Myth Merchant Films)

11

'It Felt Like Redemption'

In January 1975, while hanging around the JDL office, David picked up an exciting piece of news: Artuković was rumoured to be planning an overnight visit to his brother's house in Sherman Oaks.

David saw an opportunity. His mind began spinning with the possibilities. Another JDL member, Mike Schwartz, had also heard the rumour, and the two of them put their heads together and started plotting. It didn't take long, which was good, because they only had two days to prepare.

David wanted to make sure no one was hurt, especially Andrija Artuković himself. To scare him as he lay sleeping would be awesome, to let him feel a taste of the terror that he'd inflicted upon so many. But David was clear: Artuković must not be hurt. He needed to remain healthy, to stand trial, to be sentenced. David was certain that a trial would mean a death sentence because of the gruesome crimes detailed in the Yugoslav court documents.

Schwartz agreed with everything David suggested. This was comforting because David wondered if Schwartz actually had a brain in his head. The last thing he wanted was for this bozo to start coming up with ideas of his own. He was a funny guy, Schwartz. Irv Rubin seemed to have taken him under his wing, apparently after finding him loitering in a park, smoking dope. Maybe Rubin wanted to help the young Texan turn his life around or something, but whatever it was, Schwartz now followed Rubin around like a little puppy dog. He roared with laughter at all of Rubin's jokes, which were, David had to admit, pretty funny. Schwartz nodded enthusiastically at almost every word Rubin said. The guy brought brown-nosing to a whole new level. But he seemed 100 per cent committed, even if his commitment to Jewish causes was nearly as new as the new year itself.

David put the final touches on his plan. He had started to think of himself and Schwartz as a cell of domestic terrorists, a notion that he shared with Schwartz. The idea seemed to appeal to him, and David elaborated upon it, making sure that Schwartz understood the need for secrecy. Trust between cell members was paramount.

The next night, David drove his van over to Sherman Oaks to do a reconnaissance mission. He liked what he saw. John Artukovich's house was at the top of a hill on a quiet street. The lots were large, with trees for privacy. The house had a carport, with a new Mustang II parked in it. David wondered briefly if the Mustang belonged to Andrija Artuković. But even if it did not, no matter. As David and other JDL members had observed before, any member of the family would be a reasonable substitute to terrorise.

Instinctively, he knew what he had to do. There was no question that he would choose a Molotov cocktail. It was what the Warsaw Ghetto resistance fighters had done, and David wanted to pay homage, to honour their spirit.

David examined the distance from the road to the car. Less than 50 feet. It should be a simple matter to throw the Molotov cocktail and run to the car.

Over the next twenty-four hours, David imagined the scene, playing it over and over in his head. Schwartz had promised to secure a getaway car, relieving David of the risk that his own van would trace the crime back to him. They would meet at the JDL office at 10 p.m., drive to the valley, terrorise the family and make a quick getaway. And then wait. Wait for the fallout.

David could almost hear the sirens as he imagined the fire trucks and police cars speeding to the scene. The family huddled inside, knowing that the safety and security they'd always known had gone up in flames. News reporters would pick up the call on the police scanner and rush to interview the family. And then, the truth would come out. In David's mind, there was no question of the outcome. The fact that Artuković was living his cosy life in Surfside wasn't a secret. It was more like an open secret. But now, it would be news. Bombings of buildings, aeroplanes and cars always made the news. The media would want to know what was behind the attack. News reporters would dredge up the whole horrible truth about the 'Butcher of the Balkans'. And after all these years, the truth would come out. The world would hear that a high-ranking Nazi was alive and well in the United States, free to visit his brother at this very house in Sherman Oaks. There would be a public outcry. And finally, Artuković would be sent back to Yugoslavia to answer for his crimes. David dreamed of attending the trial, which he thought of as a 'mini-Nuremberg'.

In his fantasy, he never stopped to examine his own obvious blind spot. For almost three years, he'd been writing letters demanding justice. No one cared. He didn't ask himself the tough question: why would they care now?

There was only one question on David's mind. He'd been asking it of himself for the past two days since he'd heard the rumour of Artuković's visit to Sherman Oaks. Tonight, as he dressed carefully in loose-fitting, dark clothing and slipped on his Star of David pendant, David asked himself the question again: 'Am I failing the law, or is the law failing me?' The answer was always the same. The law had failed him. If the law had been working as it was supposed to, Artuković would have been deported for entering the United States illegally under a false name. If the law had been working properly, Artuković would have been extradited back to Yugoslavia to answer for the 770,000 deaths he ordered. Instead, the highest officers in David's beloved America had turned a blind eye. More than a blind eye. Some legislators had perverted justice even further by using America's own laws to protect this mass murderer. Countless others had ignored David's own pleas.

Man's law versus God's law? There was no question in David's mind. If this monster was to be brought to justice, it was up to David to make it happen.

The law had failed him. Now, he would let destiny take its course. He would answer to God.

The Chevy Nova that Schwartz got from God-knows-where was ten years old but was by no means a jalopy. Whoever owned it had looked after it really well, and if David weren't so nervous, he would have asked Schwartz where he got the car. But his stomach had been in knots all day and the smell of gasoline from the 5-gallon can in the back seat was making him slightly queasy.

David rolled down the passenger window to catch some air and was taken aback at how cold it was. Los Angeles had not really warmed up since the blast of cold weather that came in with the new year, and tonight the temperature had dropped again.

David was too wound up to really feel the cold. Committing a crime, a felony at that, was not something he had ever expected to do. He was an Explorer Scout, for heaven's sake, part of a search-and-rescue unit that volunteered with the Sheriff's Department.

To David's relief, Schwartz, flake that he was, had done a good job. He had shown up on time at the JDL office, having secured the car, found the 5-gallon gasoline can and filled it. He'd picked up the two quart-sized beer bottles he and David had prepared together in the backyard of the JDL offices that night. They had stuffed rags in the gasoline-filled bottles, one to throw and one for a spare.

Schwartz got out of the car and proceeded to pull on a pair of gloves. Gloves? Who knew he had it in him?

David opened the door and got out. Something was wrong. He could feel it. He and Schwartz had barely spoken all night, and if Schwartz was having second thoughts, he wasn't saying so.

David took a deep breath. Hesitated. He couldn't very well run up to Schwartz right now and say, 'Hang on, I don't think this is a good idea.'

Probably just nerves, David thought. 'I've never broken the law before. Maybe it's supposed to feel like this when you break the law.'

Schwartz lifted the bulky gas can from the back seat. David reached in and grabbed the Molotov cocktails. Side by side, the two JDL members walked toward the carport.

Finally, after two years of a fruitless campaign, David was taking real action. It felt like destiny. Finally, he, David, was no longer standing back, waiting for the authorities to seek justice. He would no longer be part of the problem, no longer idly allowing the 'Butcher of the Balkans' to live happily in America. After tonight, the world would know that the United States sheltered a Nazi so monstrous that he was considered second only to Josef Mengele.

Artuković's life was about to get uncomfortable. If the rumour was true and the 'Butcher of the Balkans' himself was sleeping inside his brother's house, he would surely get a good fright. David relished scaring the hell out of him.

Despite David's initial trepidation, everything was going as planned. Schwartz splashed the gasoline around the perimeter of the car until the can was empty. David pulled out the book of matches and lit the rag. He was no longer just a law-abiding citizen, an aspiring doctor, a dutiful son. He had crossed a line. Now, he was a fighter. He felt like he was in the Warsaw Ghetto, felt the spirit of the resistance guide him. He lifted his arm and threw the Molotov cocktail.

His aim was good: the Molotov cocktail landed beside the car. 'I felt such a sense of liberation,' David said. 'I felt like I was fighting for those six million Jews. It felt like redemption.'

Schwartz and David had left the car running. It was less than 50 feet away. Without exchanging a word, the two made a run for it.

There was the noise of breaking glass, the swoosh of flames, and another sound. A shout. 'Halt, police!'

Bullets were flying. David jumped into the driver's seat as Schwartz ducked under the dashboard. David felt a bullet graze his ear. Spraying glass bounced off the dashboard. Another bullet ricocheted off the back seat.

It was hopeless, David knew. But there was no way he was going down without a fight. Again, he felt the spirit of the Warsaw Ghetto resistance fighters who sacrificed themselves to fend off Hitler.

They barely made it 300 feet to the bottom of the hill. The tyres were shot out, and David could no longer steer the car. A crash. And then they were greeted by the most unbelievable sight: a crowd of cops with their guns drawn. 'Where the hell did they come from?' David thought.

With a sinking feeling, he realised why his spidey-senses had tingled when they arrived at the scene: someone had ratted them out. Cops had been hiding in the bushes, waiting for them, and there were more waiting at the bottom of the hill. Obviously, the LAPD had been tipped off about the exact time and every detail of the plan.

One cop pulled David out of the car and threw him to the ground. Another did the same to Schwartz.

'You're the one who threw the Molotov cocktail, aren't you?' a cop asked David.

'I'm not saying anything until I get a lawyer,' David replied. Schwartz didn't say a word. The cop read them their rights, just as David had seen on TV shows.

David noticed that his pendant with the Star of David was missing. Somehow it had broken off from the chain. It was his amulet. He wanted it back. He asked the cop where it was. Surprisingly, the cop didn't hesitate. He looked around, found it and handed it to David.

David and Schwartz were piled into a squad car and left sitting there while the cops talked among themselves.

David glanced at Schwartz. The two of them had never discussed what they might do if the plan went awry. In their excitement, they had not even considered the possibility.

Schwartz was staring straight ahead, unwilling to meet David's eyes. David felt sick to his stomach as he realised he'd placed his trust in a guy he knew almost nothing about. No one besides the two of them was supposed to know about the plan.

Had Schwartz, the stupid airhead, blown their secret?

★ ★ ★

At the Van Nuys police station's infirmary, David winced in pain as the nurse plucked shards of glass from his scalp. Some of the glass that flew through the car as police shot out its windows had lodged in David's scalp. He also learned that a bullet had grazed his head. The nurse had curtly pinned back his curly hair to shave the wound, and now, as she wielded her tweezers, her touch was far from gentle. But David refused to give her the satisfaction of showing how much it hurt, even as he realised that he must have been in shock to not have noticed the bleeding. Or the fact that the bullet could have entered his brain. He was still reeling from the experience of being arrested, fingerprinted and placed in a holding cell.

David then followed the officer into the booking room and sat still for his mug shot, the hair clips still holding his hair in place to expose the wound. He could imagine his mother's reaction and braced himself for her freaking out.

When the officer finally told him he could make one phone call, David didn't ask for a lawyer; he called his mother. Judith's reaction surprised him. She calmly asked if he was okay. It turned out that she was expecting his call because she had already heard a radio news report about two JDL boys arrested for firebombing a car in Sherman Oaks. The moment she heard the news, she knew in her bones that David was one of those boys.

Judith, who had stood shoulder to shoulder with her son at the protests demanding Artuković's deportation, understood David's anger. She shared it. Judith, who had sat beside David at her dining room table typing hundreds of letters demanding justice, also shared his growing contempt for the politicians who did nothing. She considered it a travesty.

And now it was David who was in jail. Not Artuković, but David. Her good boy. If the call from the jailhouse had come from Stephen, Judith would have thought, 'What now?' because Stephen had had numerous skirmishes with the law. Her youngest son, Billy, was also a problem, although through no fault of his own. Right now, Billy was in a psychiatric facility, and Judith could only pray that he would finally get the help he needed.

In the couple of hours leading up to David's call from the Van Nuys jail, Judith had thought through this new crisis, this unbelievable turn of events that had landed her son behind bars. Foremost on her mind was his safety. He had told her he was okay, but the police had shot at the car, and Judith wouldn't believe he was okay until she saw him with her own eyes.

Judith, who had fled Nazi Germany and built a life for her family as a single mother after her divorce from Harry, was no stranger to crisis. She knew that this crisis, like the windstorms that whipped in off the Pacific Ocean, would build. Her first mission would be to get David out of jail and safely home. After that, she'd need to marshal support from whomever and for whatever was needed. And after that, she'd need to get justice for her son. His goal was to become a doctor. He couldn't afford to have a criminal record.

Judith knew the road ahead would be long and difficult, but she would do whatever she had to do. David felt like an extension of herself, a ferocious warrior fighting for justice. For Jews. As much as Judith despaired that David had committed a crime, she also felt an overwhelming surge of pride. His life's mission had been getting justice for a mass murderer, a monster who killed children with the same bloodthirsty hatred that killed Judith's family.

Now it was Judith's turn to fight for David.

She'd have to call in every favour from every powerful person she knew.

She started with the rabbi, but his reaction shocked her: far from being sympathetic, he wanted nothing to do with the JDL and strongly disapproved of the firebombing. It took some persuading, but the rabbi eventually called a lawyer, explained that Judith had no money to pay him and asked him to work for free. Judith made a frantic call to the lawyer; he agreed to meet her at the courthouse and suggested she use the equity in her house to cover bail.

Judith jumped into her car and turned on the radio, hoping for more news about David as she fought traffic for the hour-long trip to the courthouse in the San Fernando Valley. The sight of her son in prison overalls sent a chill down her spine. And when the clerk began reading the charges, Judith could hardly breathe.

David and Schwartz were charged with four felonies. The wording of the first count, a violation of the Dangerous Weapons Control Law, sounded ominous. The two young activists might have thought they were seeking justice. But the stark language of the law made it clear how their actions would be treated:

Willfully, unlawfully and feloniously possess, explode and ignite, and attempt to explode and ignite a destructive device and explosive with intent to injure, intimidate and terrify Mr. and Mrs. John Artukovich, human beings, and further did commit the above act with the intent to wrongfully injure and destroy property, to wit, a dwelling at 16011 Meadowcrest Road, Sherman Oaks.

The second count was a felony for possessing the explosive. The next two were arson charges, one accusing them of trying to set fire and burn the Artukovich house and the next for setting fire to the car. Bail was set at $10,000 each for David Whitelaw and Mike Schwartz. With no family in Los Angeles, Schwartz had no one to call for immediate help.

Judith didn't waver for one instant. Despite her struggle to make ends meet since her divorce, she put up her house as collateral so that not only her son but also his accomplice would be set free.

Being released on bail was only the first step, however. If convicted of all four felonies, David could be in his thirties by the time he was released from prison, and he could kiss his dream of becoming a doctor goodbye.

David and Schwartz parted company outside the courthouse with barely a glance. They had hardly spoken to each other after their arrest and it seemed to David that Schwartz could have expressed considerably more gratitude to his mother for getting him out of jail.

David was still wondering how the police knew about their plan to firebomb the car and had a niggling feeling that Schwartz had exposed their secret plan. David's suspicion about Mike Schwartz proved to be well founded: word had spread quickly around the JDL office that Schwartz had gotten drunk the night before and shot off his big mouth about their plans. Irv Rubin now suspected that a mole had infiltrated the JDL.

Worse was yet to come: Schwartz had barely walked out of the court-room when he boarded a plane for Israel. David was disgusted that Schwartz didn't have the guts to face a judge. More so, he couldn't fathom how he could be irresponsible enough to skip town after Judith had put up the money for his bail: 'When I called my mother from the Van Nuys jail, she didn't hesitate for one moment. Schwartz had no family in Los Angeles to help him. The way my mother saw it was that he was a Jewish boy, and he was in trouble. She got the same kind of help for him that she got for me.'

Judith, with no experience with the criminal justice system, never considered that by signing the papers, she risked losing her house. It had seemed like a legal formality. It never occurred to her that Schwartz would flee the country, leaving her with a $10,000 debt against her house for his bail.

In addition to coping with her one good son's arrest, Judith was now about to lose her house. Her home at 1772 South Crescent Heights would be the third she'd lost since fleeing the Nazis almost forty years earlier. It was an especially bitter pill to swallow. Her first home was stolen by the Nazis, the second was seized after Harry's business failures led to bank-ruptcy and now this. For the single mother, busy with volunteering for the organisations helping Billy cope with his mental illness, the house was an oasis of stability.

The Spanish-style villa, built in 1931 in the Pico district with a dis-tinctive red tiled roof and arched entrance, was close enough to the neighbouring Fairfax district for Judith to carry on with the life she cre-ated after the divorce. In a middle-class neighbourhood that was racially mixed, the house had palm trees in the front and a large backyard. Shortly after moving in, Judith had pumped up the security by placing bars on the windows and a gate at the front. Since it was a custom order, Judith splurged on incorporating a Star of David into the design. The wrought iron fence not only made a proud statement about her Jewish identity, but it was also a comforting symbol of the freedom she enjoyed living as a Jew in the United States.

The prospect of losing her house was too much for Judith to bear. Never since coming to the United States almost thirty years earlier had she felt so vulnerable. So alone. Her dear friend, Rabbi Max Nussbaum, had died a few months earlier. And the new rabbi made it clear she couldn't rely on him. The lawyer he provided was prepared to do the bare minimum: an advocate for David he was not. And David needed more than an advocate. He needed a champion, someone who could match Judith's own zeal. Judith, used to conquering the world on her own, had to admit that she now needed an advocate, too. She needed someone to stand up for her, to fight to save her home. She turned to the only friendly voice she could think of: a talk-show host who occasionally took her calls. His name was Phil Blazer. Judith was counting on him to listen to her plight.

Blazer was just beginning to enjoy fame in Jewish media circles. He had come up through the ranks in the time-honoured way of radio personalities, starting as a 'go-for' at a small station and moving gradually into on-air roles. In 1964, he cut his teeth in Minneapolis-St Paul on a show at KUXL, a radio station that played religious programming in the morning and rhythm and blues in the afternoon.

Blazer was alarmed that his show about Jewish issues, *B'nai Shalom*, might be cancelled when the station was taken over by a new owner-manager, Bob Smith. Smith was already a cult figure under his stage name of Wolfman Jack, legendary for his on-air howl and distinctive, raspy voice. Blazer soaked up Smith's lessons on the broadcasting industry, including the one that struck him most: on-air hosts possessed power.

Following in his mentor's footsteps, Blazer bought a radio station and a newspaper in Los Angeles and established his own marketing niche in the Jewish press. His newspaper, *Los Angeles Jewish News*, was an immediate success and Blazer quickly expanded to a national edition, called *The National*.

Tall, athletic, affable and still in his thirties, Blazer threw his tremendous energy into building his business. But his first love was always behind the microphone, and no matter what other demands his business placed upon him, Blazer protected his gig as a late-night talk-show host. If listeners wanted to keep the conversation going after the show wrapped, so much the better.

One of the listeners who frequently called in and wanted to talk after hours was Judith Whitelaw. Blazer sensed that there was more at stake for Judith than simply discussing the topic of that night's show. He felt her loneliness emanating through the phone line and concluded that his programme was a lifeline of sorts for her.

'She was a very angry woman,' Blazer recalled. 'She was very angry about the Holocaust and what Hitler had done to the Jewish people. You know, everyone talks about the horror of six million Jews being murdered. And it was. But there are also the ones who survived and their children. They're damaged, too. When I talked with Judith Whitelaw, I could hear her pain. She passed that pain on to her own children. And she's not alone. There's a whole generation, and now two generations, of people hurt by the Holocaust.'

In Los Angeles, with a Jewish population trailing only Tel Aviv and New York, Blazer had gotten to know countless Holocaust survivors. He wanted to help them, and their families, in any way that he could.

Blazer's own motivation to fight for Jews stemmed from an incident in his adolescence in the San Fernando Valley: 'I played on a Van Nuys high school baseball team. My father had an offer one day from the coach, asking if my dad could host the team for a practice. We were getting ready to play, and my father was called over by another coach from a different high school, and I could hear the guy screaming at my dad, "You have to leave the field." And my dad says, "Why?" And he says, "Because you're a dirty Jew." My dad didn't say a word. But I was standing next to my dad, and I never forgot it.'

Blazer made a pact that no child on his watch would ever feel the pain that he felt that day on the baseball field. He promised to find his own unique voice to make it happen.

Blazer became an activist for Jewish causes. Like Irv Rubin, Blazer was a warrior. But unlike Rubin and his militant JDL tactics, Blazer fought as an appealing collaborator, using his flair for gentle persuasion to bring people onside. One of his first acts was to use his TV show as a platform to spearhead a fight against Standard Oil after its chairman, Otto Miller, spoke out against US support of Israel. 'I went on television and told our audience it was time to rip up their Standard Oil credit cards. I told them to send it to me, and I'll send it to Otto Miller. Thousands of credit cards came in, all shapes and forms. [People cut]

Jewish stars into their credit cards. It made the *CBS Evening News with Walter Cronkite*.'

Blazer won the respect of a wide range of people for his positive approach to activism. Jews and non-Jews, young and old, tuned into his programme. Among his young fans was David Whitelaw, who circulated Blazer's newspapers through the Jewish Students' Union on the campus of Los Angeles Valley College.

Blazer had never met David Whitelaw, but he classified David as a second-generation Holocaust victim. It was evident to Blazer that David, having grown up with a mother devastated by the murder of her seventy-six relatives, would bear deep emotional scars that transcended time and his own experience.

Blazer understood why David was drawn to the JDL. Blazer had met Irv Rubin several times and liked his witty personality. He did not like the JDL's tactics and he didn't like guns, but he couldn't bring himself to share the same contempt that many Jews felt for both Rubin and the JDL.

He had never met Judith Whitelaw, either, but when she would phone him at the end of his broadcast, Blazer felt such compassion for Judith as a Holocaust survivor that he allowed her to rant over the telephone, providing little more than a listening ear. But when she called him distressed that her son had been arrested and that she was about to lose her house, Blazer knew that he had to do more than just listen.

He did the thing that he did best: he told their story. Phil Blazer became the advocate that David needed, using his platforms of radio, TV and newspapers to tell the David-and-Goliath story of the young Jewish man fighting for justice against one of the worst war criminals in America.

The news of his arrest spread quickly through David's wide circle of friends. His high school friends, led by Gayle Freiburg, called to offer support. David's friends from Los Angeles Valley College, Mitzi Mogul and Gary Levin, mobilised their campus friends. Gary and David, an unlikely pair who gravitated to each other as opposites, had become the best of friends. Gary, enrolled in a business management programme, was such an indifferent student that he liked to joke that he was 'studying space management', or in other words, just taking up space. David, striving for academic excellence to guarantee his admission to medical school, saw beyond his friend's comic veneer: 'Gary is rock solid. I could not ask for a more loyal friend.'

Gary, the son of a pharmacist who expected him to enter the family business, had never known anyone in trouble with the law. His parents were appalled, both by the crime David had committed and also by his involvement in the JDL. They ordered Gary to stay away from David.

'No way,' said Gary. 'That's no way to treat a friend.' He called David up for coffee. Gary promised to be there for him, no matter what.

David, unsure of what to expect from the justice system, joked that Gary could visit him in prison. 'I'll be there,' promised Gary.

Both of them hoped it was a promise he wouldn't have to keep.

David's own father took a dim view of David's crime. Harry, like Gary Levin's father, was a 'law-and-order guy', a Second World War veteran astonished at the social chaos and violent insurrection of the 1970s. It was beyond Harry's comprehension that his own son had become an activist who took the law into his own hands.

David tried to take his father's disapproval in his stride, philosophically acknowledging Harry's point of view. But still. 'Your dad is your dad. You want him on your side. It really hurt my feelings.'

David tried to keep his life as normal as possible while he was out on bail. He continued to work his night shift at the eight-track-tape factory, a mind-numbingly dull job that offered a paycheck and the chance to listen to rock and roll while he worked.

David had gotten the job thanks to a friend who also worked at the factory. Working side by side with her every night, David had come to understand that she wanted more than friendship from him. It was clear to him that she would like to have a romantic relationship, to become the steady girlfriend that David hoped to have. David liked her, liked her a lot. But whether it was his head space at this time, or the chemistry just wasn't right, David couldn't return her feelings. Things had become a little awkward between them, but she wasn't the first girl that David had to let down gently, and he knew she wouldn't be the last. Not that girls and dating were uppermost on his mind, anyhow, as he waited for his day in court.

Graduation from pre-med, let alone finishing junior college at all, seemed like a distant possibility now that he was facing four serious charges. The prosecutor could go easy on him and treat two of the charges less seriously as misdemeanours, or he could throw the book at David and treat them as felonies. If that happened, David was facing serious jail time: he could be looking at twenty years behind bars.

One day, out of the blue, David received a call from one of the cops who had arrested him. The LAPD member asked him to meet for lunch. He opened the conversation by telling David that he was lucky to be alive. The forensic report showed that one of the police bullets struck the crossbar of the Chevy Nova's bench seat. The crossbar saved David's life: had it not been there, the bullet would have gone straight through his back and into his heart. 'He was doing the good-cop routine, trying to get me to talk. But he hinted that they might charge me with attempted murder. I wouldn't tell him anything. But I had no idea of what to expect. Of what might be coming next.'

The prospect of being charged with attempted murder was alarming. David never intended to hurt anyone, and it had never occurred to him that firebombing the car might cause the fire to spread to the house. The Molotov cocktail that he'd thrown had damaged the car, but apparently, the flames had also charred the siding on John Artukovich's house. If the prosecutor charged him with attempted murder, David could be facing a life sentence.

The experience was unsettling, made more so because David didn't have a lawyer. 'My whole legal representation was so precarious. One day it was the lawyer provided by the rabbi, another time it was the public defender. Another time it was the lawyer who was on retainer with the Jewish Defense League. Every time there was some court procedure, I'd be represented by someone different. I had no lawyer to advocate for me.'

Every day, David rode his bicycle from his home on South Crescent Heights to Los Angeles Valley College in Valley Glen. It was a demanding ride, pumping his legs for all they were worth, up the winding hills of Laurel Canyon, weaving in and out of LA's notorious traffic. On the way home, David biked through Coldwater Canyon, a reverse forty-five-minute journey that consumed his focus as he raced downhill, only to tackle the uphill challenge at the other end of the canyon.

His muscles burning, lungs bursting, David leaned into the ride, grateful for both the physical and mental diversion. He tried not to think about the fact that he might soon be locked up. He couldn't bear the thought that simply breathing the air outside, smog and all, might be a privilege that he would lose.

David was trying to remain positive and upbeat, but he was coping with deep disappointment. His father, abandoned himself as a child, seemed to have turned his back on David when he needed him most. Stephen and Billy were in their own worlds. David wasn't surprised but it still hurt.

He was also feeling abandoned by both the Jewish community and the JDL. The community action that David had expected had barely materialised, despite the publicity. Some support, such as that of Phil Blazer and Murray Shapiro, the principal of David's Hebrew school, was unwavering. But many Jews either shrugged or downright disapproved. David understood their disapproval of his breaking the law, but he couldn't see how they could remain indifferent to Artuković's crimes. Part of their antagonism toward him no doubt stemmed from their feelings about the JDL.

Two of the key figures threatening his future were Jewish. Bryon's Bail Bonds threatened to call in the $10,000 bail if Schwartz didn't show up for his next court appearance. Furthermore, the owner had made it clear to Judith that she would also have to pay any expenses the bail bondsman incurred in trying to find Schwartz, expenses that could run into thousands of dollars. He was deaf to Judith's appeal that he give a Jewish family a break.

The other Jew with control over David's fate was Deputy District Attorney Gerald Cohen, who was rumoured to want to make an example of David and Schwartz. Cohen's motivation, apparently, was concern over the surge of terrorism in Los Angeles, especially with the Symbionese Liberation Army (SLA). It had been one year since the SLA had kidnapped Patty Hearst and only eight months since the newspaper heiress had made an audiotape declaring that she was joining her kidnappers. The SLA had been robbing banks around California and, in May 1974, had been involved in a shootout with LAPD officers which left six SLA members dead.

Another source of dismay was the JDL. David had a gut feeling that Irv Rubin and other JDL leaders had helped Schwartz escape to Israel. It seemed highly suspicious that Schwartz would have come up with both the plan to escape and the money to do so on such short notice. For one thing, Schwartz struck David as a total space cadet. And, for another, he seemed almost indigent. David would later learn that Schwartz's parents were well off but that Schwartz was estranged from his family.

Schwartz had not seemed at all religious to David. He seemed to be looking for a cause, caught up in the prevailing 1970s attitudes of the other self-proclaimed revolutionaries, and the JDL conveniently fit the bill. Judaism had little, if anything, to do with it. David wondered if Schwartz only began to embrace Judaism when he joined the JDL. And even then, David thought, Schwartz was only trying to impress Irv Rubin.

David couldn't help but roll his eyes at the idea of Schwartz suddenly wanting to make a religious pilgrimage, or *aliyah*, and become an *oleh*, an immigrant of Israel. Under Israel's Law of Return, all Jews have the right to immigrate, however the rules require that they not endanger the security of the state. David hoped Israeli authorities would refuse Schwartz's visa considering the wanted poster issued by the LAPD, offering a $1,000 reward for a fugitive 'considered armed and extremely dangerous'. And furthermore, Israel and the United States had an extradition treaty in place. It was possible that Israel would send him back to the United States to stand trial. David hoped this would be the case, although he had found Irv Rubin lukewarm to the idea. Rubin was supposedly a friend of Judith Whitelaw and David found it strange and disturbing that his loyalties seemed to lie with Schwartz, who had placed Judith's home in jeopardy.

In David's own conversations with Rubin, the JDL leader had seemed guilty when he talked about Schwartz. He implied that if David had wanted to escape, he would have helped him too. David, however, was adamant that he did not want to escape. He was prepared to be held accountable for his actions and hoped that his trial would attract the right kind of publicity to spur Jews to take action to bring Artuković to justice.

David and Judith held Rubin in high esteem. Judith didn't want to believe anything negative about her friend. But David had his doubts. As far as he was concerned, Rubin had stabbed him in the back. 'It was never anything I could put my finger on, but Irv always looked sheepish about Schwartz. I wanted to know the truth, so I asked him if he had helped him get away. He was evasive, saying something like, "No Jew should ever go to jail for a Nazi." He knew that Schwartz would have done time because he had a rap sheet, so I think he used his connections and called upon wealthy supporters for the money to get Schwartz to Israel.' If he ever saw Schwartz again, David vowed to get to the bottom of his sudden desire to become an *oleh*.

David was also on his own as he contended with the notoriety that came with his arrest. Phil Blazer's media coverage was sympathetic, as was that of another Jewish journalist, Herb Brin. Their coverage focused on the fact that Artuković was a war criminal living freely in California. It was the kind of publicity that David expected when he set out to draw attention to Artuković.

But the wire service reports, including the Associated Press and United Press International, revolved around the facts of the firebombing. The wire stories were carried in newspapers across the country and the *Los Angeles Times* ran a story on page two that listed David's and Schwartz's addresses. The *Times* story quoted Irv Rubin as saying that the JDL didn't 'tell them to do it, but we sympathize with the action'.

Overall, the coverage was balanced. And most encouraging was the last paragraph in the *Times* explaining that 'Artuković had successfully fought efforts to expel him from the United States for the past 15 years. However, the Immigration and Naturalization Service is reported to be "once again looking into the possibility of ousting him".'

David stopped and read the line again. He felt a flash of pride. Could it be true that his Goliath would finally meet the fate he deserved? If the federal government is finally getting serious about kicking Artuković out of the country, thought David, his mission had been successful. He had taken risks so enormous that it was only now that it was finally sinking in. The car could have exploded and hurt, or even killed, members of the Artukovich family. David himself would have been killed if the bullet hadn't bounced off the car's back seat. And the charges he was now facing could ruin his life. But if it all meant that Artuković might be brought to justice?

David had no doubt about what he'd do if he had to relive that night.

He'd do it again.

WANTED

TODD MICHAEL SCHWARTZ
aka: Mike Schawrtz

M/Cauc 5'10" 145 lbs. Hazel Eyes Brown Hair DOB: 4-15-53

(wears cowboy boots, hat and levis)

Former member of the Jewish Defense League and may still have
contacts with this group

FELONY WARRANT NO: A131783

COURT: Los Angeles Municipal Court
                          Division 114 (failed to appear for Trial)

CHARGE: Arson (Firebombing of an automobile)

WARRANT HELD BY: Los Angeles Police Department
                          Criminal Conspiracy Section
                          Information in NCIC

Special attention to Narcotics Details

CONSIDERED ARMED AND EXTREMELY DANGEROUS

FOR INFORMATION LEADING TO HIS ARREST AND RETURN TO CALIFORNIA JURISDICTION - TELEPHONE:

Collect to (213) 749-1175, Frank Richards

$1000.00

REWARD

Los Angeles police issued a wanted poster for David Whitelaw's accomplice, Mike
Schwartz, after Schwartz fled to Israel. (Mitzi Mogul/Myth Merchant Films)

12

'Man's Law or God's Law?'

It had only been thirty-eight days since the fateful day when David was arrested, and on this Friday, 7 March 1975, his legal fate would be set.

Judith breathed a sigh of relief as their group approached the Ventura County Courthouse. In the past month, she'd called every friend and supporter she could think of to demand they come to court. She was convinced that a massive display of support would impress the judge. It would cost nothing but time, and she felt it was the least people could do after her son risked his entire future to bring Artuković to justice.

She was pleased with the outcome. She'd managed to pull together a sufficient crowd to fill the courtroom, and as they headed up the steps, she smiled in appreciation. David permitted himself to feel a twinge of hope. By the end of the day, he'd be going into the weekend with a better sense of what his future might hold. He hoped that this Friday night would be different from the last five and that when his mother lit the Shabbat candles, her prayers would be offered with relief and gratitude. If all went well, the charges against him would be dropped.

For the first time, David was confident in his lawyer. Mitch Egers was the JDL's lawyer who had represented David after his one and only previous brush with the law, following his arrest with several other JDL members for disturbing the peace at the Russian ballet. On that occasion, Egers had easily persuaded the judge to drop the charges.

Now, facing charges that could result in a long prison sentence, it was especially helpful for Egers to be able to argue that his client had no previous criminal record. David, who had spoken with the lawyer several times at the JDL office, liked him a great deal. He also admired Egers for his commitment to Jewish causes. Tall and bespectacled, with full lips that were smiling more often than not, Egers exuded an air of kindness and decency. Taking his seat beside Egers at the defence table, David felt that he was in good hands.

Egers had explained to David that today's court appearance was for a preliminary hearing, required in every felony case to determine whether the evidence is strong enough to go to trial. Both Egers and the prosecutor would be paying close attention to the witnesses, assessing their testimony for gaps and testing them to see how well they might perform at a trial. Egers planned to call only one witness: John Artukovich. David looked around the courtroom. Andrija Artuković, the real criminal who should be on trial, was predictably not in the courtroom. No doubt he was hiding in his gated community. To David's knowledge, Artuković had made no comment about the firebombing.

David was heartened by the show of support in the courtroom. His mother was surrounded not just by her friends, but by David's, too. Gayle had organised their friends from Fairfax High, and Gary was there with a group from college. Irv Rubin came with a couple of JDL members in tow. David wished his own family could have come. But Billy was a patient at Camarillo State Mental Hospital, and Harry and Stephen were away at sea.

There was one glaring absence, however: Mike Schwartz was nowhere to be found. By not showing up for this crucial court appearance, Schwartz had made two things clear – David was on his own, and Schwartz didn't give a damn that Judith would lose her house because he reneged on the $10,000 she'd put up for his bail. The thought made David feel sick.

All rose as the Honorable Leila Bulgrin entered the courtroom and took her seat at the bench. The judge held a commanding presence. Appointed to the bench fifteen years earlier, when she was only 35, Judge Bulgrin was a no-nonsense woman known for her marksmanship. She was an avid gun collector who posed for pictures of herself proudly showing off her rifle.

At 10.04 a.m., Judge Bulgrin called for the session to begin. She fixed her clear gaze on David. 'David Bryan Whitelaw. Please step forward, sir.'

David stepped forward, and the judge spoke directly to him again. 'Is that your true name?'

'Yes, it is, ma'am.'

The judge determined that David understood his rights. The next couple of minutes flew by in a blur as the judge moved on, her voice a rat-a-tat of legal jargon as she read the charges into the court record:

Count One charges each of the defendants on January 29, 1975, with a violation of Section 12303.3 of the Penal Code in connection with in effect possessing or exploding or igniting certain destructive devices and Mr. and Mrs. John M. Artukovich at the dwelling house at 16011 Meadowcrest Road, Sherman Oaks, at which the alleged offense happened.

Count Two charges each of the defendants on January 29 with a violation of Section 123.02 of the Penal Code in connection with possession of a destructive device on a public street, near private habitation.

Count Three charges each of the defendants on January 29 with arson, in violation of Section 447a, and names the same address as that set forth in Count One.

Count Four charges each defendant on January 29 with willful and malicious burning of personal property, in violation of Section 449a, and names the object of the fire as an automobile, the property of the same victims who are set forth in Count One.

'All right. Would you like to proceed, Mr Cohen?'

David stared at Cohen, mystified that, as a Jew, he had taken on this case. 'How can a Jew turn against another Jew and take the side of a man they called the Himmler of Croatia?' he wondered. As Cohen, slightly hunched and with a flattop haircut, stood to call his first witness, David got the feeling that Cohen would be approaching his task with more zeal than was absolutely necessary.

Judge Bulgrin sent the other witnesses away from the courtroom so that they would not hear each other's testimony. David, with his back to the courtroom, heard their names but could not see them. He heard the names of Andrija's brother, John Artukovich, and Charles Ross, the LAPD cop who had taken him to lunch and told him he was lucky to be alive.

Cohen called his first witness: Lucille Artukovich, the owner of the car that Schwartz and David had firebombed in the middle of the night.

Lucille Artukovich. David could barely absorb that the woman on the stand was Andrija Artuković's sister-in-law, a woman who had been part of his life since he first entered the country. How many family dinners, how many holidays had they enjoyed together since then, wondered David, as he thought about his own family's empty seats at celebrations.

After asking her to formally state her name and address, Cohen asked Lucille where she was on the night of 29 January 1975. Lucille testified that she was asleep in the bedroom when she was awakened at 2.20 a.m. by an explosion.

He then asked what she did after hearing the explosion.

'Well, I got scared to death and jumped out of the bed to find out what was happening. I thought possibly it was the same thing as before.' She was referring to the drive-by shooting on 11 December, six weeks earlier. But Mitch Egers objected to the reference. Judge Bulgrin agreed. Score one for David.

Cohen then asked if Lucille had heard anything else.

'Immediately following the explosion, there were shots fired. I heard those also.'

Cohen asked what Lucille did next.

'I went from the bedroom into the living room and into the foyer to see if there were shots that were shot like before.'

Egers jumped from his seat. 'Excuse me!'

Again, Judge Bulgrin ordered the 'like before' reference to be stricken from the record.

Lucille continued her testimony. 'I then went into the kitchen and saw through the back window that the car was on fire.' She went through her steps, detailing every move as she walked through her house in the middle of the night, looking for the source of the explosion. 'I opened the door, but I didn't go outside because it was on fire and I was scared to go out, that something would happen.'

She only opened the door after a police officer extinguished the fire with the garden hose sitting outside and knocked on her door.

Lucille went outside to look at the car. 'It was quite damaged. The paint had become quite liquified, I guess you would say. It was all running. And all underneath, it was burnt.'

'Did you take the car somewhere following that date for repair?'

'We had the Ford people come and tow it away. We did not start the car. We were afraid of starting it, that it would probably explode.'

Cohen then went on to make a case that the fire scorched the house, which could have led to injuring the people inside.

Egers tried to object, but Judge Bulgrin was firm. She allowed Lucille Artukovich to describe the fire damage to her house.

When it came time for Egers to cross-examine Lucille, he asked her whether there was a person named Andrija Artuković at her house that night. The answer was no. Did Artuković use her house as a mailing address? 'Not to my knowledge.'

Egers asked whether Andrija was a frequent visitor to her home.

'Not frequent. Once in a while.'

'More often than, say, once a month?'

'No, I wouldn't say so.'

'How often? What would your estimate be?'

'Oh, maybe two, three times a year.'

Later, the same questions were posed to John Artukovich when he took the stand.

'In the one year prior to January 29, 1975, how often was he a visitor to your house?' Egers asked.

'He has never been in my house,' answered John Artukovich.

'Before January 29, 1975?'

'No.'

'Never been in your house?'

'Never been in my house in Sherman Oaks.'

'You are a hundred per cent positive of that?'

Prosecutor Cohen jumped up to object that Egers was being argumentative.

At this, there was an uproar from the back of the courtroom. David tried to crane his neck to see what was going on. 'Irv and the JDL members wanted to do a little rabble-rousing,' David said. 'My mother was also very vocal in the courtroom. The judge was not impressed.'

Judge Bulgrin ordered quiet. 'I don't want any reaction in the back of the courtroom. You are causing a distraction. I will have none of that.'

John Artukovich, having contradicted his wife's testimony, was dismissed. No further questions.

As a member of the LAPD for twenty-five years, Sergeant Charles H. Ross was a savvy witness, coolly answering questions and sneaking in a sarcastic tone when he could get away with it. Under questioning by Cohen, who had called Ross as a witness, Ross kept a straight face when asked about his tone of voice as he and his partner chased Schwartz and David.

'And in what manner were you calling to them?' asked Cohen.

'Calling to them to halt, that they were under arrest and that we were police officers,' answered Ross.

'And what tone of voice were you using at that time?'

'Tone?'

'Yes.'

'As to volume?'

'Yes.'

'We were yelling at them.'

Ross didn't offer the fact that he and his partner, Sergeant Dale Baker, began shooting at the car with their service weapons. Nor did Cohen ask. It was not until David's lawyer had his chance to cross-examine Ross that the veteran cop admitted to shooting the car full of bullets.

'After you saw the flames, did you try to go to the area of their vehicle to stop them prior to the reaching of the vehicle?' asked Egers.

'As I said, we ran out into the street and were yelling at them,' answered Ross.

'You were yelling towards their car?'

'That's correct.'

'They drove off?'

'That's correct.'

'You fired bullets at them?'

'That's correct.'

'They didn't fire at you, did they, sir?'

'Not that I'm aware of, no.'

'How many officers were firing at them?'

'Two.'

Egers focused most of his cross-examination on two areas of the LAPD's actions that night: why eighteen police officers were following the two JDL members, and whether Ross had tried to prevent them from firebombing the car.

'Did you make any effort whatsoever during their journey across the street to the carport fifty to seventy-five feet away to identify yourself, make your presence known or stop them in any way?'

'No, sir,' replied Ross.

'What was it that you saw Whitelaw carrying, I'm sorry, Schwartz carrying?'

'A large, bulky object.'

'You were there because you expected that they would violate some section of the Penal Code, weren't you?'

'I was there in the event that they did,' Ross coolly replied.

'You surely suspected they might,' said Egers. 'Otherwise, you wouldn't have been there?'

'You want me to give my opinion of the JDL?' Ross shot back.

'No,' said Egers. 'I want to know whether you suspected they would violate a section of the Penal Code.'

'I have no way of knowing,' answered Ross.

The red and yellow gasoline can, which Ross described as the 'large bulky object' that Schwartz was carrying, had been entered into evidence. Also entered into evidence was a photo of the broken bottle and charred piece of cloth which had contained the Molotov cocktail. Ross testified that there was a second bottle containing a flammable liquid on the scene, but it had not been broken.

Ross testified that he and his partner were among eighteen officers following Schwartz, starting at 8 p.m. on 28 January. They watched him go into a house and later drive to the JDL office, where he was joined by David. One unit followed the two JDL members, while Ross, Baker and another LAPD member, identified only as Sergeant Zimmerman, made their way to the Artukovich home in Sherman Oaks.

Egers was curious about the number of officers involved in the surveillance and the reason Ross directed his own unit to the Artukovich home at 16011 Meadowcrest Road.

'I take it, then, that you had an informant who told you about a crime that was going to be committed imminently, is that right?' Egers asked.

Prosecutor Cohen objected to the question as irrelevant. Judge Bulgrin overruled, allowing Egers to continue.

'You had an informant, sir?'

'No,' answered Ross.

'Did you have a wiretap and listen to a telephone conversation which revealed to you that a crime was going to be committed?'

'No, sir.'

'What was the reason eighteen people were following these young men?' Egers pressed. 'Was it based upon some information you had received?'

'No. My particular squad, Criminal Conspiracy, is assigned to watch the JDL, and periodically we surveil them.'

Egers wasn't buying it. 'My specific question to you, sir, is this: did you have information about a crime that would be committed that night, that is, the night of the 28th or the morning of the 29th?'

'No, sir.'

'Because of a periodic surveillance, eighteen officers were watching these two young men?'

Ross was growing impatient. 'As I explained ...'

He was interrupted by Judge Bulgrin, who didn't like Egers's tone. 'Wait a minute. That really is not a question. It is a statement.'

Egers was becoming testy, too. 'Did it sound like it had an exclamation mark rather than a question mark?'

Bulgrin ignored his sarcasm. 'Rephrase it. It gets to where you are chewing back and forth. Go ahead.'

'Did you have eighteen men observing these two people, Whitelaw and Schwartz, because of a periodic surveillance?'

'Yes, basically,' replied Ross.

Egers, wondering to himself why an army of police officers would come from two different directions, pushed the point. Ross explained that a shift change had been planned, but the surveillance was stepped up instead because 'an unknown person entered and left the home of one of the announced leaders of the JDL'.

'As the surveillance progressed,' he continued, 'other units around the city joined in. I think I was with three or four cars over at West LA Station when it started in Granada Hills, pardon me, Chatsworth.'

Egers, who knew that JDL Leader Irv Rubin lived in Granada Hills, switched tack. 'Sergeant, did you have any information from any source besides the ones that I may have asked you about, such as wiretaps or telephones or informants, that a crime would be committed that evening?'

'That a crime would be committed?'

'Yes,' said Egers.

'No, sir.'

Egers decided to let it go. 'That cop is lying,' he thought, with surprise.

He wondered why Ross would lie. 'Obviously, it was not a shift change,' Egers said later. 'Obviously, it was an informant.'

More than forty-five years later, Egers still vividly remembers the courtroom scene. 'The question is, why were the police lying? That leads to the next question. They're lying because they want to protect somebody. Why would they want to protect somebody? They want to protect somebody because that person is on the inside, not an outsider who heard or observed something. They didn't want the informant known. Well, why didn't they want the informant known? They either didn't want David to retaliate, or the informant was still a good informant and working on other situations related to Jewish Defense League activities.'

Egers filed away the testimony for the time being, thinking that he would get to the bottom of it at the next phase of proceedings. However, he didn't know if there would be a next phase for him – he had only been hired to represent David for the preliminary hearing. Egers hoped he would be retained to represent David. He found him bright and personable. With David's good character, clean record and the fact that no one was hurt, Egers could make a strong defence. But whether he would represent David again depended on whether the Whitelaw family could pay him. Mitch Egers had a rule: he never worked for free if he didn't condone the crime. Firebombing a car, risking people's lives? He couldn't condone that. To his mind, it was a far different matter from a citizen's right to peaceful protest. In his opinion, peaceful protest was a wonderful part of democracy. But taking the law into your own hands? Never.

The attitude of his lawyer was an eye-opener for David. Not everyone would ask, 'Did he fail the law, or did the law fail him?'

Another eye-opener was that the nice-guy cop who'd taken him to lunch was also one of the cops who shot at him. When Ross had told him he was lucky to be alive, he hadn't observed that it was because his own bullet had missed.

★ ★ ★

Deputy District Attorney Cohen argued that the two JDL members had tried to burn down the Artukovichs' house. The fact that they set fire to the carport, which was attached to the house, was in itself an attack on the house.

But Judge Bulgrin was not convinced. 'I feel that the arson count is inappropriate here, looking at the photographs and hearing the testimony,' she said. 'The thing I am thinking of is the attempt here was geared towards the car. It is true there was a flagrant disregard as to possible other damages which could result from a burning automobile. That's true. But is that sufficient to support an attempted arson charge?'

Judge Bulgrin reduced the third count from arson to attempted arson. It was a victory for David, one that could reduce the number of years he could spend in prison.

Egers tried to make a case that all of the charges should be dismissed. But, after hearing from the fire chief, Sergeant Ross and Lucille Artukovich, Judge Bulgrin had made up her mind. 'At this time, there is sufficient evidence to support these counts.'

She called on David to stand.

'It is appearing to the court that the offences as charged in this complaint, with the exception of Count Three which will be a violation of Section 451a of the Penal Code, have been committed and there is sufficient cause to believe that you are guilty. You will be held to answer to each and every one of those charges.'

And with that, David's hope of living a normal life came to an end. From here on in, he would be fighting to stay out of prison while Artuković walked free.

The hearing that changed the course of his life lasted precisely 116 minutes. In less than two hours, David's journey through California's criminal justice system had been set on a punishing path.

Judge Bulgrin set his arraignment for two weeks later in the Superior Court in Van Nuys on 21 March 1975, at 8.30 a.m. She allowed David to remain free on bail.

The judge issued a warrant for Michael Schwartz's arrest. David knew that Schwartz would not be arrested. Rumour had it that he was already living on a kibbutz in Israel. Judith was on the hook for $10,000, money that she didn't have. Money raised through the equity in her house that could have gone to defending David. With no money to hire a lawyer, David had a sinking feeling that things would not turn out well for him.

His destiny had compelled him to obey God's law, not man's law.

Yet man's law was holding him accountable while allowing Artuković to remain free. Where was the justice in that?

★ ★ ★

David's next significant court date was almost three months later, on 14 July 1975, nine days before his twentieth birthday.

The time between his last court appearance and this one had not gone as David had hoped. His lawyer, once again provided by the temple, had persuaded him that there was no point in fighting the charges against him.

David had imagined a 'mini-Nuremberg' type of trial with publicity that would draw attention to Artuković's crimes. He had committed the crimes as a publicity stunt, after all, and was counting on attracting enough press coverage to expose Artuković. His own David-and-Goliath fight might just capture the public's imagination so that finally, after almost thirty years of the good life in California, Artuković would be held accountable.

His lawyer made it clear that David's imagined scenario was highly risky. Not only might the press coverage not materialise, but it also might not go his way. And risking a trial, with the evidence of being caught in the act, could land him in prison for years.

His lawyer warned him that jail time was almost certain. He urged him to plead guilty, counting on his clean record to get a short sentence. 'There was a feeling that the district attorney wanted to make an example out of me because of Patti Hearst.' The kidnapped newspaper heiress had continued to evade police since her kidnapping more than a year earlier. As David was heading to court to enter his guilty plea, Hearst was still at large, robbing banks and engaging in extortion.

Having agreed to plead guilty, it was with a feeling of resignation that David appeared before Judge Harry V. Peetris for the first time.

Again, the prosecutor was Deputy District Attorney Gerald Cohen, acting on behalf of The People versus David Whitelaw.

David held his breath and waited to see what would happen. But Judge Peetris wasn't ready to determine his fate. He wanted more information about David, requesting psychiatric and probationary reports. He assigned a deadline of six weeks for the lawyers to deliver the reports that would determine whether David would go to jail, and, if so, for how long.

Judge Peetris set David's sentencing date for 3 September 1975.

* * *

It was with a heavy heart that David sat down at his mother's breakfast table to type another letter on her portable Smith Corona. It seemed especially cruel that this very table and this very typewriter, which David had used in his dogged campaign to bring Artuković to justice, were now being employed to help him stay out of jail.

Writing in his own defence, David typed the date: 22 July 1975. In one day, he would turn 20, leaving his teenage years behind, his uncertain future as a criminal ahead.

'Now that the guilt has been established, I would like to explain something about the motive(s),' David wrote. 'There was a car firebombed for which I was arrested. It was firebombed via a Molotov cocktail. The car is owned by a man named John Artukovich. John Artukovich, born in Yugoslavia, is the brother of an alleged Nazi mass murderer named Andrija Artuković.'

Using the same argument that he used in his letters, David listed Artuković's genocidal crimes and his history of evading deportation and extradition:

As I had written beforehand, I was going to establish a motive for you so that you might further understand the nature of this case. With all the information that has been given, it should be known that I am the product of a European mother. She is Jewish. She was also born in Germany. At the hands of the Nazis, 76 of her relatives were murdered in the concentration camps. Since early youth, this grim fact has been drummed into me. Also, I attended Hebrew School for over 10 years, of which a large part of their curriculum dealt with the horrors the Nazis committed in the extermination of Six Million Jews. Through my years as an adolescent I was compelled to heavily investigate for myself just what really happened. It seemed necessary that I find out whether or not such an era inhibitory such as that of the Hitler Era was really as ghastly as it was always so vividly described to me. As a youth I found out a great deal about the atrocities that had occurred. At the same time a great disappointment came to my attention – How few Nazi war criminals were ever punished for what they had done.

As time progressed I found my way into the Jewish Defense League. It seemed just the outlet for me to express my dissatisfaction. Although I was never violent nor an overt activist I liked the way the J.D.L. had been reputed to be.

Before the date of the bombing, I had been involved with the Jewish Defense League for about one year. During that year it seems my dissatisfaction had become greatly intensified. My dissatisfaction had slowly become some form of hatred and left me with a feeling that my Mother's 76 relatives and the approximately 80,000 Jews that perished at the hands of Artuković should be avenged. It was through J.D.L. that I learned so much about Andrija Artuković. Although I may have become militant at that time I still believed (and still do) that some conventional means could extradite Mr. Artuković. Many times there had been attempts to see that Andrija Artuković was extradited. They had all failed. There had even been legislation suggested in Congress, made to protect him. It seemed that Andrija Artuković was impossible to prosecute. There had been lawful protests in front of his Surfside residence which only ended with threats of arrest, for reasons I failed to see as legal. Seeing that there was not any apparent conventional method for dealing with this individual, and also noting that it was futile to attempt any dialogue with Andrija Artuković, himself, I decided to use an unconventional means of confrontation expressed against his brother John Artukovich.

It seemed to me at the time I fire-bombed John Artukovich's automobile that if I could not get directly at Andrija Artuković that his brother John would be a most adequate surrogate.

With all the mounting frustration and anguish I felt for what happened to the Jewish people thirty years ago my fire-bombing seemed like a very justifiable act on the car belonging to John Artukovich, the brother of Andrija Artuković.

David further promised to obey all laws, to stay away from the JDL, to comply with any court or probation orders, and to live a productive and morally upright life. 'I will do nothing that will infringe upon the rights of others and recognize that each and every American has the inherent right to live in safety and security.'

★ ★ ★

Phil Blazer wrote an editorial in his newspaper, *Israel Today*, with the headline 'Where Is The Justice?':

> David faces a long jail term for throwing a small explosive at the auto-mobile of John Artukovich, brother of Nazi war criminal, Andrija Artuković. There really was never any question whether David threw the bomb or not. The problem is that he had an 'over-dose' of Nazi Holocaust, of stories told him when he was a child by his mother. When it comes to Nazis, David is simply not 'stable.' It is easy to understand since David lost 76 relatives in the camps and ovens.
>
> So, you figure that the prosecutor agreed to 'temporary insanity.' Wrong! [...] David pleaded guilty and is now a felon. His personal record blemished by an act of frustration and anguish. We are not con-doning bomb throwing but we ask the courts whether this was a fair and equal verdict?
>
> David Whitelaw is now a criminal and where is Andrija Artuković? He is in Surfside, California at 'home.' But where is the justice? Artuković was responsible for the slaughter of thousands of Jews and Serbs. He entered the United States under an assumed name illegally. Where is the justice? Artuković is free and David Whitelaw is not. Where is the justice?
>
> We address the courts and ask them who in the District Attorney's office is now meeting with the US Justice Department to carry the Whitelaw case to the end? For again, the illegal entry into this country by Andrija Artuković perpetrator of mass murders has been introduced as evidence. Where is the justice?'

Judge Peetris was not swayed, and he decided David should go to jail. On 3 September 1975, he sent David to county jail for three months for a psychiatric examination; sentencing would follow immediately on 3 December.

Judith fought back tears of anger. How was it possible that her son was being led away in handcuffs while Artuković remained free? She was not going to allow it to happen. She vowed right then and there to find a way to set her boy free.

★ ★ ★

His feet and arms shackled, David was chained to half a dozen other prisoners and led into a minivan with bars on the windows. He stared straight ahead to avoid making eye contact with the other prisoners during the sweltering forty-minute drive from Van Nuys to the Men's Central Jail on the eastern edge of downtown Los Angeles.

If being transported in the sheriff's van was not enough of a shock, there was also the fact that he was being jailed for three months to undergo psychiatric testing. It was the last thing David had expected because he had already submitted to four hours of doctors probing his emotions. They, in turn, had submitted reports to Judge Peetris, which on the whole, tended toward the positive.

The psychiatrists had dug deep. The first, Dr Michael Coburn, had dredged up every last detail about his family life. Under his emotional microscope, David disclosed things about his family that made him feel disloyal to even think about. He had told Dr Coburn that the reason he went to New York was 'to get away from his mother', whom he described as a 'melodramatist', although David had to admit that Judith would agree with that herself. She would not be pleased, however, to know her son called her a martyr. A warrior, yes, but not a martyr.

David painted a picture of his father as quiet and introverted, leading the psychiatrist to the damning conclusion that Harry and David had never developed a meaningful relationship. David could see why he thought that, but the psychiatrist didn't know the back story of Harry's abandonment as a child. It didn't help that Harry seemed to be parroting the pattern of abandonment himself since he'd been pretty much AWOL since David's arrest.

Dr Coburn had pushed until David dug up dirt on Stephen, admitting his anger with his brother for his alcoholism and dropping out of school. David called Stephen a 'part-time bum' and told the psychiatrist about the time his brother threatened him with a knife. Also, David didn't hold back on his anger about Stephen forging cheques in David's name and stealing from him.

David hadn't said anything bad about Billy, but simply told the heartbreaking truth about his little brother's emotional problems. Billy's sad life was nothing to be ashamed of; the poor kid was now in the Camarillo State Hospital because he had become violent in his teens and was mostly a threat to himself. His mother had returned from dropping Billy off, exhausted and traumatised. Billy had put up a fight, resisting admission to the hospital and wailing heartbreakingly when Judith left him.

About himself, David had offered the opinion that he was somewhat neglected. However, he stoically pointed out that he did not feel that way. 'He had no school problems, had plenty of friends, and when his parents were divorced, it was not consciously traumatic to him,' Dr Coburn wrote.

The doctor quoted David as telling him, 'I really didn't have a chance to be a child. Often, I had to be a mediator in fights (between his parents).'

'The defendant never even knew the names of his father's parents and his father would never talk of them. His mother was continually speaking of her own losses in World War II Europe, and was to a large part responsible for psychologically preparing him to become involved in his activism.'

David thought Dr Coburn didn't seem to get the significance of either the damage of the Holocaust or the fact that Artuković was a war criminal, but the report was mostly fair and overall, David came across as a decent and intelligent person, if emotionally immature. The doctor seemed to blame the influence of the JDL and Judith more than David himself for the firebombing.

Dr Coburn noted that David felt 'betrayed' by Schwartz and had now developed 'a broader view of the world':

Psychologically, it would be unlikely that he would again be involved in organized anti-social or destructive behavior. He may still take a part in expressing his views verbally and politically but would appear to be more likely to express those views in the context of more normal or usual 'political' behavior as opposed to physical activity or violent behavior.

There does not appear to be a predictable or detectable pattern of involvement in any potentially dangerous or assaultive behavior. After the public reaction, which was devoid of any real support for the act, he faced the 'de-conversion' often experienced by young activists when their previously idealistically held beliefs are found to be merely a reflection of their own limited viewpoints and are not shared by the world.

There was a lot of stuff in that report that David didn't agree with, especially the idea that he was some kind of immature weakling who couldn't think for himself. But David thought the salient point was surely Dr Coburn's conclusion that he posed no threat to society. Unfortunately Judge Peetris hadn't come to the same conclusion.

The sheriff's van arrived at the enormous garage of the Los Angeles County Men's Central Jail and began ascending several flights of the spiralling entrance to the admitting section.

It was not David's first trip to the county jail. He'd been brought here on the night of his arrest for disturbing the peace following the Russian ballet. But on that occasion, he was part of a larger JDL group sharing a camaraderie as they were led to a holding tank to be processed, then released in a couple of hours on their own recognisance. This time, there would be no immediate release. This time, he was among criminals.

A deputy opened the van's door, and each prisoner slowly and carefully stepped out into a line of uniformed, armed guards. 'No one had to tell us not to make any sudden moves. It was understood that you wouldn't want to do anything stupid.'

Under the watchful eyes of deputies, the chained prisoners lumbered and clanked into the receiving area. David was handed a folded sheet, a pillow, a pair of blue jeans and a blue denim shirt with 'Los Angeles County Jail' emblazoned on the back. Next, paperwork. Mug shot. Fingerprints.

A deputy escorted him to his cellblock, stopping at each of the many doors, waiting for them to be opened electronically. The stench was overwhelming. Urine, faeces, vomit, sweat, disinfectant, chemicals, other scents he couldn't identify. Then there was the noise. Bedlam. Men screaming, crying, yelling obscenities. Abusive language flying from guards and inmates. 'It was a madhouse.'

The door opened, and David was shoved into a cell with five other men. He recoiled from the sensory assault on his nose as he took his place next to men whose hygiene was in various states of decline. He glanced at the toilet in the corner. He didn't even want to think about using it, imagining its condition after being shared by six men, the indignity of relieving himself in front of their eyes.

There were four bunks; two of the six prisoners would be sleeping on the floor. David looked at the floor covered in grime. As the last person to enter the cell, it was obvious that he was lowest on the pecking order. David knew that the floor would become his bed.

The other prisoners, all African American or Hispanic, were covered in tattoos. Daggers with a drop of blood dripping from the tip, skulls, an intimidating array of artwork that ran from their chests up to their necks. David, so proud of being a Jew, was thankful that his name didn't sound Jewish. 'I wouldn't want to be a Goldstein or a Rosenberg in this snake pit. God forbid they find out you're a "dirty Jew".'

David kept his mouth shut and tried to ignore the five pairs of eyes staring at him. He made up his mind that if anyone asked him what he was in for, he would say only one word: 'Murder.' One thing he'd learned in Brooklyn was to exaggerate your toughness. The thought crossed his mind that the experience of fighting his way every day through the throngs of toughs and bullies of Coney Island would serve him well for the next three months in jail.

Three months. Already, David was losing a sense of time. The overhead fluorescent lights were glaring, the cinderblock and bricks adding to a disorienting sense of time and place.

David felt that life as he knew it had come to 'a cataclysmic halt'. 'Oh my God, what the hell have I done?' he asked himself. David knew that he had crossed a line and that he would never be the same again.

Retreating to the coping mechanism of pretending that everything would be fine, he sat down on the floor and began to compose a letter to his mother:

Dear Mother

Hi! How are you? I love you very much and miss you!! Do not worry about me. I am getting along just fine! As you can see, I could not wait to write to you!! I am writing very small to save space. I only have a small amount of paper! The food is very satisfying and most appetizing. The people I am sharing a room with are very sociable, quite intelligent and accommodating!! As soon as I was able to settle myself, I requested a Rabbi!! Please, I urge you, go to Temple and make the best of the High Holidays! Do not worry; I will do my own praying. I am doing a great deal of praying. When I pray I feel at ease. At this time I only have ONE person on my mind! That is YOU – Not women, school or work, only YOU!!! I'm not worried about myself. (What a silly person to worry about, right?) Only YOU! And when I have a moment, I think about some of the absolutely fantastic and wonderful friends that I am so lucky to be blessed with. When I think of my great friends and what a wonderful mother I have, I can stay strong and keep my hopes up.

Eventually, exhaustion overcame him. David put his pillow on the filthy floor, lay down, pulled his sheet over himself, and fell asleep.

The next day, 4 September 1975, he resumed writing the letter he'd started the day before:

> It's not bad here. My room is empty at this moment except for me and that is nice. I am enjoying this privacy. I slept excellent last night. And I woke up to very pleasant breakfast of scrambled eggs, sausage, bread, jam, scalloped potatoes, a bowl of cornflakes and coffee. Now, can you beat that for a breakfast? I don't even like to eat that well at home! It is also nice that they 'pipe' music through the halls. They play one of my favorite radio stations.
>
> I've just learned that I'll be at this facility until Tuesday. So if anyone needs to get into contact with me, I'll be here!

The Jewish High Holidays were approaching. Rosh Hashanah, the Jewish New Year, would be celebrated in two days, followed ten days later by Yom Kippur, the holiest day of the year in Judaism. Despite his falsely upbeat letter to his mother, David was heartsick at being away from his family and religious community.

But more alarmingly, he had heard a frightening piece of news from his cellmates about their neighbours in the next cellblock. Of the 5,000 inmates housed at Men's Central Jail, it was the presence of these two prisoners that made David's blood run cold. They were two men of about his own age, being held for the murder of the leader of the National Socialist Liberation Front, a Nazi organisation. The prisoners were Nazis too, members of a rival organisation called the National Socialist White People's Party.

They were accused of murdering Joe Tommasi, who had broken away from the National Socialist White People's Party to start an organisation that was even more radical. The members of both groups dressed in the same way, wearing brown uniforms in the Nazi style of the Second World War and red armbands with black swastikas. Tommasi, 24, had angered the rival party with his constant taunts, such as driving past their headquarters in El Monte, about an hour east of David's home in Los Angeles. The JDL had organised several protests in front of the old farmhouse used by the National Socialist White People's Party.

David had occasionally attended public meetings of both groups of Nazis, sometimes protesting outside and sometimes causing mischief. He was scared that the two Nazis now in jail with him would seize the opportunity to kill him, especially since they were already facing murder charges.

On 7 September, his first Friday night in jail and the first night of Rosh Hashanah, David used his daily ration of one sheet of yellow foolscap to write his will. 'To be read if anything should happen to me,' he wrote. His will was not a traditional last will and testament bequeathing property. Instead, it was 'written for the people listed below as a tribute to their sincerity, loyalty and love.'

He began:

Dearest, sweetest Mother. I love you with all my heart and soul. You are the most wonderful Mother any son could ever possibly ever have. I love you very deeply and I cherish you.

To my dearest wonderful Father: my love for you is only comparable to that of Mother's. I know I was not always such a great son but I tried. I love you very much and could not get a more wonderful Father. Please do not forget that I love you very deeply.

To my dearest, wonderful, loving Mitzi. In all my life I have never met a girl as wonderful as you! Your dedication, loyalty and love will always have a special place in my heart. You were always there when I needed you. You're a rare and wonderful person. I'll always love you. Thank you, Mitzi.

To my dear loyal friend Gary, I want to thank you for everything you have done for me. You were loyal and consistently proved your friendship.

To his friends who raised money for his legal defence, David asked that they donate the money to help out his mother. 'You are tremendous individuals. I will never forget just how kind, good-hearted and genuine you were to me in the short time I knew you. Thank you for being my friends. I will never forget you.'

Anticipating his imminent death, David wrote, 'this entire situation has caused untold grief. Not just for myself but my wonderful friends and dear parents. It tears me apart to think of the misery this may finally bestow.' He asked all of his friends for one last favour:

Please, please console my grieving parents during this crisis in their lives. My parents have suffered so terribly much. Please try to ease their suffering. It hurts me so bad that they may have to go through this. I don't want them to suffer, please. Thank you very, very much.

David also wrote a note to anyone who might read his will. 'But please, everyone must understand that I did not want to injure anyone. I only meant to bring this issue to public light. I did not want to hurt anyone, please believe me.' David began to pray silently.

As long as he was well behaved, David was allowed a visitor every day. Judith joked that she would play the role of social secretary and manage his calendar so that his friends would all be able to spread out their visits.

On one of her first visits, Judith was terrified to learn that the Nazis accused of killing Tommasi were in the same cell block as her son. David, working hard to earn his 'tough guy stripes', tried to play down the threat. He wanted it understood in the jail that he wasn't complaining. 'I didn't say, "Oh Mommy, I'm peeing my pants, help me."' Nonetheless, there was no appeasing Judith. She rushed home and called Phil Blazer.

Blazer described what happened next in his newspaper column:

Mrs. Whitelaw, shocked and excited, asked me for help. It seemed that she had visited David earlier that day and had learned that his life had been threatened. Those Nazi killers of Tommasi, the Nazi leader from El Monte, are in a cell right next to David and they said they are going to kill my boy ... right there in jail.

Phil Blazer immediately called Deputy District Attorney Gerald Cohen to tell him of the threat on David's life and to demand action. 'He seemed rather shocked and hurriedly put me in touch with an inspector, Russ Sletmoen. Within hours, I received confirmation from Deputy Garcia at the LA County Jail that David had been moved to another part of the jail and in a cell by himself.'

Although Cohen had helped on this occasion, Blazer found the behaviour of the deputy district attorney towards David to be unduly harsh. Blazer was scathing in his criticism, starting with the fact that Cohen allowed Judge Peetris to send him to jail just before the High Holidays. 'I received a telephone call today from David's mother telling me how depressed he was, praying in his cell and the difficulty he had in obtaining a prayer book,' Blazer wrote:

> Without any forethought or compassion on Sept 3, the court took custody of David and placed him in L.A. County Jail. This was just days before the High Holidays. 'Why couldn't you have let David be at home with his family for the holidays,' I asked. 'We just didn't think of it,' Cohen replied. 'We could have arranged for it.'

Criticising Cohen for 'taking a direction that was much too severe', Blazer issued a challenge to the district attorney to deal with Artuković:

> A killer of thousands of Jews and a known illegal immigrant is living it up in Southern California.
>
> We have a project for Gerald Cohen and his fellow Jewish colleagues in the District Attorney's Office. We ask them to spend their free hours collecting documents on the Artuković case and then start to lobby against your counterparts in the Justice Department. *Israel Today* will help as will many of our colleagues. And after that we can talk further about all kinds of 'Law and Order.'

★ ★ ★

David didn't realise that the timing of his incarceration had an uncanny parallel to Artuković's own journey in the California justice system. It was twenty-four years earlier, in September 1951, that Artuković had been locked up for the first time at Men's Central Jail in downtown Los Angeles.

Jail time was excruciatingly boring. Now that David was moved away from the Nazis, he was kept in isolation. It was for his own safety, but it felt like punishment nonetheless. He longed for his radio, the friendly voices of the DJs and the music that kept him from feeling lonely since he was sent away from home for the first time back in 1966 when he moved to New York. He told his mother how much he missed his radio.

The next time she came to visit, Judith brought a photograph of the radio. 'Look what I brought for you,' she said, holding up a photo of the radio and pressing it to the glass. David touched the photograph through the glass as if he were visiting with a long-lost friend. He memorised every detail, every button, imagined how the mechanical digital clock's numbers would make a clicking sound as they moved into the next minute, the next hour.

When David returned to his cell, he drew a picture of the radio from memory so that he could cherish the anticipation of hearing it. It was a bittersweet moment, longing for the day when he could lose himself in his programmes, allowing himself to dream of the bigger world out there. Back when the world out there meant all of the unlimited possibilities and not the world outside the prison walls.

Back when he was not all alone in the world, with a real radio, and not just a picture, to keep him from feeling alone.

True to her word, Judith organised a visiting calendar for his friends, making sure that there was no overlap. Gary Levin defied his parents and came to visit; Gayle Freiburg flew into action and organised friends' visits and care packages. Gayle always included postage stamps so that David could write back:

Dear David, Hi

It's been a busy day. It seems I will be doing housework until I'm 999 years old.

I usually don't start on my homework until 8 o'clock. I had an appointment for a manicure but then at the spur of the moment, Dear Daddy decides he wants to go to the butcher shop.

I think about you and can't help worrying sometimes. I talk to your mom almost everyday. Yesterday, she was just so tired that she went to bed at 5 o'clock just to rest a little. She wouldn't take the phone off the hook for even a minute because she thought she might get a phone call concerning you. She's such a sweetheart. I've aways liked her and now I've become even more fond of her. Now I know what she's really like and you're lucky to have her.

I'm going to see the Elton John concert this Saturday at Dodger Stadium. I hope he's as good as last year. I'll send you something soon!

Feel better [heart drawing] I'm sure you'll get this letter after our visit. It's not full of too much new news but I want to keep in touch. Love, Gayle.

The stories he heard from other prisoners were far from reassuring. When David moved from isolation, he was housed in Charley Block, or C Block, where he began to meet more prisoners. There was only one other Jewish prisoner who entered David's orbit, an accountant named Arnold Nudelman. He and David would discuss Judaism, and as David got to know him better, he found it hard to believe that Nudelman could commit a crime. David didn't know what Nudelman was charged with, but in talking with the quiet, soft-spoken, bespectacled 30-something professional, David thought his arrest must have been one of mistaken identity. Later, David learned that Nudelman was charged with raping and stabbing two 14-year girls who were hitchhiking. The girls were in critical condition in hospital and Nudelman was accused of rape and assault with intent to murder. 'Whoa!' thought David, 'In this insane place, people are not what they appear.'

David had already learned to give a wide berth to another prisoner, the 'Skid Row Slasher'. When he first met Vaughn Greenwood, David was struck by his small stature. 'But he'd slash your throat as quick as he'd look at you,' David learned. Greenwood was charged with murdering eleven down-and-out alcoholics living on Skid Row in downtown Los Angeles over an eleven-year period.

More infamous newsmakers became David's neighbours on C Block a couple of weeks later. When Patty Hearst was captured by the FBI in September, two founding members of the Symbionese Liberation Army were sent to the Los Angeles County Jail. Russ Little, 25, and Joe Remiro, 28, were accused of murdering Marcus Foster, the superintendent of Oakland schools. David was highly curious about the SLA, especially since Patty Hearst was supposedly the reason the district attorney wanted to make an example of David. However, David never got to speak to the SLA founders because whenever Russ Little and Joe Remiro were allowed out of their cells, they were each escorted by four officers.

The mother of one of his friends arranged for newspapers to be delivered to David's cell. Mitzi Mogul's sister, an attorney, also used her clout to have books delivered. David heard that books were forbidden because drug dealers would smear heroin on the pages. Once the paper was dry, the drug was invisible, but it could be rehydrated and sold or used.

The newspapers and the books were an unheard-of perk that gave David's spirits a tremendous boost. His mother brought a used copy of *Gray's Anatomy* and David immersed himself in preparing for medical school. He studied for ten to fifteen hours a day and began making drawings of the human anatomy. In a letter to his mother, he remarked, 'At this rate, I'll be able to pass the exams when I get out.'

But looming over the optimistic focus was the impending assessment by the prison's chief psychiatrist, set for 3 October 1975. Dr Robert Flanagan's reputation was well known: he was notorious for being a tough interrogator who showed no mercy. If Dr Flanagan determined that a prisoner's prognosis for rehabilitation was not favourable, he'd make sure the judge had every piece of information needed to lock the guy up for a long time.

After a month behind bars, David was already feeling dehumanised. He couldn't bear to think about the crushing impact on his spirit if Judge Peetris decided to lock him up for years.

He was already getting a taste of the soul-destroying routine of being incarcerated in a real prison. A week earlier, he had been moved from Los Angeles County Jail to the California Institution for Men, one of the oldest and largest prisons in the United States. Located on farmland near the city of Chino in San Bernardino County, it was colloquially known as 'Chino'.

The 35-mile trip out to Chino on a sheriff's bus ought to have been distressing because David was being sent to a real prison, not just a holding facility like Los Angeles County Jail. He could only imagine how tough it would be to join the population of hardened criminals. And who knew whether his friends would be able to make the trek such a long way to visit him?

But David was so happy to be outside the walls of Los Angeles County Jail that he pushed aside the impending despair building in his heart. Instead, he fixated on the view from the window of the sheriff's bus, drinking in every detail of the landscape. 'One of the hardest things about being in jail was never seeing the outside world. You don't know if it's dark outside or light; you don't see people moving around. For me, with my love of nature, it was excruciating.'

As the brush turned increasingly sparse, the mountains took hold and the desert grew closer, David pressed his nose to the window of the bus. The hills took him back to his days as an Explorer Scout when he and other idealistic young men trekked through the woods, testing their mettle. David, with his love of the ocean, had expected to join the marine branch of the Explorers. But the forest drew him and, like the destiny that led him to firebomb the Artukovich car, he felt propelled along a path.

Feeling lonely and lost on the sheriff's bus, David grimaced at the irony that his Explorer unit had been welcomed by the Los Angeles County Sheriff's Department to help locate hikers who had become lost. His was a search-and-rescue unit whose leaders trained the young men to find people who might suffer hypothermia. Sitting around the bonfire beside their lean-to tents, David and his fellow Explorers absorbed the woodsmen skills they would likely never use. 'How to eat a snake if you had to, how to defend yourself against mountain lions and bears, how to use twigs to build an encampment.'

The Explorers turned him into a 'tree hugger', albeit a Republican one. But mostly, the Explorers made him stronger physically and gave him a greater appreciation of God's good earth. The strength in his heart, and in his legs, could be credited both to the Explorers and his long bike rides through the canyons. What he wouldn't give now to feel his calves and lungs burning from the exertion of pedalling up the canyon's hills.

David's joy at seeing the outside world plummeted to an abrupt halt as the sheriff's bus arrived at Chino. This was the California Institution for Men.

Chino proved to be difficult. The guards, like their counterparts at Los Angeles County Jail, seemed to have a knack for keeping prisoners off balance emotionally. David was starting to conclude that their ability to rattle prisoners stemmed from some kind of sixth sense that inmates were growing too comfortable. As soon as David adjusted to one cell and one routine, he'd be moved. David prided himself on his own chameleon-like talent for fitting in, but it seemed to be working against him in prison because he was moved around continuously.

It hadn't taken long for the white supremacist neo-Nazis to discover that a member of the JDL was in their midst, and David was moved to an isolation unit for his own protection. Kept in isolation, David would look forward to the one tasty meal of the week, pancakes. As he heard the food cart trundling toward his cell, David would sit up, Pavlovian-fashion, in anticipation.

When the guard would slide open the slot, David would be waiting for the tray and plate, both made of cardboard to prevent them from becoming dangerous weapons if thrown. Speed was of the essence on pancake day because the watered-down maple syrup would turn the delicious cakes to mush if allowed to sit too long. David hated to wolf down his food, but in a couple of minutes flat, he'd return the empty plate to the tray.

Mostly, it was the boredom that got to him. And the lack of natural light. What was happening out there? Who was supporting him? Had any rabbis spoken out in his favour?

There were bright spots. Phil Blazer came, bringing the kind of news that David hungered for, and asking David questions to help him tell the stories to garner support. His friend Gary Levin came as often as he could, defying his parents' demand that he stay away from David. Making the 70-mile round trip was risky because Gary lied about where he was taking the family car. If his father noticed the odometer, there would be hell to pay. But Gary, bless his loyal soul, always came to kibitz and made David laugh with his non-stop jokes. Gary liked to mock him, reminding David that one day he would be released from prison, whereupon he would continue to have equally bad luck with the ladies. Gary, aka 'Swamp Man', would be there for him, ready to step right up and do the sweet talking for him.

David loved Gary's banter, but he was wrong about women. The opposite was true. It seemed to David that the women he considered nothing more than friends often wanted more than a platonic relationship. Even his old friend from Fairfax High School, Gayle Freiburg, was sending hopeful, romantic vibes his way. Gayle mailed him a steady supply of care packages that included Snoopy and Hallmark card books. David found the books kind of corny, but he was so overwhelmed with Gayle's relentless cheerful affection that he devoured the little books over and over again. The thought that Gayle might have a sexual interest in him made him feel squeamish because David loved her as a sister.

Even more distressing were the attentions of his friend from college, Mitzi Mogul. She ran a high-octane, one-woman campaign with an energy that rivalled his mother's. Mitzi's family was well off, with a network of influential friends and celebrities. Mitzi didn't bat an eyelid at calling them up to ask for donations as she set out to raise money and public awareness about David's case. She and her mother came to visit every Sunday, getting up early to beat the traffic from their home in West Hollywood, bearing gifts, and lingering at Chino for as much time as permitted.

Mitzi's mother was the only parent of his friends to show support. She believed in David and empathised with Mitzi's desire to be there for him. However, Mrs Mogul drew the line at letting 18-year-old Mitzi visit Chino on her own. She struck a deal with Mitzi: she would drive her to the prison and supervise her visits. There would be no private conversations.

But David wished they could have a private conversation because he wanted to ask Mitzi how she felt and let her know where she stood. He had tried to talk with his mother about his concern that he was leading Mitzi on, but Judith was dismissive. This was not the time to be thinking about girls. It was clear to Judith that he and Mitzi were not a good match, and even if they were, David needed to focus on medical school. He had never promised her anything more than friendship, so why should he worry if she wanted more?

But the next Sunday, as Mitzi fretted over David's pallor, he worried that he would break Mitzi's heart. He made an impulsive and painful decision, one that would hurt them both. He flatly told her to stop coming.

She did stop coming. David lost one of his biggest champions and closest friends. It would take decades for the rift to heal. And many years passed before David came to understand that he had developed a pattern of rejecting women, one that came as a direct result of his childhood trauma. The Holocaust hadn't just broken his mother's heart; it had left David with an inability to trust in love. His father, too, had taught him to be wary of emotional attachments

As a child, David had seen into the emotional wound in his father's heart. Now, as a young adult, he saw how his father would overreact to any feeling of rejection, perceived or real. With time in prison to think about his family dynamic, David had contemplated the scars they all carried from their childhoods. All of them, Judith, Harry, Stephen, Billy and himself, were hurting from wounds passed on from the previous generation. It hurt David that his father had never come to visit him.

Later, he would learn that Harry did come to visit one day. But Harry hadn't realised that he needed to call ahead and sign up on the prison roster. The day Harry arrived at Chino, he was turned away because David had already received a visit from Rabbi Nisson Shulman, who also served as a chaplain to the US Navy.

When David met him in the reception area, the rabbi was dressed in his full navy dress uniform, with the Star of David embroidered on the lapels. His navy whites seemed to sparkle in the drab prison. Rabbi Shulman winked and leaned in to tell David: 'I dressed like this to get you some respect.' David smiled at the rabbi's wisdom and thoughtfulness. He was right. The guards looked at him with new respect after that.

Unbeknown to David, the rabbi's visit would reverberate unhappily with Harry. When the prison authorities turned Harry away, he flew into one of his characteristic temper tantrums and blamed David for shunning him. Harry was still angry with him for committing a crime that landed him in jail. He had not offered any support and David knew that it took a lot for his father to overcome his own disappointment to make the trip to Chino.

It hurt David that he had not been able to see his father. But it hurt even more to think that Harry would believe that he'd choose to see the rabbi over his own father.

But the visit from Rabbi Shulman had bolstered David's spirits as he braced himself for the appointment later that week with the prison's chief psychiatrist, Dr Robert Flanagan.

The appointment, scheduled for Friday afternoon, would be the most important step to date in his journey through the justice system. From speaking with other prisoners, David had learned of Dr Flanagan's ominous nickname, 'CIM Charlie', or California Institution for Men Charlie, a reference to his track record for sending men to prison. In David's case, the psychiatric assessment was ordered by Judge Peetris, and Dr Flanagan's report would carry considerable weight in deciding whether he'd be sent to prison and the effect on the rest of his life.

David wasn't prepared for Flanagan's warm manner as he began to poke around the territory of laying bare the Whitelaw family's secrets.

The psychiatrist remained poker-faced, never once exhibiting a reaction as David began his story. The Holocaust. Seventy-six relatives. His mother's bitterness. His brothers' problems. The divorce. The JDL. The shocking news that a mass murderer known as the 'Butcher of the Balkans' was practically a neighbour.

Flanagan gently pressed David to tell him more about the war criminal. David started with the numbers: 770,000 people. 80,000 Jews.

'What do you believe that he did?' asked Flanagan.

'He ordered his henchmen to pour caustic acid into the food of children. His soldiers were so cruel that when German Nazis came to inspect the camps, they asked Hitler to intervene because the Ustasha's cruelty was out of control. People reported seeing hundreds of bodies floating in the Sava River past their homes.'

Flanagan took notes, encouraging David to continue.

David hated voicing the horrors. But he knew that his only chance of freedom was to convince Dr Flanagan that he committed his crime as a last resort to bring Artuković to justice. To prevent him from receiving 'biological amnesty'.

And then, having methodically laid out his history lesson, David now needed to explain his anger over his own country's protection of this monster. David, the Explorer Scout who copied George Washington's 'W' in his own signature, could not hide his rage that his beloved America provided a safe haven to a man who signed the death warrants, who designed the camps.

As he spoke, it was obvious to David that Flanagan did not believe a word he said.

David was inconsolable. He called Phil Blazer to plead for help. If there was anyone with the clout, not to mention fighting spirit, to help him, it would be Phil.

He wrote to his mother, imploring her to find supporters who could make his case directly to Dr Flanagan. David was convinced that the prison psychiatrist thought he was delusional and 'threw a bomb randomly at some stranger's house, not really knowing who it was'. He warned Judith that without the right supporters, Chino would become 'my new home'. David had never felt so desperate in his entire life. But, as it turns out, he was in for a big surprise.

13

'I've Never Been So Ashamed To Be Roman Catholic'

On Monday morning at the California Institution for Men, David was called unexpectedly. '3555827, now!'

The prison guard opened the cell door and ordered him to report to the inmate recreational centre. David couldn't imagine why he was being sent to the centre that served as a games room, and while nothing of the atmosphere of Chino was pleasant, it was the least uninviting room in the ugly sea of prison grey.

His spidey-senses were vibrating. And when the guard gestured for David to walk to the centre alone, without the usual escort, he knew something was up. 'One of the ways you survive in prison is by paying attention to every little detail. You develop antennae to pick up on any minutiae that's changed.'

As he approached the room, he could see a shadowy figure behind the door. It was Dr Flanagan.

David registered the fact that Dr Flanagan was waiting for him. And then he registered another fact: Dr Flanagan was smiling. 'Hi David, how are you doing?'

David's prison antennae zoomed to high alert, attuned to the slightest variation in the atmosphere. Inwardly, he processed the change in Dr Flanagan, the smile, the friendly tone, Flanagan calling him by his first name. 'David? Not Whitelaw? Not 3555827?' This was different. Something really was up. Something important.

Dr Flanagan gestured to one of the stainless steel chairs welded to the floor. 'Please sit down.'

'Please?' David silently repeated, processing Flanagan's words, and wondering to himself: 'You're saying "please" to me? What's with the courtesy?'

Flanagan looked at David for a long moment before he spoke. 'I didn't believe you when you told me about this war criminal,' Flanagan began.

David held his breath. He couldn't believe his ears. The psychiatrist went on to explain that there was something about David's story that rang true. It had nagged at Flanagan all weekend. He decided to call a buddy who worked for the Immigration and Naturalization Service. Flanagan had thought it wouldn't hurt to give him a call to check out David's claims about Artuković. When he learned that David's claims were true, he was shocked. When he learned that Artuković had ordered the slaughter of children, had sanctioned mass murder in the name of God, he was horrified. When he learned that the Vatican had issued false papers to help him escape justice, his entire being flooded with shame.

'I'm ashamed of this country,' Flanagan said. 'I've never been so ashamed to be Roman Catholic.'

David fought back tears. He could barely comprehend what Flanagan said next: 'I'm going to do everything in my power to get you out of here.'

David felt all of the tension seeping out of his body, like air out of a balloon. Dr Flanagan, aka CIM Charlie, was a very good man. And a very good man to have on his side.

Dr Flanagan's report was thorough and concise:

MENTAL STATUS: This is a bright if somewhat immature young man who is without evidence of mental disorder as such. He is impressionable, and espouses idealistic motives which is not unusual for young persons of intellectual stature. He was swayed by extremist propaganda and exercised poor judgment. His recent experiences have had a sobering and maturing effect on him. He expresses appropriate regret and remorse for his ill-advised behavior. He is capable of profiting from experience and shows no pattern of destructive or assaultive behavior. It is considered highly unlikely that he will re-offend in this manner.

PSYCHIATRIC DIAGNOSIS: (318) No mental disorders.

PROGNOSIS: Favorable.

RECOMMENDATIONS: Probation. It is advisable that terms include the requirements he disassociate himself from the Jewish Defense League and other extremist organizations, that he continue his university work and maintain acceptable grades, and that he not possess dangerous weapons or explosives. Since his arrest he has received counseling through the Jewish Committee for Personal Service. It is advisable that he continue with this counseling.

Dr Flanagan's report was supported by David's probation officer, Frank Urbach, who pointed out that initially he had 'seriously considered recommending time in custody'. However, the character references, psychiatrists' reports, consultation with senior probation personnel and David's own statements had persuaded him to change his mind.

'He is apparently a good student, a good worker, and active in school and civic affairs,' Urbach wrote:

His motivation for his involvement was to gain notoriety and 'gain the world's attention.' He was responsible for placing a Molotov cocktail in the carport of a home owned by a local resident, who is reportedly the brother of an individual regarded as a war criminal, and whom the defendant and his associates felt should have been deported. The probation officer feels that the defendant is sincere in stating that he had no real intention to harm anyone, but only gain exposure for his 'cause.'

The defendant now appears to be aware of the folly of his rationale for becoming involved in the present offense and is aware of the serious ramifications of his behavior. Furthermore the defendant has had no recent association with the JDL which he feels has 'betrayed him.' It is the writer's feeling that the defendant has some justification for these feelings and that members of the organization duped the defendant into believing that his actions were appropriate.

Urbach expressed his opinion that 'time in custody would serve no useful purpose' and recommended a fine, restitution to the victim and supervised probation. He outlined a list of eighteen conditions and submitted his report to Judge Peetris.

The Associate Superintendent of the California Institution for Men, Bob Bales, also reported to Judge Peetris that the staff at the prison in Chino 'is unanimous in making a recommendation for probation'.

Bales offered nine reasons for setting David free, reiterating the findings of other criminal justice officials that David was unlikely to commit another crime, that jail had had a sobering, maturing effect on him and that his crime 'was highly situational and apparently provoked by outside influence'.

But the prison's associate superintendent also raised two other important points, based on his experience from inside Chino's walls:

Members of prison groups, (Nazi, Aryan Brotherhood) have threatened Mr. Whitelaw and if he is retained in prison he would need to remain in protective custody, thus negating normal program participation.

Confinement at this time in his life would interrupt and possibly terminate his long-range planning for a medical career.

The support from key influential people, such as the chief psychiatrist, prison staff and probation officers was certainly promising. However, none of it would matter if Judge Peetris sided with Deputy District Attorney Gerald Cohen. And Cohen had made it quite clear that he would be satisfied with nothing less than prison time.

David's fate would be decided on 3 December 1975, two months to the day of his first interview with Dr Flanagan. In the meantime, his treatment in prison improved. The warden, Bill Mooneyham, took him under his wing and provided the intellectual stimulation David missed.

The first time David was summoned to the warden's office, his antennae soared into high alert, seeking out nuanced clues about what this new situation might mean. He was greeted by Mooneyham, a tall, thin wisp of a man with salt-and-pepper hair and a crisp moustache on his chiselled face.

Warden Mooneyham's manner was beyond polite. It was positively deferential as he welcomed David into his office and invited him to take a chair. As with Dr Flanagan, the solicitous treatment was hard for David to process.

'Would you like some coffee?' the warden asked as a prison 'trusty', a prisoner entrusted with special tasks, stood nearby, ready to take his order.

Even more mind-boggling was Mooneyham's next question. 'Would you like cream and sugar?' Okay, now David knew something extraordinary was happening because prison coffee was served black. 'The joke went that you could have your coffee any way you wanted, as long as you wanted it black.'

As the trusty brought a tray with the coffee, Mooneyham revealed the purpose of this appointment. 'David,' he said, 'tell me what you think of the situation in the Middle East?'

Mooneyham was intensely interested in world politics. He was genuinely interested in David's take on the Israel–Arab conflict. But more to the point, he had learned from Dr Flanagan that David was a bright young man who craved intellectual stimulation.

Mooneyham didn't tell David explicitly that he approved of his Nazi-hunting activism. It was only later that David learned that the prison warden had his own feelings about the Nazis. Mooneyham, a veteran of the Second World War, was part of General Dwight D. Eisenhower's army that liberated Dachau concentration camp. As the Allies advanced toward Germany, the Nazis began moving prisoners from other concentration camps into Dachau, just north of Munich. By the time Mooneyham's regiment arrived on 29 April 1945, there were more than 60,000 prisoners in Dachau, many of them near death. Furthermore, the army found thirty railroad cars filled with bodies. Another 7,000 prisoners had been forced into a death march from Dachau; those too ill or weak to walk were shot.

Having liberated Jews from a concentration camp, Mooneyham was all too keenly aware of the atrocities committed in the other camps across Europe. It stuck in his craw that Artuković, who oversaw the building of Croatia's camps, was living in the United States that his regiment had fought to protect. It was to keep the world safe from mass murderers like Artuković that Mooneyham had risked his own life. And now this war criminal, who had signed the death warrants for 770,000 innocent children, women and men, was free.

Mooneyham, with the experience of the Second World War seared into his soul, would not let his Nazi-hunting prisoner suffer unduly. Every week after that, he called David into his office for a discussion of politics. He always served coffee with cream and sugar. The warden's affection deeply touched David, especially after Mooneyham told him one day that David reminded him of his own son.

'Mr Mooneyham, I'm not like your son. I'm 3555827.'

David was surprised at the warden's irritated reaction to David's reciting his prison number. 'Horsefeathers,' he said in a sharp tone that David had never heard before. 'You're no more of an inmate than I am. Your only crime is that you got caught.'

Dr Flanagan also continued to be an ally. He brought David a new copy of *Gray's Anatomy*. David so immersed himself in the medical text that his eyesight became strained, partly because he wasn't allowed to exercise outside. He also ended up with such a severe case of haemorrhoids, thanks to the prison diet, that he couldn't walk and had to be transported to the prison's hospital on a gurney.

The food in the infirmary was better, and David was treated to daily sitz baths. But, best of all, Dr Flanagan made a point of checking on him every day. As with Mooneyham, Dr Flanagan wanted to engage in long conversation with David. 'He would sit on my bed and ask what I thought of an issue, not so much asking my opinion but more like he was seeking my advice.'

The chief psychiatrist was curious about David's abiding faith. Flanagan confessed to David that he sometimes wished he could be a better Catholic.

All his life, David had been a sounding board for adults who seemed to rely on him as a counsellor. David had been little more than a toddler when his mother would pull him close, curling him up beside her to listen to her stories about the Holocaust. Pouring out her emotions as she tried to come to terms with the horrors and the loss of her seventy-six relatives just over a decade earlier, David learned that the best way to comfort his mother was simply to listen.

It was the same with his father. Harry never talked about the childhood wounds that had scarred his soul. Rather he would lean on David, who was barely in kindergarten, to talk about his problems with Judith. David listened neutrally, never expressing sympathy for his mother, even though he had shared the rawness of her heart. What mattered to David was that Harry was trying. He wanted to be a good father. Judith clearly didn't think so, but David could see in his father's face and hear it in his voice that he wanted to do his best. He just didn't know how.

In Brooklyn, Herty had shared her fantasies that her mother was still alive in Germany, living in hiding and longing for a reunion with the daughter she lost when the Nazis ripped her from Herty's side. David listened. In his heart, he knew that the Nazis had murdered Herty's mom. And it seemed to him that deep inside, Herty must know that, too. But yet, he would never say anything of the sort. He listened, offering little more than a gentle presence to express his empathy.

In David's teens, Billy turned to him too, craving the attention and kind words that seemed never enough to soothe the signals firing his tortured brain.

It seemed to David that even his own mentors talked with him as an equal. Miss Ewans, offering him her personal copy of *Mein Kampf*, conveyed that his attention meant a lot to her. His religious teacher was attended to by several young people from the temple, but it was David whom she considered destined to best use the knowledge she passed on.

Irv Rubin, too, talked with him as an equal, affording David a respect not extended to the others. David's partner in crime, Mike Schwartz, for example, seemed to be a project for Rubin, someone he wanted to save from wasting his life smoking drugs in the local park. Rubin took a paternalistic tone with Schwartz, while he engaged with David, seeking his input.

And now, the prison warden, Bill Mooneyham, wanted to know what David thought. David was flattered, even though he couldn't figure out what he had to offer this Second World War veteran who had liberated Jews from Dachau.

But Dr Flanagan? The chief psychiatrist, aka CIM Charlie, sitting down on the side of David's bed and asking his advice? The irony was mind-blowing. 'Me, the inmate, counselling the prison's chief psychiatrist? Man, you couldn't write a funnier scene.'

Still, though, David was moved. He felt honoured that the two extraordinary men thought him worth their attention. Maybe destiny had brought these men into his life for reasons that he would eventually come to comprehend.

★ ★ ★

David's spirits were buoyed by how prison life had changed for him. But his future still hinged on persuading Judge Peetris that he deserved to be freed.

To David's great disappointment, his David-and-Goliath story had not become a cause célèbre. Maybe his bombing was just the latest in a long list of terrorist actions for causes that the public didn't care about. Or maybe journalists considered Artuković a non-story, accepting that after he'd won his court battle, he was here to stay. Maybe they, like Artuković's neighbours in Seal Beach, thought it was time to let the old man die in peace.

In Yugoslavia, though, it was a different story. The Yugoslav press covered the firebombing and kept the David-and-Goliath story alive. For the small Jewish population remaining in Yugoslavia and the Serbs, Artuković's crimes were still a fresh memory. Like Judith herself, they carried the images of slaughtered relatives. Not just static photographs, but vivid memories of a loved one's physical quirks, a lopsided smile, an impish wink, the scent of their perfume. People in Yugoslavia cared about justice for Artuković's 770,000 murdered victims, even if mainstream America did not.

Judith was determined to make them care. She wrote to newspapers and magazines. She would bend the ear of any journalist who would listen. She hoped journalists would become another weapon in her battle to win justice for her son.

Anyone she'd ever met who had any kind of clout, Judith called on. Her cousin, Horst Schiftan, was the Consul General of Honduras. Surely a man with his contacts could help. But the most powerful and connected person Judith knew was her old sweetheart from Germany, Rudy Sternberg. Rudy was now Lord Plurenden in the British House of Lords and a billionaire recognised by the queen for his role in rebuilding Britain's economy after the war. Judith sat down and wrote him a letter, appealing to him as a person whose family was also devastated by the Holocaust. She included a copy of Phil Blazer's story with the headline 'Where is the Justice?'

Judith asked him, as she did of all of her contacts, to write a letter of support to Judge Peetris. It was a modest request, one that Lord Plurenden considered too modest, as he explained in his immediate reply. He promised instead to involve the White House.

The White House. Maybe the White House, which had ignored David's letters demanding justice for Artuković, would pay attention to Lord Plurenden.

In the meantime, Judith went to war on her own. She waged a full-blown campaign to free David. She fashioned a 'Free David' sign out of wood and set up a table on Fairfax Avenue. She organised a group of friends to take turns sitting at the table in shifts, day and night. Her table had newspaper clippings, pictures of David, stories about Artuković and a petition to sign. The first signature was from Judith herself. She mobilised her friends to write letters to Judge Peetris, testifying to David's fine character and cementing the message that he had community support, a crucial factor in keeping criminals from re-offending.

'She was a real pest,' said Phil Blazer with a chuckle. 'As well she should have been.'

Blazer kept the story alive by publishing letters from David's supporters, as well as from David himself. Blazer even tried to track down survivors and their families to tell the stories of Artuković's camps, in the hope that their eyewitness accounts would shame the United States Justice Department into deporting Artuković.

Blazer's newspaper, *Israel Today*, published a poem written by David in prison called 'Their Eyes', a haunting dedication to the six million Jews who died in the Holocaust. The poem, Blazer was certain, would also give his readers a snapshot of David's mind, troubled as it was by Jews who suffered and his desire to seek justice for them:

There they stand, rain or snow, heat,
They stand, they must … or
Their eyes, their eyes
Dark, deep hollow
Their eyes speak. No! They do not cry – they scream
They tell stories
Each story different … yet alike
Different? You were only a number
Why should you be different?
Yes, they stand, they must
Starved, wretched, naked
Pleading to be heard
Dazed, stultified, they cry
They cry bitterly to deaf ears
What did they see?
The buildings – large – 'efficiens'
Why hasn't his wife come out yet?

When will his son come back from there?
A 'shower' only takes a moment.
What is that large ravine for?
Why are his mother and father standing in front of it?
They stand – they fall,
Their eyes, dark hollow sockets
They stare into oblivion
What do they see?
They reflect two thousand years
Their eyes, they are ablaze
Their eyes defiantly kindle an ancient flame
Yet, so many flames were extinguished
Did they weigh 86 or 68?
Who could tell anymore?
Their eyes, they stare
They are solemn – they are awesome
What did they see?
Fathers, mothers, sisters, brothers, aunts, uncles, cousins … children
There are always children
So tragically many children
Their eyes cry no more
Their glands too swollen to dry
Their eyes turns to pleas
They turn to screams
What do they see?
Towns, villages, cities, nations
Decimation
Yet they stand – they must
Starved, naked, tortured
Yet they stand – a mighty rock
Their eyes, deep, dark and hollow
Yet they glow
Their glare defiantly and furiously
There are flames in their eyes
– Six million flames
Six million flames
Six million flames crying

Do not forget! Do not forget!
Do not forget – we were six million flames
– Snuffed out!

David's voice, and his story, became well known to Blazer's audience. Phil Blazer had sworn to Judith that he would stay on top of David's story.

Israel Today ran an editorial cartoon showing the scales of justice tipped out of balance and with the word 'Justice' rendered apart with a jagged line in the middle. The cartoon covered two columns, with an entire page of the newspaper devoted to letters of support for David.

David wrote a personal letter to Phil Blazer, which the newspaper printed for all to read:

Dear Mr. Blazer:

I just received a copy of ISRAEL TODAY. What can I say? I have absolutely no faith and no hope in the Jewish people. Thank you for giving me a spark of hope. As lonely as life gets, being confined to an 8 ft. by 10 ft. prison cell virtually 24 hours a day, I was glad for once that I was alone when I received your paper. My emotions were pretty strong. I propped your paper up against one of my walls in my cell where I can always see it, so that I can be reminded that someone is out there who gives a damn.

I fully realize that what I did is not an easy thing for some people to understand. But thank you for understanding. I seem so isolated from the 'outside' world that I forgot there were compassionate and understanding human beings still around. You don't see much of that on the 'inside.' You know being in prison begins to become a somewhat dehumanizing process. After a while, I began to almost lose respect for myself. I thought at times that perhaps I really am a criminal. But I keep fighting that thought. After your newspaper came, I really cannot tell you just what it did to me. I am so overcome with your 'guts' that my entire outlook has changed.

Mr. Blazer, I know this letter sounds a bit 'melodramatic' but it is somewhat difficult a thing to avoid. It isn't meant to be melodramatic – it's exactly what I am feeling now and I just have to say what I sincerely feel.

I cannot thank you enough for everything you've done. You've really given me hope. You really are a man amongst men.

With love of Israel,
David Whitelaw
Chino State Prison.

Phil Blazer also ran stories about Judith's fight to save her house. Mike
Schwartz was still a fugitive, hiding in Israel. A poster had been issued for
his arrest, warning that Schwartz might be armed and dangerous. Also,
that narcotics might be involved. The United States started extradition
proceedings to bring him back, but Israel refused to release him.

Blazer's newspapers carried stories that were picked up by other Jewish
newspapers from across the United States. Donations began flowing into
the newspapers, asking the editors to pass the money along to Judith
Whitelaw. The amounts were not large: $5, $10 in cash, cheques for $20
or $25. Most donors asked to remain anonymous.

David's gratitude for the publicity his case was receiving was over-
shadowed by anxiety that the attention might put him and his family in
harm's way. His mother was on her own, alone in a house whose address
had been published several times in various newspapers. Several times she
had received hate mail addressed to David.

Judith, in full battle mode, spent every waking moment trying to drum
up support for David with her petition and letter-writing campaign. She
also wrote articles herself and submitted them in the hope of publication.
When journalists came calling, Judith was happy to oblige with interviews
and supporting material. As an advocate, she was only rivalled by Phil
Blazer. But Blazer had a media empire and a Rolodex full of influential
contacts behind him. Judith was a one-woman force of nature, visible on
Fairfax Avenue at her table. When some newspapers began publishing letters of rebuttal from Artuković's supporters, who protested his innocence,
David begged her to cool it:

Mother, these newspaper articles are going to ruin me in the *National
Tattler*. *Israel Today* or *Jewish Heritage* – Fine. But the others are going to
ruin your Son!

Unfortunately, in your sincere desire to help your son, I am afraid
you will ruin him. I don't want any part of Artuković or his comrades!
EVER!

I want no more interviews. I want you not to associate with
Mr. Rubin and his cohorts (in the Jewish Defense League).
Your son's future is at stake!
Love,
David,
Chino State Prison.

Judith ignored his plea. Give up fighting for her boy? Not until she drew
her last breath.

Phil Blazer held Judith in the highest admiration for her relentless
efforts to free her son. But he said the call he received one day from her
elevated his respect even more. 'She had connected with Vincent Bugliosi.
He was a big attorney.'

Vincent Bugliosi was the most famous lawyer in Los Angeles, and one of
the most well known in the United States. The country had been gripped
by his prosecution of Charles Manson, the cult leader who masterminded
a killing spree, including the murder of the actress Sharon Tate Polanski.

Bugliosi had managed to persuade a jury to convict Manson of murder
even though there was no evidence that he had carried out any of the
killings. It was the latest victory in an almost perfect record: as a prosecutor with the Los Angeles district attorney's office, Bugliosi lost only
one felony case. He persuaded the jury at 105 felony trials to convict the
accused and sent twenty-one killers to prison.

Now he was on the other side. Bugliosi had left the district attorney's
office to go into private practice, defending criminals instead of sending
them to prison. He had built on his fame prosecuting Manson by
co-writing a book, *Helter Skelter*, about the Charles Manson family. The
book had become a best-seller, and now a TV movie was in the works.
Bugliosi was a star. A celebrity. Judith knew she couldn't afford even an
hour of his time.

According to Blazer, Judith was undaunted. She called up Bugliosi and
booked an appointment. Then she called Blazer and asked him to come
with her. She might need his negotiating skills to help get Bugliosi to
represent David. For free.

The next time Judith visited David at Chino, she was beaming.
Brimming with miraculous news. Judith's prayers had been answered, and

then some. Her son was now blessed with the best lawyer in Los Angeles. 'It was such a great sense of validation when someone like that, of such brilliance, sides with you. This guy had been a public prosecutor, a brilliant legal mind. He had never treaded lightly on anything. I felt like a million bucks.'

Having a superstar lawyer attracted even more publicity. Judith used Bugliosi's name to pitch interviews, reasoning that the commitment of a high-profile lawyer would reinforce David's case. Her campaign consumed much of her time and she passed up one of her visits to Chino.

David would hear snippets from visitors about where Judith had appeared and what she had said. The stories, told third or fourth-hand, were often exaggerated or distorted. One story, David saw for himself: a schmaltzy centrefold in the *National Tattler*, a tabloid fond of photographing family members holding a picture of their (usually dead) beloved. When David saw the photo of Judith with 'big, sad eyes', hugging his photo, he flipped.

He took his allotted sheet of prison foolscap and socked it to her:

Nov. 13, 1975:

Dear Mom,

I'm very unhappy that you did not come and visit me. I can get along without the visits but somehow I need to know concretely what is going on. All I hear is bits and pieces, if nothing.

I absolutely insist on NO publicity WHATSOEVER. Not one scrap. You do not realize the tremendous damage it will do to me. You are not going on any TV shows or any of that other GLAMOROUS garbage. OR ELSE.

Also, you tell Mr. Bugliosi if it's publicity he's seeking – then hire PHILLIPS. I want NO publicity. If I must give Bugliosi publicity I refuse it – I would rather pay cash to PHILLIPS.

I do not know what it takes to sink into your head. NO PUBLICITY AT ALL. I swear if I have found that you have pulled some more crap like that AGAIN – I will take drastic action to STOP you. I am very serious. I am tired of you not listening to me or anyone else. Everyone I talk to says the same thing, the more PUBLICITY the more DANGER.

You tell Bugliosi – NO PUBLICITY AT ALL. OR THE DEAL IS OFF!

I hope you come to visit me soon. If you get PUBLICITY, you'll be
visiting for many years to come!
DO YOU UNDERSTAND?
It is going to drive me crazy if you don't STOP, I swear!
David,
Chino State Prison.

David knew the reference to Phillips, a lacklustre lawyer who had represented Judith in her divorce, would drive home the point. Feeling
increasingly edgy in his tiny cell at Chino, it seemed to David that his
mother had become more than a little starstruck. It was one thing to fight
for her son, but David thought she was a bit too caught up in the romance
of the David-and-Goliath story. To him, it seemed like Judith was relish-
ing the glitz and glamour, enjoying her moment in the spotlight.

For David, who had chafed at being treated like a husband and sadd-
led with the responsibility of being the man of the house, Judith had
crossed a line. This was no time to be writing 'loving son' letters. He felt
justified in writing a letter that pulled out all the stops, unconsciously
mimicking the tone and language that, as a child, he heard his father use
against Judith.

David's frustration grew, and he felt left out. His mother and Bugliosi
spoke frequently, working together on the facts and nuances that the
lawyer needed to build his case. But Judith didn't deliver information
about every conversation or every incremental detail, and David was feeling in the dark about his own future.

That all changed the day he met Vincent Bugliosi for the first time.

The lawyer turned heads when he walked into the prison for his meeting with David. Bugliosi, confident and glamorous, wearing a well-cut
suit and carrying an elegant briefcase, had an aura about him. He exuded
power. David could feel the eyes of guards and prisoners looking from
Bugliosi to David, back to Bugliosi and back to David. Some of the prisoners might even have been on the losing side of Bugliosi, ending up in
prison as a result of his shrewd prosecution before he switched sides to
practise as a defence lawyer. The question in their eyes was easy to read:
'Who is this guy, and how does he rate Vincent Bugliosi to defend him?'

David himself was awestruck. 'I thanked him for coming and called
him Mr Bugliosi. He told me to call him "Vince".'

David told Bugliosi that he'd read *Helter Skelter* and was intrigued by the Charles Manson case. Bugliosi began to chat about 'Charlie Manson' and David listened, enthralled with the inside glimpse of Bugliosi's rarefied legal world.

Bugliosi's down-to-earth manner, gentle and direct, melted away all of David's anger with being left out of planning his defence. Bugliosi grew animated, his expansive personality washing over David, leaving no doubt that he understood why David felt compelled to bring Artuković to justice. Bugliosi understood that Artuković was a mass murderer. He understood David.

Bugliosi's biggest challenge was that he was coming late to the case. Had he known about David's case sooner, he could have advocated more strongly. The best he could argue at this point was for David to be released on probation. Working in his favour were the letters from Dr Flanagan and the probation officer, which also recommended probation.

'So this is what it's like to have a real legal champion,' David thought, in wonder, as he recalled the other lawyers who had represented him since his arrest. 'Bugliosi wasn't just a high-powered lawyer. He was a moral defender, too. I knew that he would fight for me, morally, legally and politically.'

It felt like a turning point.

★ ★ ★

David's heart was in his mouth for the ninety-minute, early morning drive from the California Institution for Men in San Bernardino County to the Superior Court of California in Van Nuys. His court hearing had been moved up by six days to 25 November 1975, thanks to Bugliosi's legal magic. Six days. It didn't sound like much in the big picture. But a hearing six days earlier might mean that he would get out of jail six days earlier. Almost a week, an eternity in his isolation cell.

His heart soared with elation as he peered out the window of the sheriff's bus, revelling in seeing daylight again. He watched people going about their everyday lives, commuting to work, running to cross the street before the light changed, the mundane to and fro that he yearned to experience. In his darkest moments, David feared he'd never be part of that life ever again, that he would somehow get lost and disappear in the vortex of the system.

But today was a day of hope and confidence that he would be getting out. Miraculously, one of the best defence lawyers in the country would be fighting fiercely for him. David dared to hope that his hard work studying medical textbooks would pay off. His aspiration to become a doctor was within reach.

The courtroom was packed with allies. Judith was there, surrounded by David's friends, thanks to Gayle's mobilisation. His friend Suzie Berliner, herself the daughter of a Holocaust survivor, felt incredulous as Vincent Bugliosi stopped in the hallway to chat with Judith and the friends gathered around her. 'He was very unassuming, very casual. He was such an accomplished attorney, and this was so soon after the Manson trial that I was shocked he was David's lawyer.'

But Bugliosi quickly dispelled any questions lurking in the minds of David's friends. He was upfront about his admiration for David and his personal reasons as a Roman Catholic for taking on the case. Bugliosi was seeking redemption. 'He was enthusiastic about helping David. He told me that he felt that he owed to the Jewish people as an Italian to try to make up for what the Italians did during the war. He was a fantastic human being.'

With Bugliosi in his corner, David's supporters were in high spirits as they entered the courtroom. Surely the man who persuaded a jury to send Charles Manson and his cult to prison four years earlier would easily persuade Judge Peetris to let a good Jewish boy like David go free.

It would come down to the judge. He could send David away for up to ten years, or he could exercise leniency and grant probation, meaning David would be free as long as he behaved himself. David, appearing before Judge Peetris for the third time, prayed that this would be his last.

Judge Peetris, with thick grey hair parted neatly on the left and wearing aviator-style glasses, stood out among his peers for his unusual career path. He had graduated from the University of California with a degree in accounting. But when the Second World War broke out, he signed up and served in a counter-intelligence section of the FBI for the next five years. Even after rising to the Los Angeles County Superior Court, Judge Peetris had continued to provide service to the FBI.

With his background, Judge Peetris's thinking could go either way on the question of bringing Artuković to justice. On the one hand, who better than a former FBI counter-intelligence officer to fully grasp the magnitude of Artuković's crimes? On the other, the FBI considered the JDL a terrorist organisation. Judge Peetris might very well share the law enforcement fraternity's prevailing views about self-styled 1970s revolutionaries. Both the LAPD and the FBI ran ongoing surveillance on such groups, from peaceful labour activists to the violent extremists who strutted around toting guns, robbing banks and exploding bombs. Whether Peetris would be inclined to favour David seemed to be a 50-50 proposition.

Bugliosi began to speak, citing David's character as a model prisoner with no previous criminal record, an ambitious and intelligent young man, whose crime had not hurt anyone and was not intended to injure. As Bugliosi spoke, David watched Peetris, looking for any sign of reaction in the eyes behind those large glasses. 'This judge would make a damn good card player,' David thought as Peetris's expression never flickered.

The prosecutor, Gerry Cohen, was easier to read. Cohen was methodical in restating his case against David. He demanded jail time, saying that custody was required for punishment of David's crime, for endangering the safety of John Artukovich's family.

Bugliosi called David to the stand, banking on David's own oratory as the key to swaying Judge Peetris.

David took the stand and began. 'Your Honour, I'm sorry I broke the law. I'm not sorry for why I broke the law. But I do believe that it is incumbent upon me, as it is with all people in a civilised society, that we do our best to follow the law or we cannot have a governable society. I understand that, and I appreciate that, and I always have. But there comes a time in a human being's life where at some point they come to a crossroads where they have to choose between man's law and God's law. And I believe without hyperbole that this was something demanded upon me by the law of God and not the law of mortal men. That a monster like Artuković is living amongst us. When I've tried everything within the confines of the law to see that this monster is deported and it's failed, that I was left with my back up against the wall to make a choice that I neither relish nor encourage others to follow. But, your Honour, I feel that the one question that is forced upon us to ask is, as I see it, "Did I fail the law by breaking it? Or did the law fail me by allowing this monster to live here?"'

David wanted Judge Peetris to know that he understood that it was wrong to break the law. 'Your Honour, I want you to know I understand psychologically, socially, morally, in every way, that you can't have a civilised society where people cobble together their own law systems. That's anarchy, and I'm not one of those types. But knowing that, your Honour, surely you might appreciate that a guy like me, knowing what a guy like him was like, what would run through the mind of a person like me, an otherwise essentially decent person which I've always believed I am.'

After David finished speaking, Judge Peetris called for a short break. At one point, he called Bugliosi into his chambers for a brief conversation.

When court resumed, Judge Peetris asked David to stand to hear his sentence. David couldn't believe his ears when he heard the verdict: one year in jail, to be followed by five years probation. Stunned, he heard that he would be given credit for the eighty-four days served to date. David was being sent back to jail for nine months and six days.

His mind struggled to accept what had happened. 'I thought Vince Bugliosi was invincible.' But even as he thought this, he had a sinking feeling that the outcome was the one predicted all along. Cohen, and Peetris, too, wanted to make an example of him.

The bailiff appeared at David's side to escort him to the minivan waiting to return him to his cell at Chino.

Bugliosi crooked his finger towards David and gestured for him to step closer. He leaned in and spoke gently. 'It was almost a hushed undertone, and I remember verbatim to this day what he said. He said, "Now, David, I know this didn't go the way you would have wished it would go. But there's one thing I have to tell you. After you were done, Judge Peetris called me into his chambers. He wanted to talk to me. And I want to tell you what he said. Judge Peetris said that in all of his career on the bench, he thought your defence was one of the most eloquent he'd ever heard from a defendant. And he was very moved by you. He wanted me to tell you that. If that's any consolation to you, he was very touched by what you had to say. I want you to remember that." It's been more than forty years, and Vince Bugliosi's words still ring in my ears.'

It did make David feel better. Somewhat. But he was heading back to Chino, not going home to prepare for medical school. He would be a prisoner, not a student, for what felt like an eternity.

The bailiff slipped the handcuffs on David and led him away.

Vincent Bugliosi vowed to keep up the fight. He let Judith and David know how much he appreciated knowing them. He presented Judith with a copy of his book *Helter Skelter* and wrote the following inscription:

To Judith Whitelaw,

One of the most wonderful persons I have ever met. I can't express to you the sorrow I have for the tragedy you have experienced in your family. I want you to know that I will do everything in my power to help your fine son come back to you very soon and to become a neuro-surgeon in the State of California.

My very warmest personal wishes always, Vincent Bugliosi.

★ ★ ★

After two weeks at Los Angeles County Jail, David was moved to a new prison, Wayside Honor Rancho near Castaic, about 42 miles northwest of downtown Los Angeles. From the I-5 Freeway, both the lush green farm fields and the signs pointing to the 'honor ranch' created a deceiving impression. The prison housed 5,000 prisoners in maximum, medium and minimum security sections. It was the second largest prison in California, and even though the word 'honor' in the name implied that prisoners were allowed to roam freely on the farm, nothing could have been further from the truth.

Thrilled to see daylight, David's morale improved further as the minivan pulled off the freeway and into the farm. 'This is beautiful,' he thought, imagining being allowed outside to work in the fresh air, surrounded by nature.

But as the minivan made its way deeper into the complex, a feeling of foreboding overcame him. And inside Wayside, the atmosphere was anything but bucolic. As David was paraded down the long corridors with their institutional lighting and horrific smells, he thought of Jews being herded into concentration camps. Their shock after learning that deportations and the prospect of work camps would turn out to be much more frightening and threatening. He imagined Artuković's victims, forced into the grey bunkers of the camps. The children separated from their parents under Artuković's watch only to perish in the children's camps.

Artukovic's victims, the children poisoned with caustic acid. David felt an overwhelming sense of despair as he was escorted to his cell. 'This was not a concentration camp. I'm not saying it was Auschwitz. Far from it. And I would never diminish or disrespect anything about their experience in the Holocaust. But that feeling of being brought to a strange place that looks so beautiful on the outside, only to find out how awful it is once you're there, I couldn't help but think of concentration camps.'

He was placed in what was called 'Super Max', the highest security wing of the prison. 'They said it was for my own protection, but I felt like they were doing it to torment me. It felt like I was on death row.'

The colours were an awful steel grey and concrete. His thin mattress was placed upon a steel bed. His cell was perpetually cold, and David would huddle up in his prison blues, pulling his blankets tight in a futile attempt to get warm. He was trusted with a razor and allowed to shave, but he was only permitted a shower once a week. 'Sitting in your own stink for days. Ugh.'

But it was the emotional cruelty that bothered him most. David had witnessed cruelty and brutality at Los Angeles County Jail and at the California Institution for Men. But the staff at Wayside seemed outright sadistic. As the Christmas season set in, they piped Christmas music over the public address system, including one of David's favourites, John Denver's hit 'Back Home Again'. Imagining playing his guitar, David would hum along, 'Hey, it's good to be back home again. Sometimes this old farm feels like a long-lost friend. Yes, hey, it's good to be back home.'

'They would just blast this over the loudspeakers, over and over and over again, just to torment us. You're sitting in this miserable cell that looks like something out of Devil's Island. And there's this song about home blasting over the speakers.'

'Sadistic bastards,' David thought as the poignant song played for the umpteenth time. Watching some of the inmates who looked as if they were about to break down into tears, David grimly set his heart into a cold determination. He'd be damned if he'd let the bastards break his spirit.

He remembered the songs sung by Jews in the death camps. 'This one song, "Die Gedanken Sind Frei", helped me keep it together. The message is that you can lock me up, but you can't lock up my thoughts.'

He wrote to his mother on 14 December 1975, carefully omitting the painful details of his life at Wayside:

Dearest Mom,

Hi. I just wanted to let you know that I am fine and everything is going well. So don't worry about me, my state of being is excellent. I want you to do me few (other) favors. You know the protest letters and pleas that were written on my behalf by a group of medical doctors? Please make a photocopy of their letters. It is very important to me spiritually to know what men in medicine had to say on my behalf.

The day starts so early and with so little to do it goes very slowly. That is why I look forward to visits so much. They really are the highlight of my day. And that is the truth. But do not worry about me because I am doing just fine! Don't let my 'grubby' appearance frighten you! I have asked of my friends to watch over you and take care of you in this time of stress. Don't worry, they will all do a great job helping you out. They are all great friends!

Please have people visit me. You know how important it is to me. Since I can be visited only ONCE daily, schedule people to come visit so that they will not be turned down when they get here! I'll write you soon and often. With all the love in the world!

Love, your son, David

David was discouraged to receive a letter from his father, which included a note from Billy, saying that they had tried to visit but weren't able to get in. 'I made several trips to see you and due to the visiting system, I was unable to make contact with you. Although I spent at least 2½ to three hours to find out I could not see you.'

Harry was still angry about the time that Rabbi Shulman had gotten in to see David instead of him and made a point of harping about it again:

I might just as well have not been there. Some day I'll discuss this with you.

Sorry I don't have much very to write about that will cheer you up but that's the way it's always been with our family.

Right now I have Bill with me and he is doing very well. I will ask him to write a few lines:

Dear David, we went to see you but couldn't see you. I feel pretty bad about you being transferred but I wish you good luck with your studies and I hope you'll make it. I'm home for the Christmas vacation and had a very pleasant visit with Dad. I went to see Stephen on the ship, finally shipped out. I'm going to school and trying to express myself and taking some courses.

Well, I'm going to close this letter and hope you get out soon.
Love, Bill.

Harry added a postscript: 'I think he has improved a great deal. Hope we can all be together real soon. Love, Dad.'

Two days before New Year's Eve, David was abruptly transferred from Wayside Honor Rancho prison to Los Angeles County Jail. He quickly scrawled a note to his mother:

Dec 29, 1975,
 Dearest Mother,
 I am NOW at: LA County Jail. Again.
 They transferred me tonight!
 Come soon!
 Always with deep love,
 Your son, David … in transit

Back in the Men's Central Jail, David was sent to the maximum security wing and placed in isolation for his own protection. And once again, he fell under the protection of a man who would become a mentor.

Raymond Gladden was a muscular, 6ft 7in African American, arrested for his part in a kidnapping. When he first met David, he laughed at his surname. 'Whitelaw? You kidding me? White and law, the two things Black people hate most.'

At first, David was intimidated by Ray, but as they got to know each other, they developed a friendship so close that Ray began to feel like a big brother to him. He guessed Ray to be in his mid-to-late twenties, only a few years older than David but so worldly that he seemed older. 'He was in solitary confinement because for reasons that I never knew he was considered high-risk. In jail, prisoners in solitary would be allowed out to stretch their legs on the balcony. We called that break "Freeway Time". Other prisoners would leap at the chance for some exercise after sitting all day in their cells. But not Ray. The second they'd let him out of his cell, he'd made a beeline for my cell and would plop his ass right in front of me.'

Ray was from Maryland and had no family to visit him in jail. David's feelings of closeness toward Ray were reciprocated. He felt as if Ray had adopted him as a little brother, so protective was he of the prison newbie. 'Sometimes, I would look at him and think that I'm glad he's on my side,' David said. 'I wouldn't want to be on the wrong side of him.'

In jail, where prisoners aligned themselves on racial lines, Ray's friendship with David was risky. 'It took guts for him to talk to me like that. There was no mixing of the races. The Aryan Brotherhood attracted the white guys, the Mexican gangs, the Latinos, and the Blacks stuck with the Black gangs. Approaching me in plain sight with everyone watching probably could have gotten us both killed.'

Ray was curious about David's drawings of anatomy and the story behind his treasured gift from Dr Flanagan, his copy of *Gray's Anatomy*. When David explained that he was studying to prepare for medical school, Ray became more than David's protector. He became his number one cheerleader, reinforcing the message by always referring to David as 'Doc': 'You're really something, Doc, do you know that? You've really got it together.'

And, just as he had with Warden Mooneyham and Chief Psychiatrist Flanagan, David found himself mentoring Ray. Like them, Ray seemed to be seeking a spiritual connection, asking about his faith. 'I can still hear his voice now, telling me how impressed he was with Jews. He'd say, "I wish my people weren't so divided. I wish we had it together they way you Jews do."'

Every day, Ray would demand to know what David had learned that day, serving as a sounding board and a source of inspiration.

Ray showed off pictures of his beautiful fiancée back in Maryland. 'When I get out of here,' Ray would say, 'I'm going to marry that girl, and I'm going to become a chef. I won't be coming back to this place ever again.'

'Good for you, Ray. I know you'll do it,' David replied. He wondered about Ray's own childhood, whether he'd grown up in a stable home. But like Harry, Ray wouldn't talk about his childhood. And having learned from his father about the pain of opening that wound, David asked no questions. He could only hope that whatever had happened to Ray wouldn't ruin his chances for a successful relationship with his beautiful fiancée.

Ray asked lots of questions about David's family and told him he couldn't wait to meet his mother. 'He always asked after my mom, always calling her "your beautiful, sweet mother".'

David told his mother about his brotherly friendship with Ray and Judith promised that when David was free, she'd come back with him to visit Ray. Acting on the same impulse that led her to put up her house to bail out for Mike Schwartz, Judith felt compelled to help Ray. When it came to people who had no family, Judith had a soft spot. She wanted to help.

* * *

As the anniversary of the firebombing approached, David decided to go on a thirty-day hunger strike to protest his own incarceration while Artuković was free and enjoying his nightly walk on the beach. When the food cart came around, David accepted the tray that was slid under the door. But he refused to eat anything and would toss whatever food could be tossed to inmates in neighbouring cells.

But Ray and others quickly figured out what he was doing. They warned him that if he openly claimed to be on a hunger strike, he would be locked up in the 'ding tank'. It didn't sound like a good place to go, and when David pressed further, he learned why. In the wing for mentally ill prisoners ('dings', short for dingbats) prisoners were tied to their beds with restraints. David definitely did not want to end up there. But he still wanted to protest, so he made a silent pact with himself. The world didn't have to know, but God would know.

His weight started to drop. When his mother visited, David would hunch over, trying to slink down a little behind the chest-high glass to hide his body from her. It didn't work. Judith called Bugliosi to tell him that she was uneasy about David's health.

Bugliosi immediately asked Judge Peetris to grant a hearing to allow him to request a modified sentence for David. The hearing was set for 23 January 1976.

Judith kept up her publicity campaign. She had, of course, defied David's wish to stop talking with the press. And with Bugliosi's star power attached to the case, Judith's 'Set David Free' table on Fairfax Avenue attracted no shortage of volunteers. Her friends, staffing the table day and night, had managed to get 1,200 names on a petition. Along with letters attesting to David's character, Judith had an impressive dossier to present to Judge Peetris.

Some key members of the Jewish community had rallied round, including a wealthy Hungarian refugee named Frank Horny. He donated hundreds of dollars to cover Schwartz's bail and held fundraisers at his Mid-Wilshire home to keep Judith from losing her house.

David wrote the thank-you notes from the list that his mother brought him, checking off each name as he went. Some of the names were unknown to him. But one of his donors was Murray Shapiro, his former teacher at Hebrew School and a decorated Second World War veteran. Mr Shapiro let it be known that he considered David a hero, one who was being prosecuted unfairly. His cheque was extravagant for a man on a teacher's salary with kids in university.

It brought David great comfort to know that in the outside world, there were some people who cared about him.

Phil Blazer was one of them. He came to visit David at each of the jails, bolstering his spirit with his larger-than-life presence, quirky sense of humour and unwavering support. In the face of his own father's rare visits and open disapproval and older brother Stephen's complete absence, Phil's loyalty meant a lot to David.

Phil was a true champion, filling an emotional void and providing tangible support. Phil Blazer, like Gary and Gayle, Bill Mooneyham and Dr Flanagan, Vincent Bugliosi, and even Ray Gladden, were all looking out for him as if they were family. It reminded him of the feeling he had in Brooklyn. *Mishpokhe*. Family. Clan.

★ ★ ★

Bugliosi came for a visit on 13 January 1976. What he saw so disturbed him he could find only one way to describe it: 'Cruel and unusual punishment.' He feared that white supremacists would murder David.

Bugliosi wanted David out of prison. Now.

Judith wanted him out, too. Besides worrying about her son's physical and mental health, she had confided to Bugliosi that Harry had stopped supporting the family. After everything that Judith had been through, she now had serious money problems to worry about.

The next day, Bugliosi sent an appeal to Judge Peetris. The hearing was still ten days away. Bugliosi made his case in advance in writing, arguing that David should be released immediately after the hearing on 23 January:

(1) Because of threats made upon the life of David Whitelaw while in custody, his further incarceration not only constitutes cruel and unusual punishment since David Whitelaw is forced to remain away from his co-inmates, but constitutes an ever-present danger to him of death or great bodily harm.

In his supporting documents, Bugliosi detailed the threats against David from the Aryan Brotherhood, a neo-Nazi group. He cited comments from prison staff at both Wayside Honor Rancho and Los Angeles County Jail describing the threats:

While at the county jail, there is a 'keep away' on him which means that he is not permitted to co-mingle with the general inmate population. I was informed by Los Angeles County Sheriff Gordon Caron on January 13, 1976, that a 'keep away' is on David Whitelaw because of the threats on his life by the Aryan Brotherhood.

David Whitelaw's mother, Judith Whitelaw, who visits her son on a regular basis, has informed me that David Whitelaw's health has been impaired by his isolation in custody and she is very concerned about his welfare if the incarceration continues.

The two problems which present themselves if incarceration continues are the cruel and unusual punishment of someone being isolated in custody, and because of the threats of the Aryan Brotherhood, continued incarceration constitutes a danger of death or great bodily harm to David Whitelaw.

(2) David Whitelaw's mother, Judith Whitelaw, is without any present means of support and needs her son back home with her so that he can become employed and contribute toward her support.

A second and independent reason for modification of sentence is that the defendant's mother, Judith Whitelaw, has no means of support.

Since 1969, and up until a few months ago, her husband was paying her $400 a month on a voluntary basis for her support. Within the past few months, for some reason, perhaps attributable to the problems of David Whitelaw, the father has decided to divest himself of any association with the family and had discontinued making support payments to Mrs. Whitelaw. The payment on Mrs. Whitelaw's home is $209 per month, her savings have been depleted and she desperately needs her son, David, back home with her so that he can acquire gainful employment and contribute towards her support.

Pursuant to that, declarant will furnish this Honorable Court on January 23, 1976, four (4) separate offers of employment for David Whitelaw upon his release from custody.

One of those job offers was from Phil Blazer. He was impressed enough with David's writing from prison that he figured the young man would make a fine addition to his newspaper's journalistic ranks.

But despite Bugliosi's sense of urgency, at the hearing on 23 January, Judge Peetris refused to release David, saying he wanted more information. He also wanted to hear from Judith Whitelaw about the claims Bugliosi made. He set a new hearing date for 18 February 1976.

David would remain in the Los Angeles County Jail until that hearing was over. Another twenty-six more days. For all of David's faith in Bugliosi, it was another plunge on the emotional rollercoaster of prison.

★ ★ ★

On 18 February 1976, just over a year after her son was arrested, Judith had a chance to testify in court. She welcomed the day, hoping that a mother's pleas would finally convince the judge that David deserved to be set free. His life might depend on it.

Judith admitted to the judge at the California Supreme Court that her own welfare depended on David; she needed her son to be gainfully employed and contributing to the household. Harry no longer provided financial support, and without David's income, Judith couldn't pay her bills.

Judge Peetris remained impassive. He said he needed more information and set a date for another hearing.

Phil Blazer listened to the proceedings in disbelief. It was incomprehensible that Judge Peetris remained unmoved by David's plight. The Aryan Brotherhood was threatening to kill him. Prison guards had sworn to Bugliosi that, given the opportunity, the Brotherhood would certainly kill him. Prison staff and officials alike supported David's case to be released on probation.

And now, Judge Peetris was stalling again, oblivious to Judith's own financial dependence on her son. Blazer furrowed his brow, his journalistic gut telling him that something fishy was going on. Blazer decided to get to the bottom of this story. He started to work his contacts. What was up with Judge Peetris, anyhow?

One of Blazer's friends, Barbi Weinberg, told him she knew the judge extremely well and that she felt this intransigence was out of character. 'I asked her if she would speak with the judge,' Blazer said. 'Barbi Weinberg is one of the most respected leaders in Los Angeles. I asked her to get to the bottom of it.'

A few days later, Blazer's friend called back. 'I was shocked by what Barbi Weinberg told me,' Blazer said. She alleged that Judge Peetris had nothing against David but he couldn't stand Bugliosi, whom he considered a showboat. 'Barbi told me she asked the judge a question: "What if David Whitelaw was represented by a new lawyer? Would you let him go free?" She said that Judge Peetris said nothing and just smiled. But it seemed that he might.'

Blazer shook his head in disbelief. 'I'm supposed to fire Vincent Bugliosi? You can't be serious. I'm a nobody from Burbank. Not to mention that Judith Whitelaw sees him as David's saviour.' But he heard her message loud and clear: 'If you want David to get out, it's what you have to do.'

'Oh great,' said Blazer. He couldn't even imagine the conversation.

The conversation was unpleasant enough that it stands out in Phil Blazer's memory forty-three years later. 'I'm a totally non-confrontational person and I'm no legal beagle,' Blazer says. 'I knew that Bugliosi was no pussycat. And he was representing David at no cost.'

Blazer suspected that part of the reason Bugliosi had embraced David's case was for the publicity to help his campaign for district attorney. And in fact, when Bugliosi did run for DA a few months later, he listed his pro bono defence of David as one of his acts of public service.

Blazer was brief and to the point when he met with Bugliosi: 'We're moving on to a new lawyer because we think the judge will favour David if he has a different lawyer.'

Bugliosi stood up. He was equally brief and to the point. 'I don't agree with it.' He walked away.

David didn't learn of the real reason Bugliosi had taken a step back until months later. All he knew was that a new lawyer would be coming on board. When he signed the paperwork substituting the new lawyer, he saw that Vincent Bugliosi was listed as co-counsel. His new lawyer was named Marvin Part. Bugliosi agreed to remain in the background. Part would argue the rest of the case to Judge Peetris.

Marvin Part was far from a low-profile lawyer. He had attracted front-page coverage for his own role in the Charles Manson trial. Part had been appointed to defend Leslie Van Houten, one of five women charged along with Charles Manson. As such, he had gone head to head with Bugliosi in the courtroom as the prosecutor drilled away at Van Houten on the witness stand.

Bugliosi and Part might have been legal rivals, but they also had a lot in common. They had worked together at the district attorney's office prosecuting high-profile cases, and each had made a name for himself as a creative writer. Along with his son, Part was one of the writers for the show *Superior Court*, while Bugliosi was a best-selling author.

They both enjoyed a laugh as well. Part once wrote a hilarious skit about the Charles Manson trial called 'The Family that Slays Together Stay Together', lampooning the publicity-seeking, theatrical legal flair of lawyers like Bugliosi.

As Marvin Part and Vincent Bugliosi prepared their arguments for the hearing on 27 February, David was reluctant to get his hopes up. After so many disappointments, he despaired of ever getting out. It would be thirteen months, almost to the day, since David was arrested and for six of those months, he had been behind bars. His life had been altered in ways that he still didn't fully grasp.

Part appeared before Judge Peetris on 27 February 1976 to argue the case Bugliosi had prepared. The strategy to change lawyers proved successful, and Judge Peetris accepted Part's argument that David should be released on probation. He ruled that the eighty-four days that David had already served was sufficient punishment.

'I breathed the biggest sigh of relief,' David recalled. 'I can't begin to describe that feeling of relief.'

The deputy district attorney who had seemed out to get him walked over to the defence table. Gerald Cohen extended his hand to David. 'I almost recoiled. This Jew who went after another Jew for trying to bring a Nazi to justice. But I realised that it took guts for him to walk over to the defendant's table. I took his hand and shook it. He said, "Good luck, son."'

David would be set free. But not just yet: the paperwork could take up to a week. David had learned that the cliché about the wheels of justice turning slowly was certainly true.

Justice was taking a long time. Not just for David, but also for Artuković. In 1976, when David won his freedom, Artuković had already been free for eighteen years. It was in January 1959, when David was not yet 4 years old, that a judge ruled that Artuković was free to stay in the United States. And, of course, he had been free before that for another eleven years when he entered the United States on a false passport provided by the Vatican.

Contemplating his own freedom, David vowed to keep fighting to end Artuković's. Judith, too, had been galvanised by her son's imprisonment. She was more determined than ever to help David resume the battle against Artuković. Judith promised that as soon as he was ready, she'd stand by his side, shoulder to shoulder once again, to fight for justice.

★ ★ ★

As the prospect of being released in a few days loomed brightly, David allowed himself to fantasise about seeing his friends again, to kibitz over a coffee, or riding his bike over Laurel Canyon. To listen to his radio in the peaceful seclusion of his bedroom, free from the cacophony of prison. To eat food cooked by his mother. Real food, food that meant love.

He longed to see the ocean again, to take a long drive in his own car along the Pacific Coast Highway. 'There's something meditative about watching the ocean, especially at night when the moon is shimmering on the water. Listening to the sound of the waves crashing. I looked forward to parking the car and just feeling the tempestuous sea stirring my soul.'

David was feeling anxious about what the future might hold, whether he could still become a doctor. 'What's waiting for me now?' he would think. 'What's waiting for me now that I'm a convicted felon?'

As the days counted down, David started to mentally tick off the 'lasts', the last time he would walk in shackles, the last time he would eat a jail-house breakfast, the last time he would take a weekly shower, the last time he'd use the harsh prison soap or shave with a cheap disposable razor, the last time he'd dress in prison blues.

He allowed himself to dream of what it would be like to be clean, really clean, to be able to take a shower every day and to shave with a decent razor.

And to dress in clean clothes. Clothes that he chose himself, from his own closet. He admitted that he inherited his parents' vanity and looked forward to being a sharp dresser once again. To choose clothes to match his mood, clothes that would be suitable for whatever he was up to that day. And the days, themselves, each one holding its own promise. A new day, each unique. He would have to regain his health, though: his hunger strike had taken a toll, and he'd lost 60lbs.

He was conflicted about how he wanted to celebrate his freedom. Part of him wanted to hold a party, to pull in all of the loyal friends who had stood by him. His victory was their victory, too. But part of him just wanted to go home, give his mom a hug and retreat to his bedroom and close the door.

Undecided, and unsure of when he would be released, David wrote a letter to his mother, telling her he would need new clothes. And, just as he had on the night of the firebombing, David chose his clothing carefully. His instructions were specific: 'A nice, open-collared shirt and bell-bottoms. No cuffs!' He also asked her to arrange for him to stop at a friend's house to shower. 'I don't want to show up smelling bad!'

As the day grew closer, a feeling of sadness would sometimes creep up on David. Living among prisoners had taught him something about himself. His own life had been far from easy, but he'd had a roof over his head, food on the table. He knew what it was to be treated with love and respect. People with the stature of Phil Blazer, Vincent Bugliosi, Dr Flanagan and Bill Mooneyham had advocated for him.

The inmates he'd gotten to know in prison seemed to admire him. Ray Gladden seemed to tether himself to David as a moral compass. 'Don't get me wrong. I'm not saying I didn't want to leave. But part of me felt like I was abandoning those guys. It was like I was their link to normalcy.'

Ray had been like a brother to him, a person who risked his own life by violating the jail's unwritten rules about mixing with other races. Ray was a warrior, just like David himself. If Ray had lived in Brooklyn instead of Baltimore, he could have been one of the African Americans David faced, his fists clenched, walking on the Boardwalk. David thanked the destiny that brought Ray into his life at this time, not earlier or later when the opportunity to bond would have been lost.

Their friendship transcended race. Ray's thoughtful questions about Judaism demonstrated that he harboured none of the insidious stereotypes that led to the violence in Brooklyn. David, having immersed himself in a world that reinforced his Jewish identity, valued Ray's friendship as a gift. He felt as if he'd seen into Ray's heart, had felt the courage that could only come from purity.

Without knowing what had happened to Ray as a child, David could only imagine the experiences that shaped his pure and brave heart. Ray had an empathy that was truly inspiring. David made a pact to visit him in prison. Anticipating walking into the jail's visiting area would undoubtedly bring back traumatic memories, but his loyalty to Ray eliminated the option of chickening out.

Ray's friendship was a gift that must be repaid.

★ ★ ★

It was Phil Blazer who met David at the reception area of the California Institution for Men at Chino, smiling as he handed him a new set of clothes. Judith had decided that it would be best if she waited for David at home because she wanted to keep their reunion private. She knew there would be tears on both sides and, emotionally reserved German that she was, Judith wanted no witnesses.

When David saw Phil Blazer, he laughed. He looked even more anxious than David felt. 'He was as nervous as an expectant father,' David says with a chuckle.

On the way home to the Whitelaw house on South Crescent Heights, Phil talked excitedly about bringing David home to his mother. 'He was just nervous and shaking with excitement about it. He was just beside himself he was so excited.' Overwhelmed with gratitude for the help, David was touched even more deeply to realise how much helping him had meant to Phil. 'It was really something to see how excited he was about it. He took this case to heart with every inch, every fibre, of his being.'

Somehow David found the words to express his gratitude. 'I will always be in your debt,' he said. Phil was more than a champion. He'd gone far beyond what David could have expected from a blood relative. He was *mishpokhe*.

Driving up to their Spanish-style bungalow, David felt as if he were vibrating with emotions. His mother and Billy were waiting at the gate. Stephen and Harry were both at sea. Billy, now 15 and living in a group home, had come home for the day to welcome David back.

Judith, shocked at how skinny her boy was, wrapped her arms around him. Such intense feelings made David think a single thought: 'This must be what it feels like to come home from the war.'

Coming home from an actual war was something that David would never feel: while he was in prison, the Vietnam War had ended. David had been willing to serve: on his eighteenth birthday, he had reported to the military recruiting office, allowing his name to stand on the draftee list.

At the end of the war, Bob Dylan came to Judith and David's synagogue, Temple Israel of Hollywood, to sing in celebration. It was a performance that David missed. Just one more thing on a list of opportunities missed while he served time in jail.

Phil Blazer, the man who had bolstered David and Judith every step of the way, looked on as mother and son embraced. He was witnessing a scene that was a long time coming: It had been nearly fourteen months since he'd received that first desperate phone call from Judith Whitelaw.

In Phil Blazer's long track record of high-impact activism, the joy of this deeply personal fight stood out. He had acted on an instinct to help a kid traumatised as a second-generation victim of the Holocaust. His special affinity with Holocaust survivors had already shaped Phil's destiny, too.

★ ★ ★

Judith didn't throw a party to welcome David home. She knew that his emotional state, and perhaps even his physical state, were not up to it. A party could wait. She gave him space. She did what she knew was guaranteed to warm his heart: she showed her love by cooking a big kettle of chicken soup with matzoh balls. 'I think that was symbolic for her. I had lost my freedom because I was a Jew so I think she wanted to welcome me home with food that is identified as Jewish. Plus, she wanted to fatten me up.'

The radio that Judith bought for David while he was in prison was waiting in his bedroom on the bookshelf below a line of carefully arranged books. On the bottom shelf was the model of the boat his father had given him in childhood, the *Santa Ana* replica that David considers his 'Rosebud'. Directly above the radio was David's copy of *Mein Kampf*.

The radio became his new companion. 'I absolutely loved that radio. When I was in prison, the image of the radio represented a defining value. It was my mom's way of telling me that I had good things to look forward to in life. And when I came home, I felt like I was repatriated with the radio and also with my bed, my bedroom, all of the comforting things that represented home.'

David turned the radio to his favourite music station and cranked up the rock and roll.

★   ★   ★

David's obsession with Artuković didn't lessen now that he was out of jail. If anything, now that his own fate was no longer uppermost in his mind, David began to brood anew about Artuković. In prison, David often asked himself: 'How does this make sense that I'm in a tiny cell and this monster is free? How does it make sense that he can go to barbecues, hug his kids, walk on the beach?'

Now that he was at home, David dwelt further on those questions. He told his mother that he was feeling anti-social and wanted to be alone, to retreat to his bedroom and think about the injustice that his prison term had failed to address. 'This just can't be,' David thought. 'Why did I go to prison when he's free? The gods must be laughing. Six million Jews must be screaming for justice.'

David was emotionally drained from being locked up. He longed for the camaraderie of the JDL and would have loved to be part of their ongoing actions against Artuković. But the terms of probation prohibited him from associating with the JDL. Sometimes he would encounter Irv Rubin, who was in the habit of stopping by Judith's house for a cup of coffee, even though his visits could have landed David back in jail.

David was far from ready to give up the fight against Artuković. He just needed time to regroup and to figure out his next steps.

★ ★ ★

David resumed his studies at Los Angeles Valley College, biking across the canyon every day and attending summer classes to catch up. His life was like that of most of his friends, except for the weekly visit to his probation officer and the fact that he was paying restitution to Lucille Artukovich for her car. Day-to-day life had returned to normal.

A few weeks later, Judith threw a party. Among the people who signed the guest book were Vincent Bugliosi, Dr Robert Flanagan, the chief psychiatrist at Chino, and Bill Mooneyham, the warden, and his wife, Dell. The Mooneyhams had already invited Judith and David for dinner at their home. 'My mom and Dell became close friends. When they had us over for dinner, it made me realise just how special my relationship with Mr Mooneyham had been. I'm pretty sure the prison warden wasn't in the habit of inviting former inmates to his home.'

Judith's party guests included the friends whose emotional support had helped David feel connected to a normal life in the lonely days in prison. And David never forgot how he counted on them to fulfil the wishes of his last will and testament written during his first weekend at Los Angeles County Jail. 'In some ways, prison was a positive experience. People were so good to me. My champions really fought for me. Interestingly enough, the people who fought hardest for me were all Roman Catholics, Dr Flanagan, Mr Mooneyham, and Vincent Bugliosi,' he says, drily adding, 'The only Catholic who ever caused me problems was Andrija Artuković.'

★ ★ ★

Vincent Bugliosi became a constant in David's life. Etched in his memory is a long walk that they took together when Bugliosi stopped by after work one day. 'He was still wearing his work shirt and suit pants, but he'd taken off his tie. This one time, I'll never forget it. He put his arm around my shoulder, and we walked around the block, those are long blocks, and we talked. He wanted to know what I thought about my life and what I wanted out of life. He just kept asking me gentle questions and listening carefully to my answers. He never pressured me, but I know that he really wanted me to become a lawyer. It's a beautiful memory. I loved that man.'

Later, Bugliosi ran for district attorney against John Van de Kamp. Judith put her energy into volunteering for his campaign, drumming up votes and raising money. She hosted a party for him in her backyard. 'It was a great party. Bugliosi was the talk of the town.'

Bugliosi thanked Judith publicly and privately, always saying that it had been an honour to defend David. To show how much he valued Judith's work on his campaign, he invited her and David to high-profile events hosted by celebrity supporters. One of them was Hugh Hefner, the founder of the Playboy empire.

David applied to the University of Southern California. One of the people he asked to write him a letter of reference was Judge Peetris. He received an affirmative response from both: Judge Peetris wrote the letter and David was accepted at USC.

Life was back to normal. David was happy.

Except for one thing: Artuković was still free.

14

'It Has Made Those Who Know Us Love Us More'

A phone call out of the blue reignited David's inspiration to fight fiercely. It came from one of his idols, Simon Wiesenthal, the dogged Nazi hunter who himself had survived Hitler's death camps.

David had come to Wiesenthal's attention thanks to Judith's activism while her son was in prison. She had appealed to her cousin Horst Schiftan, then the Consul of Honduras. He, in turn, wrote to Simon Wiesenthal, asking his advice. Now Wiesenthal was in Los Angeles, meeting with members of the Jewish community who were working to establish a human rights organisation. They were months away from opening the Simon Wiesenthal Center, devoted to fighting antisemitism.

Wiesenthal had been instrumental in providing the information that led to the capture of Adolf Eichmann in Argentina. He had devoted his life to tracking down Nazis and had become an expert on the ratlines that served as escape routes after the war. Wiesenthal estimated that 15,000 Nazis had escaped, many of them through the ratlines. Among those were Ante Pavelić and Andrija Artuković.

Pavelić, who escaped to Argentina, had died in 1959 from injuries sustained two years previously when a Serbian war veteran attempted to assassinate him. Wiesenthal kept his sights trained on Artuković, still very much alive and living in Los Angeles. 'Imagine picking up the phone and Simon Wiesenthal asks to speak with you,' David says incredulously.

When Judith had reached out to her cousin, she was asking simply that he write a letter of support to Judge Peetris. When her cousin used his influence to connect with Wiesenthal, Judith was delighted. She was even more pleased to receive a letter from Wiesenthal offering information about evidence against Artuković and providing contacts in Yugoslavia who would be eager to help. Judith took his advice and tucked away the letter from Wiesenthal as a cherished souvenir.

She and David never expected to hear from Wiesenthal again, but when he came to Los Angeles, he went to the trouble of looking up their number in the phone book. When he called to invite David to lunch, David was blown away. 'He took me to a place that was very local, very LA. He had a heavy accent. I was so proud to meet him and so nervous. I wish I'd saved the menu or the napkin even if it had traces of food on it,' David says with a laugh.

The lunch passed in a blur, so dazzled was David. Afterwards, all he could remember was that Simon Wiesenthal wanted to thank him for his activism. He praised David for his diligence and commitment. David was inspired to fight even harder, always staying within the law. Having committed a crime to draw publicity to Artuković's crime, David seemed to have finally succeeded in shining the light on Artuković.

A newspaper reporter for *The New York Times*, Howard Blum, was writing a book about Nazis hiding in America. He called David and Judith and interviewed them over the phone. He wrote about David's fight in his book, *Wanted! The Search for Nazis in America*. Serialised and syndicated in newspapers in January 1977, it suggested that the US government's official policy was to wait for Artuković to die in order to solve a long-standing embarrassment. David shuddered at the thought of 'biological amnesty' for Artuković as a government goal.

David shifted his campaign. Instead of focusing on the personal letter telling of the seventy-six relatives his mother lost in the Holocaust, David created a letter that others could adopt and send to reach more people.

Judith pulled out all the stops to join him. As with so much between them, in the matter of seeking justice for Artuković, Judith and David were one. Judith also had time on her hands. Billy's illness had become too much to handle at home, and he had been placed in a group home. Stephen was off in his own world, gambling and drinking when he was on shore leave.

Harry wasn't around much, and Judith had settled into a long-term relationship with a man she'd begun dating off and on a few years earlier.

She still maintained a close relationship with Irv Rubin, despite David's reservations about his loyalty. David felt strongly that Rubin helped Schwartz escape to Israel and could not reconcile his mother's devotion to a man who had willingly put her at risk of losing her home. David had steered clear of the JDL since his release from prison, partly because the terms of his probation prohibited contact, but also because his focus had shifted to working with Jewish organisations on campus. He tapped into a large network with national and international contacts and stepped up the fight to force the US government to kick Artuković out of the country.

Judith, bolstered by her success at gaining 1,200 names on the petition to free David, returned to Fairfax Avenue, down the street from the JDL office. Just as she had done when she was trying to set David free, she set up her table and cajoled passers-by into signing her petition. To the dozens of Jews and Holocaust survivors who stopped to listen, Judith had a strong message: the worst war criminal in the United States, the worst mass murderer, a man responsible for the deaths of 770,000 people, was about to get 'biological amnesty'.

Artuković was almost 76 years old. David heard a rumour that Artuković lived in terror of him. 'I heard that if he ever saw a young man on the beach, he'd hold up his hands and say: "Are you David Whitelaw? Please don't kill me."'

The rumour that Artuković was so terrified of David and the JDL that he barely left his home, afraid to even walk on the beach in the gated community, was tremendously gratifying. But David had no intention of trying to harm Artuković. 'That was for a judge to do. I always saw it that way. And now I wanted to speed up that process.'

At last, the tide seemed to be turning. Andrija Artuković had come to the attention of Elizabeth Holtzman, whom David had met in 1974 just one year after she became the youngest woman ever elected to Congress. He took advantage of the chance encounter to tell her about Artuković. 'She seemed really interested in getting this putz brought to justice,' David said.

Like David, Holtzman had grown up hearing stories about Jews who were subjected to violence because of their religion. 'My own mother's family came from Russia, and she grew up during pogroms,' Holtzman said later. 'My family is Jewish. I am Jewish. Growing up with those sto-ries and having been the victim of social injustice was something that resonated with me very deeply. I always felt an obligation to stand up against it.'

Newly elected to the House of Representatives, Holtzman was shocked to hear that as many as 10,000 Nazis were hiding in the United States. That number was later disputed. But until this point, only one Nazi had ever been kicked out of the United States: Hermine Braunsteiner Ryan, who had been an SS guard at two Nazi concentration camps. Ryan, described as a 'kind and quiet housewife' from Queens, New York, had been extra-dited to West Germany in May 1973 and stripped of her US citizenship.

Holtzman set out to change the laws protecting Nazis. One of them was the law which Artuković had used to stay in the United States, making the claim that he would be persecuted for 'political' crimes.

In December 1975, nearly a year after David threw his Molotov cocktail, Holtzman asked the Immigration and Naturalization Service to reopen the extradition order from Yugoslavia to bring Artuković to justice.

This time, there was no bureaucratic back-and-forth, with one fed-eral government department quietly undermining the other. The INS was blunt: Holtzman's office told a reporter for the *Chicago Tribune* in October 1976 that 'the INS does not want to open hearings and have some-one from the State Department come in and say Artuković's extradition would be a bad thing because he might be subject to political persecution. We are at an impasse.'

The *Chicago Tribune* reporter wrote:

Speculation as to who Artuković's government 'friends' were runs from former President Nixon to the CIA. According to one Washington source, Artuković may have been promised immunity for his wartime crimes in return for supplying the CIA with information on Eastern European governments and leaders. Others say he is supported by influ-ential Catholics, who remember that the Croatian state was an avid supporter of the Vatican during the war, as opposed to the Serbs, who supported the Eastern Orthodox Rites.

The *Chicago Tribune* managed to secure a rare interview with Artuković by persuading the guard at the Seal Beach gatehouse to call him on the telephone. Artuković asked the reporter to 'please go away [...] the press has always tried to hurt me'. However, the reporter persisted and asked him a few questions, including what it felt like to be called the 'Butcher of the Balkans'.

'It has made those who know us love us more,' Artuković replied. 'Never did I think such a thing could happen in this wonderful country. I have been persecuted and jailed by the Germans, the Serbians, the Yugoslavs and others. One could not imagine that one could be exposed to that in this country. And for nothing! I am not guilty of anything. I ordered no arrests and no executions.'

Neighbours spoke with the *Chicago Tribune* and said that Artuković was practically a prisoner in his own home. One woman said she used to see him walking on the beach ten years ago. 'But I haven't seen him much any more at all. Why don't you just leave him alone and let him die in peace? After all, the war is over, you know.'

Soon after, an Associated Press reporter, Holger Jensen, visited Surfside and tried to contact the Artuković family. No one would speak with him. A neighbour offered the opinion that he was a 'nice old man who loves kids. He always has something cheerful to say.'

Jensen reported that the firebombing of John Artukovich's car prompted the family to hire private bodyguards, but since then, the Seal Beach Police Department established an 'Artuković detail', which the family now relied on. 'To friend and foe alike, Artuković has the same message: I just want to be left alone. My declining years are my own.'

★ ★ ★

David enrolled in pre-med at the University of Southern California. His future looked bright. His criminal record had been partially overturned when he completed his probation and he had won a full scholarship to one of the most prestigious universities in the United States. But he soon realised that he did not want to become a doctor. Like Andrija Artuković, who had been repulsed by the sight of blood at medical school more than fifty years earlier, David also found medicine too gory. Instead, he found a passion for law and student politics. He ran for vice-president of the student council. 'My opponent made it public knowledge that I had a criminal record. But I won anyhow. By one vote!' He became president of an organisation called Americans for Safe Israel. His new contacts broadened his network, and he found new opportunities to speak publicly about Artuković.

David offered himself as a speaker to synagogues and Jewish organisations, such as the Jewish Federation Council, raising awareness about Artuković's war crimes and his freedom. He always warned them that time was running out, repeating the line that Irv Rubin had taught him: 'We need to keep Artuković from receiving biological amnesty.'

The lectures were usually followed by question-and-answer sessions. Often there were Holocaust survivors in the audience, who listened raptly and asked thoughtful questions about his fight. At the end of the sessions, they would line up to speak with him. All wanted to shake his hand; many would put their arms around his shoulders, or pat his hand, sometimes exposing their concentration camp tattoos. Calling him by his Hebrew name, pronounced Daw'vid, they thanked him solemnly for his courage and determination

Their gratitude further compelled David to keep fighting. He organised protests at the federal building in Westwood and at the State Department on Temple Street in downtown Los Angeles. Sometimes he would picket the buildings on his own; sometimes Judith would join him, creating a mother-and-son protest of two. The number of protesters didn't matter to them. Keeping the fight visible was what counted.

★ ★ ★

David was heartened that his fight to bring Artuković to justice was gaining political support, the kind of traction that would truly make a difference. But he still suffered from a hurt left over from his time in prison. His mother had never received a penny from Mike Schwartz of the $10,000 that she lost when he skipped bail.

Judith was no longer in danger of losing her house, thanks to the donations that followed Phil Blazer's stories. Thanks, too, to another bail bondsman, Sylvia Brothers, who had stepped up and taken over the bond, telling Judith to pay it back when she could. As Phil Blazer passed on the donations to Judith, she gradually paid back Sylvia Brothers. But she couldn't manage to dig herself out of the hole of debt racked up when David was in trouble with the law.

David was incensed that Schwartz had left his mother in financial trouble. In 1976 he learned of Schwartz's whereabouts through a story in *The Jerusalem Post*. Living in Israel, he was no longer known as Mike Schwartz, having chosen a Hebrew name, Tuvia. It was clear Schwartz would not be coming back. The full-page newspaper article was comprehensive, documenting the ironic parallels in the extradition cases against two people accused of crimes: Artuković and Schwartz. In both cases, their host countries refused to release them.

With the headline 'Two Fugitives', *The Jerusalem Post Weekly* editors wrote a synopsis of the story:

> Tuvia Schwartz, a young Jew who jumped bail in the United States, is currently serving in the Israel Army. Schwartz was charged with malicious injury to property and possession of a destructive device near the home of Andrija Artuković, a known Yugoslavian war criminal, who has himself resisted all attempts at extradition. Andrew Griffel traces Artuković's background and examines Schwartz's crimes, with special reference to the extradition treaty between the US and Israel and the Law of Return.

Griffel gave an edifying picture of Schwartz: less than two weeks after the firebombing, he arrived in Israel as a tourist and soon afterwards became an *oleh*. He married an Israeli girl from Kibbutz Ruhama, moved into an apartment in Beersheba and enlisted in the army. It is not clear how US authorities learned of Schwartz's presence in Israel, but in mid-September 1975, a complaint was filed against him in California for unlawful flight to avoid prosecution. As Griffel reported, two months later, the Israeli Foreign Ministry received a request for Schwartz's extradition:

> There was indignation and protest here when the possibility arose that Israel might respond affirmatively to the extradition request. The Knesset [Israel's parliament] voted unanimously to send its Law Committee four urgent motions on the matter. Several Knesset Members demanded that the extradition request be denied or that the US Congress be asked to quash the proceedings – they felt that extraditing Schwartz to stand trial for expressing his outrage against a Nazi war criminal would be unjust and immoral, and against everything that Israel is meant to represent.

Griffel pointed out that while Schwartz was exercising his right conferred upon him as a Jew under the Law of Return, there are restrictions to that law. He cited extenuating circumstances, including the fact that Schwartz had broken the law, then compounded the crime by jumping bail and forfeiting the $10,000 bail which raised the possibility of Judith losing her house.

He further drew a parallel between the extradition case against Artuković and Schwartz:

> Neither Israel nor the US, however, is obligated to grant extradition when it is apparent that the country requesting it intends to punish the wanted person for an offense of a political nature. Tuvia Schwartz's crime, committed as a protest against the American policy of harboring a Nazi criminal, and intended to bring this fact to the attention of the public, was, according to many just such an offense.

Israel decided against extraditing Schwartz back to the United States. David understood the reasons, but Schwartz was being honoured for standing up for his convictions, while he, David, was punished for the same act. It didn't seem right. Or fair.

On 3 October 1976, eleven months to the day after David was sent to jail, *The New York Times* carried a stunning report:

> Nazi War-Criminal Suspects in US Face Deportation as Drive Widens
> The Immigration and Naturalization Service, after years of delay, has significantly expanded its investigations into Nazi war-criminal suspects living in the United States.
> The effort, involving the first exchanges of files with Soviet and Israeli officials, has produced a list of 91 leading suspects, of whom about 14 are reported to be facing deportation proceedings.
> The State Department has shown signs of dropping its long opposition to the extradition to Yugoslavia of Andrija Artuković of Surfside, Calif., who was an official in the World War II Axis puppet state of Croatia and is considered the most notorious of the suspects here.

David was jubilant. It looked like justice would finally be done.

15

'Artukovic's Final Battle'

The case to deport Andrija Artuković as an illegal alien reopened in Los Angeles on 15 August 1977. It ended quickly without resolution after Artuković's lawyers argued that the judge had no power to rule on the case because it should be heard by an Immigration Court judge. In accepting the argument, US District Judge Irving Hill emphasised that his decision was based on a 'narrow technical issue' and had nothing to do with what Artuković 'may or may not have done during World War II'. The ruling bought Artuković time, allowing him to remain in the United States while his lawyers resumed their protracted legal battle. However, as Artuković's arguments were crawling through the courts, the legal ground shifted dramatically.

On 30 October 1978, US President Jimmy Carter signed a new statute. The Holtzman Amendment was entitled 'an Act to amend the Immigration and Nationality Act to exclude from admission into, and to deport from, the United States all aliens who persecuted any person on the basis of race, religion, national origin, or political opinion, under the direction of the Nazi government of Germany, and for other purposes'. The law was written by Congresswoman Elizabeth Holtzman, who had first exposed the presence of Nazi war criminals in the United States and led the fight to force the government to bring them to justice. For Andrija Artuković, it meant he could no longer claim the United States should protect him from being sent back to Yugoslavia where he would be persecuted for political crimes.

In 1979, the federal Justice Department set up the Office of Special Investigations to investigate ninety-one Nazi war criminals living in the United States. The team of lawyers and historians chose the target of its first investigation: Andrija Artuković.

The stakes had risen. Artuković was months away from his eightieth birthday. Just how much those stakes had risen was indicated starkly by the language used by US Justice Department lawyers at Artuković's next deportation hearing in October 1979. Headed by Walter J. Rockler, a former prosecutor at the Nuremberg trials, the Justice Department's legal team demanded Artuković be deported 'without further delays or manoeuvrings'. Referring to Artuković's illegal entry into the US on a six-month tourist visa in 1948, the lawyers wrote:

The 'temporary visitor for pleasure' has now stayed more than 30 years, not withstanding his record as an outstanding Nazi collaborator and director and participant in genocidal programs.

The major Nazi collaborator and prime mover of large-scale persecutions is not entitled to the continued hospitality of the United States.

Nonetheless, the case was far from over. Artuković's lawyers managed to continue stalling his deportation hearings for another three years.

In 1982, the Ninth Circuit Court of Appeals ruled that Artuković was entitled to a full evidentiary hearing. It would be up to an immigration judge to determine whether the amended 1978 immigration law could be used be deport him. By now, Artuković was 83 years old and said to be in failing health.

In February 1984, the US Justice Department requested a new deportation hearing. The State Department was on side, recommending that asylum be denied. Now that the Red Scare was over, the authorities tended to take a more critical look at Artuković's case.

The following month, five survivors of Croatian concentration camps sued Artuković. They claimed a loss of loved ones and property and described the Ustasha's atrocities.

The Artuković family fought with all their might to keep Andrija from being taken from them. On 11 September 1984, Artuković's lawyer,

Ronald Bonaparte, said he was not competent to go through with the deportation hearing. He asked Immigration Judge Reece B. Robertson to stop the proceedings. 'The problem is that at this time, Respondent is neither physically nor mentally able to testify in his own behalf, let alone confront and rebut witnesses and evidence to be introduced as part of the government's case,' wrote Bonaparte.

Bonaparte cited letters from four different doctors detailing Artuković's ailments. The first, from his family physician of twenty-five years, warned that the stress of the deportation hearing might prove fatal to 84-year-old Artuković. The doctor, George Mikulicich, said he had examined Artuković at his home a month earlier and 'had the impression that he may be approaching his terminal state'. Artuković was suffering from brain damage associated with 'advanced vascular insufficiency of many organs'. His heart and lungs were not functioning well, and he had a large aneurysm in his abdomen. Another doctor reported that surgery for the aneurysm would likely cause him to bleed to death. Furthermore, the elderly patient was disoriented, confused, suffering from delusions and paranoia.

Dr Mikulicich said Artuković required twenty-four-hour nursing care at home and that he was taking daily high doses of Haldol, an antipsychotic drug, to help manage the symptoms.

A psychiatrist, Eric Speare, elaborated upon Artuković's delusional and paranoid state. Dr Speare had treated Artuković the previous October in hospital after he had been admitted following an 'episode at home wherein he became delusional and combative, including breaking a window with a shovel':

> He believed there were agents who were after him and struck out, imagining they were on the other side of the window. In the hospital, Mr. Artuković required round-the-clock one-to-one special nursing supervision for his safety and the safety of others, especially after he attacked the woman in the room next to him, thinking she was an agent lying in wait.

Dr Speare suggested that his paranoid psychosis was partly related to brain damage resulting from a lack of blood stemming from his heart condition. But he also thought that perhaps Artuković had an 'underlying propensity' to develop paranoid psychosis because he had a history of 'episodes of severe depression. [...] The present illness might represent the other side of bipolar affective disorder.'

Artukovič underwent two weeks of treatment in hospital to control his psychosis before Dr Speare determined that it was safe for him to go home:

> As the patient's admitting physician, I was able to note that while he tried to hide his suspiciousness and delusional ideation that he occasionally could not do so and one could come to understand the degree to which his thought content included grandiose, self-referential and persecutory ideation. There was prominent religiosity, including specific delusions about his special contact with the Pope.

Dr Speare claimed that any legal proceeding, even an 'innocuous' small claims court, would further exacerbate his conditions.

Judge Robertson's reply to the request to halt the deportation hearing was swift and succinct. He wrote his response in three lines to Ronald Bonaparte:

> Dear Sir:
> There will be no change to the hearing date scheduled for September 18, 1984.
> Very Truly yours,
> Reese B. Robertson
> Immigration Judge

Artukovič's son Rad, now a 34-year-old stockbroker with a family of his own, filled out mountains of paperwork on his father's behalf. Andrija Artukovič was now legally blind and could no longer sign his own name. On 17 October 1984, Rad further appealed to Judge Robertson, asking for asylum for his father. Artukovič repeated his claim that he 'cannot return to my country of birth. I am stateless and no country would grant me a visa.'

The next month, Yugoslavia once again sent an extradition request to the United States. This time, the request included new evidence from witnesses. The former chief of the Office for Special Investigations, Allan A.

Ryan Jr, told the *Los Angeles Times* that Yugoslavia apparently believed American judges would be more receptive to extradition to a communist country than they had been during the Red Scare. 'The Yugoslav government is betting that attitudes have changed,' Ryan said, explaining that 'a court that might have been influenced by anti-communist fervor would be more objective, more dispassionate now.'

Ryan, one of the prosecutors against Artuković, described him as one of the highest-ranking Nazi war criminals, not only in the United States but in the world: 'I don't know of any other person with a higher rank who is still alive and who has never been tried.'

Ryan later went on to write several books on war criminals, including *Quiet Neighbors: Prosecuting Nazi War Criminals in America.*

★ ★ ★

On 14 November 1984, at 8 a.m., US Marshals and local police arrested Artuković at his home in Seal Beach. 'They burst into my dad's place,' Rad Artuković told the *Los Angeles Times*. 'They just came in and grabbed him and took him off by ambulance.'

Artuković was placed in the jail ward of County-USC Medical Center to await a health evaluation ordered by US Magistrate Ralph Geffen. His hospital room was turned into a makeshift public courtroom, with three reporters and a photographer crowding into the space with Magistrate Geffen and lawyers for both sides.

Eric Malnic, a *Los Angeles Times* reporter who witnessed Artuković's arraignment, wrote: 'The elderly man lay quietly on his bed during the 90-minute proceeding in the small, crowded room, indicating – despite apparent confusion at times – that he understood the charges against him.'

Ronald Bonaparte, Artuković's lawyer, described his client's illness: 'He has a number of medical complaints, including senility, an aneurysm that is ready to burst. He is nearly blind. When I think of the money and effort put into this guy instead of letting him die, it's just insane.'

On 27 November 1984, two days before his eighty-fifth birthday, Andrija Artuković was delivered to a courtroom for a bail hearing. He was swathed in blankets and slumped in a wheelchair as a Serbo-Croatian interpreter hovered, translating the proceedings. Artuković, who once spoke several languages, including Latin, could no longer understand English.

The courtroom was packed with both friends and foes. Emotions ran high among the 100 people, who included family and members of the Croatian community as well as victims of Artuković, other Holocaust survivors and officials of the Simon Wiesenthal Center. Newspaper reports described an atmosphere so tense that Magistrate Volney V. Brown Jr threatened to clear the courtroom as Croatian supporters jeered at comments made by the prosecution team and applauded when defence lawyers spoke.

The jeers were for claims from witnesses that Artuković ordered tanks to plough down a house jammed with women and children, killing them. Cheers erupted when Artuković's lawyer said, 'They've arrested an old man no longer able to speak on his own behalf.'

Magistrate Brown denied bail, saying that Artuković's condition seemed to have improved in the two weeks that he'd been in the hospital's jail ward. 'This is a very difficult decision,' he said. 'But bail is the exception and not the rule in international extradition cases.'

After Artuković was wheeled out of the courtroom and returned to the hospital, supporters and victims gathered on the courthouse steps.

Croatian Holocaust survivor Leo Handel, one of the five litigants in the lawsuit against Artuković, was interrupted as he tried to speak with reporters. 'My parents were killed, and I was tortured,' Handel said, as Artuković's supporters jumped in.

'You're lying!' they yelled. 'That is not true.'

Media reported that Rad Artuković stood a few feet away, 'vehemently denouncing' the new charges against his father. 'It's the same phony evidence they came up with in the '50s,' Rad said.

The Artuković family was not giving up. Over the next months, they would exhaust every legal means to keep Andrija in the United States. Included in their campaign were emotional appeals to politicians. For example, Artuković's grandchild wrote to First Lady Nancy Reagan. The child's name and address are redacted in a file released through Freedom of Information, but the grandchild's hand-printed letter is duplicated:

Dear Mrs. Reagan.

My grandfather, Andrija Artuković is the person from Surfside, California. He was taken from his home when I was in third grade and now I'm in fourth grade.

Some people think he was a Nazi but he never was one, and now they want to kill him.

I miss him very much.

I want him home where he belongs.

Sincerely, [Name redacted]

P.S. Please write back to me because I want to know if you really got the letter.

The family was further distressed by a judge's ruling in March 1985 that Artuković could be transferred to a US prison hospital near Springfield, Missouri. 'You've just killed him,' one of his daughters is reported to have shouted at the judge. Later, the *Los Angeles Times* reported that Ana Artuković and two of her daughters attended a special Mass held in his US Naval hospital room in Long Beach before saying their goodbyes.

Artuković was flown to Missouri on a charter flight on 15 March 1985. His family appealed to Amnesty International to intercede, claiming that he was not receiving proper medical care. According to an Associated Press story two weeks later, Amnesty International pursued the complaint but was satisfied by Artuković's treatment. His son, Rad, was not satisfied with Amnesty's conclusion. He said his father's condition was clearly deteriorating. 'He's very confused,' Rad Artuković told the Associated Press. 'He thinks he's in Switzerland.'

Artuković was returned to the Long Beach hospital in July, however, after a judge ruled that the prison was not granting the family additional visiting rights ordered by the court.

★ ★ ★

The legal battle continued until 11 February 1986, when, shortly after noon, the Ninth US Circuit Court of Appeals refused to block Artuković's extradition. Two hours later, a doctor from the federal prison at Terminal Island joined two US Marshals and two inspectors to escort Artuković in a wheelchair from the prison to Los Angeles International Airport. At 3.30 p.m. Artuković was flown out of Los Angeles, escorted by the prison physician and two inspectors on American Airlines Flight 22 bound for New York.

As the clock ticked down, his family and legal team continued to fight. While the aircraft retracing Artuković's first flight in America was en route, his family made one final appeal to the US Supreme Court.

In New York, the Yugoslav Airlines flight was waiting. Artuković's flight landed at 11.20 p.m., and everyone waited for US Supreme Court Justice William Rehnquist to decide whether the extradition should be delayed.

At 12.20 a.m. on 12 February, Rehnquist ruled against Artuković; forty minutes later, Artuković was turned over to Yugoslav authorities. The American doctor and two inspectors accompanied him on the flight to Zagreb. When the flight arrived at 9 a.m., Artuković was taken to hospital to await trial.

Back in California, his family never got to say goodbye. They vowed to keep fighting.

★ ★ ★

Artuković's trial took place in a courtroom in Zagreb that evoked the trial of Adolf Eichmann in Israel. Like Eichmann, Artuković sat in a specially built cubicle behind a bulletproof glass screen. Five judges presided. The public gallery included 175 spectators, all carefully screened, consisting of media, survivors of Croatia's concentration camps and Second World War veterans.

Listening and watching intently was Rad Artuković, who had fought for the right to attend. He was not allowed to speak with his father, who sat in an armchair, occasionally dozing off. He felt that his father's senility precluded him from having a clue of what was going on, and to him, that was an injustice in itself. As far as Rad was concerned, the entire month-long trial was 'a charade'.

His father was found guilty of ordering four separate massacres, in a thirty-two-page indictment based on witness accounts and documents. The trial heard that he had ordered 450 men, women and children to be killed by machine-gun fire because there was no room for them at a concentration camp in 1941. The following year he had ordered the massacre of the entire population of a town and most of its surrounding villages southwest of Zagreb. He was also convicted of ordering the deaths of several hundred Yugoslav partisans in 1943.

Artuković was sentenced to death by firing squad.

His family appealed, but the Yugoslav Federal Court's five-member tribunal upheld the death sentence. 'It has been undoubtedly proved that Andrija Artuković had committed war crimes,' the court said in an announcement.

Yugoslav law forbade executing a convict who was ill. A medical panel found that Artuković was not fit to be executed, so his death sentence was delayed, and he was incarcerated in a prison hospital. Rad Artuković and his sisters travelled from the United States several times to visit him.

★ ★ ★

Andrija Artuković died in prison on 18 January 1988, at the age of 88, after spending twenty-three months in a hospital prison. Forty-two years had passed since he fled Yugoslavia, and it was just shy of forty years since he arrived illegally in New York in July 1948, under a false name with a visa issued with the help of the Vatican.

The Yugoslav government will not disclose where his remains were deposited.

After winning so many battles, Artuković had lost the war. Reflecting upon his own fight, David felt gratified that his David-and-Goliath battle helped win his war.

★ ★ ★

One week later, 400 mourners gathered at St Anthony's Croatian Church in Los Angeles for a memorial Mass for Andrija Artuković. His son eulogised him: 'He believed in God (and) in his nation,' the *Los Angeles Times* reported him as saying. 'They don't come any truer than Dad. I'm proud that I'm his son.'

Rad Artuković made it his life's mission to clear his father's name. He hired historians and lobbied Congress. He demanded an investigation into the US Office of Special Investigations (OSI) because he felt they had helped Yugoslavia with its case against him. He maintained that all of the crimes attributed to his father were completely fabricated by the communists; or, that if they did occur, they were committed by other people. In some cases, he claimed that Tito's partisans themselves committed the atrocities. He accused the OSI of wilfully collaborating with the Yugoslavs 'in perpetrating a fraud'.

His courage in facing his father's foes won Rad the respect of those opponents, even as they fought him. The late Herb Brin, a legendary journalist who advocated for David Whitelaw, told the *Los Angeles Times* in 1986 that he had 'a lot of respect' for Rad, even though he considered him misguided.

Once, after Rad Artuković spoke up at an event heavily attended by JDL members, Irv Rubin came up to him and shook his hand. Rubin didn't agree with Artuković's son, but he admired his courage. It took guts to step in the lion's den, and Rubin valued courage above all else.

★ ★ ★

Artuković's wife, Ana, continued to live in Surfside until her death in December 2003, three weeks before her eighty-third birthday. In September 1986, the US government had reactivated the deportation order for Ana, who had not become a naturalised citizen since she arrived illegally thirty-eight years earlier, but her family fought successfully to keep their mother and grandmother in the country.

To her dying days, she remained proud to have been Mrs Andrija Artuković. Her obituary read:

> She lived her life with grace and dignity and endured her struggles with such faith, fortitude and love that she was an inspiration to all who knew her. Her steadfast devotion, not only to her husband but to the Croatian people is forever etched in the hearts of her family.

Ana Artuković left behind five children, eight grandchildren and one great-grandchild.

★ ★ ★

David took considerable satisfaction from the fact that Artuković had died in prison. The war criminal who had waged a 'holy war' in God's name would now stand before God and answer for his crimes.

David, who himself had committed a crime in the name of God, acknowledged the parallels between Artuković's war and his own. 'He absolutely thought God was on his side. And I was willing, and still am, to stand before God and answer for what I did.'

His faith determined David's destiny. Faith in God. Faith as a Jew. As a child at Sunday school, the story of David and Goliath had resonated with him. As a teenager, he felt compelled to take on his own David-and-Goliath battle.

He considers his role in bringing Artuković to justice the greatest accomplishment of his life. 'Right or wrong, good or bad, at least I did something I really believed in at the cost of potentially my own life. I stuck by it then. And I stick by it now. I'm at peace with my God.'

David's accomplice, Todd Michael Schwartz, was never brought to justice for his part in firebombing Lucille and John Artukovich's car. Israel refused to send him back to the United States.

One time, on a bus in Jerusalem, David felt eyes boring into his back. He turned around and met the eyes of a man who looked familiar. The man looked away and quickly stepped off the bus. 'That was him,' thought David. 'That was Schwartz.' The man was absorbed into the crowd, and David never saw him again.

Later, during the research for this book, David was furious to learn that the charges against Schwartz had been stayed. No longer a fugitive, Schwartz returned to the United States in the 1980s, settling in Houston, where his parents and brother lived. In May 1987, he married a local woman. Four months later, on 15 September, he died at the age of 34. His cause of death was not made public.

16

The Power of Love

As David considered the profound impact the Holocaust had on his family, he began soul-searching about his own childhood. How much had his own destiny, and that of his brothers, been predetermined by the sins of the previous generation?

His father's fate had been sealed when Harry's own father abandoned his first family to an orphanage, choosing to invest his limited resources in the children born to his new wife. David, who had first intuited the feelings expressed by 'sins of the father' listening to his parents arguing, now empathised with Harry as a victim, too. His conviction that Harry was fated to commit the sins of his own father was as certain as his belief that Harry's actions sprang from pain. Harry's childhood traumas had been passed down to his children, as invisible as the name Aronowitz, the name of the grandfather David never knew.

David thought of Klara, the only grandparent he ever knew. His grandmother, so harsh and cold, hurt the people she should have loved. Klara died a bitter and angry woman, so devastated by the losses of the war that she couldn't even show affection for those who survived. The Nazis hadn't just stolen Klara's business and home and murdered her family: they'd destroyed her heart, her capacity to love.

And his mother, Judith, how wounded was she? His fierce warrior, whose gift was her ability to channel her anger into action, was clearly damaged. No one knew her pain better than David, who had curled up beside her as a toddler, drinking in her 'mother's milk' of the Holocaust.

There was no doubt that the wounds to his mother's psyche, and to her own mother's, had been passed on to the next generation. Stephen and Billy were victims, too, their emotional wreckage the destiny charted one generation earlier by a madman determined to wipe out all Jews.

When David thought of the images of the Holocaust, the stories his mother told him, and those that he heard himself, the stories that hurt him the most were about children. He always felt an affinity with the children who were victims of the Nazis. Emaciated, scraping the porridge bowl with their fingers. Their eyes. Children like his cousin Herty being ripped from her mother at gunpoint. The children in Artuković's Croatia, torn from their parents and murdered in special camps, the only camps in Nazi Europe designated just for children. The Ustasha starving innocent children, poisoning them with caustic acid.

David had visited Yugoslavia several times, wanting to 'walk the blood-soaked soil of Jasenovac' for himself. He became friends with a woman, Greta Kresnik, the daughter of Jews who had survived the Jasenovac camp. There was an immediate bond between them, and as their friendship grew, David felt the pain of her inherited trauma. Greta, who affectionately referred to herself as David's 'second Jewish mother', brought the Ustasha's atrocities home to him. Artuković's crimes had gone from 'the academic to the intimate'. David's deeply personal connection to the Holocaust had grown even deeper, his appreciation for survivors even more profound.

Those who survived were a miracle, their lives a gift from God. The fact that they carried on at all, the resilience of the human spirit, flooded him with hope.

So much of David's story is about loss. Family loss. His brother Stephen never recovered from the addictions that manifested in his early teens, despite countless rehabilitation programmes. Stephen had long since been kicked out of the Merchant Marines, subsisting on odd jobs that never lasted very long. He lived in a rundown apartment in Hollywood and barely kept in touch with his family. But when he didn't call or visit during Hanukkah 1989, which began on 22 December, Judith and Harry became worried.

Harry had tried calling over the holiday season, but Stephen never answered. At first, Harry assumed his eldest son was out partying. But on 29 December, as the days passed and there was still no answer, Harry drove over to Stephen's apartment. When there was no answer, he asked for help from the landlord.

What he found inside broke his heart. Stephen had collapsed and died at the age of 39. The coroner placed the time of death as having occurred five days earlier, on Christmas Eve. In keeping with Jewish custom, no autopsy was performed. However, the coroner listed the cause of death as 'accidental overdose of barbiturates'.

Harry and Judith were too distraught to make funeral arrangements. 'My mom pretended Stephen was away somewhere. She couldn't bring herself to say that Stephen had died. And my dad was visibly heartbroken. I looked at him, and I knew he could never recover. Looking at his face, it seemed like my dad had died, too.'

It fell to David to make arrangements for Stephen's funeral. 'At the funeral, my dad sobbed uncontrollably. It was the only time I'd ever see my dad cry.'

★ ★ ★

In 2002, David buried his brother Billy.

Billy died at age 42 in a hospital where he had lingered for weeks after his heart began to fail. David was heartbroken by his youngest brother's death and by the sadness of his life. Billy had never lived on his own, gained a driving licence, bought a car or fallen in love. David gave him a full Merchant Marine funeral, fulfilling in death Billy's lifelong dream of 'shipping out'.

Six weeks after they buried Stephen, Harry passed away. The official reason was a heart attack, but David saw a broken heart. Even as he had comforted his father at Stephen's grave, David had a horrible premonition that his father would soon die, too. 'I knew my dad couldn't go on living after burying his first-born son. It was too much for him to bear.'

Harry had requested cremation. He wanted his ashes scattered in the sea. 'I told him that I couldn't grant that wish. I wanted my father near me. He smiled. He understood that it wasn't because I didn't want to respect his wishes. He knew it was because I loved him. I needed to hold on to him, to have him near me.'

In his old age, Harry seemed to realise that by favouring Stephen, he had neglected to value David. 'It was as if one day, he woke up and realised that while he was so busy making sure he had Stephen's back, that I was being responsible for the whole family. He started to slowly back away from Stephen and reached out to me. He even started to brag about me for the firebombing. He'd introduce me by saying that I'd fought to bring Artuković to justice.'

David never blamed Harry for the gaps in his parenting, and went along with him when his father sought a closer relationship. 'I never told him so, but in my heart, I knew it was too late for him to bond with me. He was trying. And I appreciated that.'

David buried his father beside Stephen. At the same time, he also bought the two burial plots beside Stephen's and Harry's graves.

Before he died, Harry had reconciled with his eldest sister, Sarah. His other two sisters remained so distant that when David called to inform them of Harry's death, one responded with, 'What do you expect me to do about it?' David, having lost his own brother only six weeks earlier, was too stunned to reply immediately. After a moment, he collected himself enough to say, 'I'm calling to tell you that your brother is dead.'

To David, his aunt's heartless reaction speaks to the everlasting damage of childhood trauma. It helps explain his father. How could Harry, abandoned to an orphanage with no parent as a role model, learn to be a parent himself?

David saw the evidence of that trauma in his father's face when, after decades of burying his past, Harry decided to visit his mother's grave. He invited David to travel across the country with him to Albany, NY, where Lena Aronowitz was buried in 1921. Her death, two days after giving birth to her fourth child, destined them to an emotional void that none of them could ever fill. 'You could see the tenderness in my dad's face as he stroked his mother's headstone. He remembered her love, and his love for her was written on his face.'

David longed to ask questions about what happened to his father and his siblings when their mother died. All he knew was that they went to an orphanage and that their father started a new family. But standing at his grandmother's grave, David knew that his father's pain was too great ever to be able to talk about it.

Even in his old age, on this sad day, Harry did not relent on the name Aronowitz. Harry forbade mention of his biological name until the day he died. David thinks his attitude explains a lot. 'I have a real soft spot for my dad. He wanted to be in the Merchant Marine, to live a life of adventure. I get it. He had to make a living. But a boy needs his dad. Boys need their dads.' David saved Harry's uniforms from the Merchant Marine, as well as his military tags and the insulated overalls that Harry wore during his time as a refrigeration technician during the war.

When he was going through his father's possessions after Harry's death, he found affectionate and racy letters from women all over the world; but even with a woman in every port, David believes Harry's heart belonged to Judith, as evidenced by the fact he saved every love letter from her, every photo of her. 'My dad was still in love with my mom. And I think she was in love with him, too. Neither of them ever remarried, even though my mom had lots of boyfriends. One time my dad told me that my mother was the most kindest, most decent woman he ever met. That always stayed with me. I think my parents were like star-crossed lovers, each of them with so many childhood wounds and emotional baggage. I feel profound compassion for what they lived through.'

Harry and Judith remained close friends, and he would visit her frequently, dropping in unannounced. 'If my mother's current boyfriend's car was in the driveway, my dad would just keep on driving. But if she was home alone, he would come in and spend a few hours. He died of a heart attack while having a nap on her couch.'

David inherited one genetic characteristic from Harry: a propensity for daily sneezing attacks. 'My dad's sneezes were almost seismic,' David says, as he braces himself for another. David doesn't know if the sneezing was passed down from his grandmother's genes on the Schorr side of the family, or from the Aronowitz side. Part of his family's tragic history is that he knows almost nothing about his ancestors. One side was lost to him when his father chose the name Whitelaw, blurring the connection to his biological family with the surname of the family who took him in briefly before the Great Depression.

David can only speculate about what might have been on his mother's side of the family by staring at photos from Germany. The dozens of relatives who crowded into the family's elegant home. Some of them, seventy-six of them, perished in the Holocaust. He'll never know if he inherited any of their mannerisms, quirks, the personal tics that other families fondly note, and sometimes joke about.

Mishpokhe. Family.

David is the only survivor of the family started by Harry and Judith in 1948 when they married under an open canopy in the Jewish custom, to symbolise the new home the couple would build as husband and wife. It was a home haunted by the ghosts of history, dragged down by the baggage of loss and grief, childhood abandonment, rejection and anger.

The Whitelaw home, with its troubled family dynamic, had left David feeling ambivalent about marriage and family. He felt conflicted about having children. He had dated lots of girls, and one of them, Hannah, he had even considered marrying. But she lived in Germany and already had children of her own. Judith cautioned him against taking on the responsibility of another man's children, of moving them to America. David listened to his mother's advice.

Now, approaching middle age, he was on the path of becoming a lifelong bachelor. Sometimes he regretted not marrying his German girlfriend. At other times, he questioned whether he was suited to fatherhood. Would he be doomed to commit the sins of his father and his father before him? Part of him wanted to settle down and raise a family, but somewhere, deep in his soul, he lacked trust. If humans could do what the Nazis did, what Artuković did, how could you ever trust another human being? Furthermore, how could you bring a child into a world that David believed was hardwired to hate Jews?

He had yet to meet a woman optimistic enough to convince him that it was safe to bring Jewish children into the world. No woman yet had been able to reassure his own inner voice that he was not too damaged to be a good father.

David felt guilty about not having children. 'Part of me felt that I had a duty to bring Jewish children into the world, to help repopulate the world with Jews, to do my share in making up for what the world lost when six million Jews were murdered. But the other part of me was conflicted about hatred toward Jews.'

His mother was pining for grandchildren. Judith had made her living for several years by babysitting other people's kids, and now she wanted to be surrounded by little ones of her own. Stephen, despite always having a besotted girlfriend, had never offered Judith any tangible hope that he would settle down and raise a family. Billy's unstable health made any kind of relationship unlikely. But David was successful, handsome and deeply affectionate. Judith thought he would make a great father if only he'd find the right woman. 'She was always talking about how much she'd spoil my children, how much she'd love to have grandchildren to spoil. She'd do this Yiddish thing, "Ach, David, I wish you had ten kids. Ach, I'd spoil them so rotten."'

Without grandchildren of her own, Judith started her own babysitting business when she was in her early 70s.

David invested his earnings in real estate and began to rent out his houses. By becoming a landlord, David paid homage to his mother, who lost two homes, and to his grandmother, Klara, who saved her family by walking away from the five-storey apartment building that provided their livelihood.

If David's story is one of loss, it is also one of love. The love of God, instilled in him by Judith. The love for his family. The transformative love showered upon him by Herty, and the love that came to fill David's own heart for the people who stood by him after he was arrested. They became like family to him, the family he chose to fill the void his biological family could not.

Lawyer Bugliosi, Prison Warden Mooneyham, Chief Psychiatrist Flanagan: all of them had gone well beyond their professional calling. They had taken him in, made him feel valued as a father might have done. When they died, David mourned their loss.

Ray Gladden had played the role of big brother and protector at the Los Angeles County Jail. He risked his life by breaking prison racial code to befriend a white inmate, a newbie with no clue about the unwritten jailhouse rules. For a person whose presence was fleeting, Ray had a profound impact on David's life. He was a champion and mentor from a different race and class, a surrogate big brother who felt like family. Sadly, David lost touch with Ray. Even though Judith had kept her promise to visit Ray in prison, one day when she went to visit, he was gone. Prison staff said they didn't know his whereabouts, leaving David and Judith to always wonder if he'd been released or moved to a different prison.

A few months after Billy died, David lost Irv Rubin, who died in prison. He and another prominent JDL member, Earl Krugel, had been charged with conspiracy to bomb a mosque and government buildings. Krugel was murdered in an Arizona prison when another prisoner hit him over the head with a concrete block, killing him instantly. Rubin was awaiting trial in November 2002 when he died after a fall from a two-storey balcony. His throat had been cut. The official reason for his death is suicide, but many of his supporters, including David, believe he was murdered.

David attended his funeral. 'I was fond of Irv. I still am.'

Of all the people who stepped up as mentors, role models, champions and friends, David held none in higher esteem than Phil Blazer, who had played all of those roles. Phil had immediately understood David's pain as a second-generation Holocaust victim the moment Judith called asking for his help. His response was visceral, a one-on-one humanitarian balm against the wounds inflicted by the Nazis.

Judith and David Whitelaw were among the first to receive the benefit of Phil's talent and energy to fight for Holocaust victims. In the coming decades, Phil became a larger-than-life guardian to countless others, using his gift for collaboration to help Holocaust survivors and even save the lives of 1,000 starving Ethiopian Jews. He died of complications from Parkinson's Disease in 2021 at the age of 76.

But the person who had embodied the essence of family through his ongoing commitment was Gary Levin. 'Gary is my brother from another mother, as that saying goes. He is *mishpokhe*, absolutely.' Gary, whose easygoing demeanour belied a spine of steel, had never wavered in his loyalty. Following his defiance of his parents by visiting David in all three jails, Gary continues to treat David as a brother.

With Stephen and Billy both dead, Gary felt David's grief that he would never know the joy of being an uncle. Gary instructed his two children, Ashley and Tony, to refer to David as 'Uncle Dave'. David recalled the children objecting to Gary's request. 'The kids didn't want to do it, because they rightly pointed out that I was a friend and not an uncle. But Gary felt sorry for me having no family, and he always included me in their family celebrations. I told Ashley and Tony that they didn't have to call me uncle, but they decided on their own to do it anyway.' David pauses, choked up. 'Ashley told me recently that if anything should happen to her father, God forbid, that she'd like me to walk her down the aisle on her wedding day. That means a lot.'

The feeling of *mishpokhe*, transcends blood.

In 1999, with David's forty-fifth birthday looming, Gary Levin and his wife Marina seized an opportunity to play matchmaker to their bachelor friend. After decades of teasing David about being 'too vain and too picky', Gary was finally fulfilling his destiny as 'Swamp Man', introducing David to a promising-looking woman.

Gary and Marina engineered a dinner with a relative of Marina's, a Peruvian woman named Edith Galvez. They had no doubt that Edith, slim and petite with long dark hair and film-star good looks, would meet David's high standards for a first date. Edith had professed that she wasn't eager to find a husband. She had plenty of suitors, but none that met her own expectations of high-quality character. Swamp Man thought it just might be a match made in heaven. 'We thought they would like each other, but you just never know, do you?' Gary said. 'We held our breath and waited.'

Their first date took place around Hanukkah and David brought Edith a white teddy bear wearing a kippah. Edith, raised a Catholic in Lima, barely knew anything about Jews or Judaism. She was intrigued. 'I wasn't really looking for any certain kind of guy,' says Edith. 'I was pretty independent. The only thing that was important to me was that the man I marry would have good values.'

They fell in love. The timing could not have been better. A month later, Judith fell ill, but by then, Edith had become part of David's life.

As he picked up Edith to meet his mother, David's heart filled with sorrow at a fate requiring him to present the love of his life to his mother at a hospital. It seemed another tragedy for Judith, who would have relished cooking a meal in her own home for the woman who had finally won David's heart. Another fateful tragedy that would prevent her from holding the grandchildren this woman might finally deliver to her.

Driving to the hospital, David suspected that his mother would immediately see Edith's gracious, kind spirit. He expected her to love Edith and Edith to love his mother. But he was not prepared for the instant bond between the two women: it felt as if each had been waiting to become best friends their whole lives.

Eerily, some of Edith's characteristics evoked Judith. They shared a birthday, 10 July. Both hated red roses. The first time David brought Edith red roses was the last, because her comment echoed Judith's word for word: 'Red roses make me sad.'

Just a few weeks after meeting Edith, Judith died of complications from a dental infection. She was 79 years old. 'Sometimes I imagine what it would have been like if my mom had lived. She and Edith would have been best friends. I'd be the odd man out, without a doubt,' David says with a smile. Edith's presence in David's life, the comfort she brought him when Judith died, was a gift. It didn't seem a stretch to consider the timing of Edith's arrival in his life as a gift from God.

David and Edith married in Los Angeles on 26 January 2003. 'We dated for three years, even though we knew we were right for each other. Let's face it, I have a lot of baggage. Edith has no baggage. And I know that my parents' marriage was doomed, through no fault of their own, because of the baggage they carried from the heartbreak of their childhoods. I didn't want to repeat that cycle.'

Their wedding was attended by 175 friends and family. David, with no blood relatives in attendance, placed photos of Judith, Harry, Stephen and Billy, to represent his side of the family. Edith's family included her parents, four sisters, two brothers, nieces and nephews and cousins. She has nineteen nieces and nephews.

The Galvez family embraced David as one of their own.

Edith converted to Judaism. Watching her pray, David is moved by her devotion and by her body language, both of which remind him of his mother. 'It's uncanny. I'm not one to talk this way, but sometimes I feel like my mother is being channelled through Edith.'

★   ★   ★

David saved the mementoes of his mother's life: the artistic dressmaking patterns and drawings that Judith made as a teenager in Germany, her father's Iron Cross and helmet, newspapers and correspondence in German, Spanish and English.

He also saved her stove, unable to bear parting with the symbol of the delicious meals that only David seemed to appreciate. 'Her Spanish rice was the tastiest, the rice the most golden, the little pieces of vegetables sautéed to perfection. I can still remember coming home from Fairfax High and smelling the Spanish rice the minute I opened the door.' He chokes up at the memory. 'I would give anything just to do that one more time again with my mom.'

David designed her tombstone, which reads: 'Judith Whitelaw, July 10, 1920 – Feb 23, 2000. Dearly Beloved Wife, Mother, Daughter and Sister. Noble, Loving and Courageous.'

Etched on the bottom of the tombstone is the logo of the JDL, the clenched fist inside a Star of David, with the slogan 'Never Again.'

David is sure that Judith, a warrior until her last breath, would be proud.

★ ★ ★

With his marriage to Edith, David gained the large family he'd been yearning for his entire life. At the age of 47, he'd finally found the love that his heart could trust. Edith was twelve years younger, and they hoped children would soon come along.

They bought a house in Malibu with a view of the ocean. Living on the Pacific Ocean was a dream come true for David. The ocean had offered solace to his father when he ran away from the orphanage in Brooklyn. The ocean had saved his mother, grandmother and uncle when they fled Germany. The ocean had given Stephen what little stability he could claim in his tortured life. The ocean had sustained Billy's hope that one day he'd ship out as a merchant mariner.

David placed his 'Rosebud', the replica of the *Santa Maria* he cherished as a childhood present from his father, on a shelf overlooking the ocean. The inchoate notion to associate the ocean with destiny had been born in his childhood home; the *Leave it to Beaver* suburb of Buena Park.

Watching the waves crash on the beach across from his house in Malibu, David would sometimes contemplate the tides of change that had washed over the world, and his own family, since the halcyon promise of the 1950s. The idealism and social turmoil of the 1960s mirrored the chaos of their family life imploding in Buena Park. The domestic terrorism during the civil unrest of the 1970s when David was sent to prison for his own act of terrorism. The reckoning of the 1980s when Artuković was finally brought to justice, ending his freedom to enjoy a nightly walk along the beach just as David did now.

Here in their house on the ocean, David and Edith had a chance to start a new legacy for the Whitelaw family. A chance to right the wrongs of the past. As a child, David aspired to become an astronaut, then a scientist, and eventually a doctor. With each, his goal was the same, to do something noble with his life. 'I will build a better tomorrow', the declaration he promised at his bar mitzvah, continued to be the driving force in his life.

He considered a career in law and academia. But he always came back to the question of how to build a better tomorrow, a better world. He decided to become a teacher. In children, David saw hope. Nurturing and moulding children gave him hope that he could prevent hatred. He taught in the toughest and most impoverished neighbourhoods in Los Angeles for thirty-three years until he retired in 2017.

'I saved every picture every child ever drew for me. And I would tell them that I was going to save them for the rest of my life. I'd make them laugh, you know, by talking about myself in the third person. I'd say something along the lines of, "You know that when Mr Whitelaw is an old man sitting in his rocking chair, he's going to have a stack this high, and I hold my hand high above my head, of all the drawings and cards you gave your teacher. Do you know why? Because each of you put a piece of your heart into making those drawings to show how much you love your teacher. And if your teacher threw them out, he would be throwing away all that love you gave him. Mr Whitelaw will never stomp on your heart like that." They might giggle, or they might look at me very earnestly, but I meant every word. And I saved every drawing.'

David never forgot the way his own kindergarten teacher, Mrs Oveson, made him feel. 'She was so nurturing. When I was thinking about becoming a teacher, I thought about how good Mrs Oveson made me feel about myself, the way she told me I was a talented artist. Every kid needs that kind of encouragement. She's the reason I decided to become a kindergarten teacher.'

In thirty-three years, David had the opportunity to pay back Mrs Oveson by boosting the esteem of some 825 kids. And, as he never forgot Mrs Oveson, he also tried to create a world that would be better for kids like his brothers Stephen and Billy. The childhood wounds of his parents were never far from his mind as he tried to build up students rejected by their parents because of addictions and abuse. Some kids were homeless; some were the young siblings of gang members who were in jail.

He tried to elevate them by giving them hope, the kind of hope that lifted the children licking the porridge bowls at Auschwitz, the hope that was lost on the children being poisoned by the Ustasha in Artuković's camps. 'I wanted to help them hang on to their innocence as much as possible. One of the best things about being a teacher is that you get to be around innocence every day. What other job lets you be full of wonder and act silly all day long? I cherished every moment of that.'

Upon his retirement, David wrote some parting words to his students: 'It is not merely enough to know math and how to count numbers, but also to count your many blessings. It is not sufficient merely to read and write well but to use your language skills to communicate important ideas of friendship and understanding and to learn about the beautiful, fascinating world around you.'

His words are born of idealism. The destiny that propelled him to wage his own David-and-Goliath battle also led him to try to prevent the childhood wounds that create anger and hatred. 'If I ever had kids of my own, I wanted that to be my legacy. To stop the cycle of hurt, bitterness, and anger that cannibalised my family. Through a twist of fate, their inheritance was one of misery. I wanted to break that cycle.'

David and Edith were not able to have children. 'We wanted our own family. I wanted the chance to leave a legacy that was full of love and hope and pride in their Jewish identity. We would have taught our children to be proud and strong, to stand upright and to fight for what you believe in.'

And as David looks back on his fight to bring Artuković to justice, idealism is the thread woven through the experience. 'It's not just my idealism; it's the idealism that I saw come out of other people. I saw in Dr Flanagan and Mr Mooneyham cynical, prison-hardened men who saw beyond my veneer. Vincent Bugliosi and Phil Blazer, who saw me as a soldier of my own convictions. All of them took a leap of faith. And I tried all my life to live up to that. Everything I ever pledged to do, I did. I've lived my life with integrity and moral conviction because I never wanted to betray that faith. And I pray to God that I never do.'

Epilogue

David's destiny, forever intertwined with the legacy of the Holocaust, took another powerful twist on 8 November 2018. On the eve of the eightieth anniversary of Kristallnacht, his house in Malibu burned to the ground.

The California wildfire skipped the neighbouring houses to the front and back, as well as on both sides of David's and Edith's house, as it raged along the Pacific Coast Highway. The flames ate up the shed where he had stored his mother's piano and stove, the happy relics of David's fondest memories of her singing German songs and cooking the meals that symbolised her love. 'I'm not sure if God is testing me for some higher purpose, but for the fire to destroy those symbols on the anniversary of Kristallnacht must mean something,' David says.

Eighty years earlier, as the Nazis rampaged through Germany, smashing and burning Jewish businesses and throwing Jewish books onto the fire, David's grandmother made a primal decision to flee. Klara Schiftan, her daughter Judith and her son Walter were only able to carry their most precious belongings. David inherited his grandfather's First World War helmet and Iron Cross awarded by Kaiser Wilhelm, along with original family photos and his mother's designs for sewing patterns. For years, he stored these possessions at his house in Malibu.

In the spring of 2018, six months before the fire, he transferred the precious boxes to a storage space in the San Fernando Valley. The move was prompted by the writing of *The Fierce* to allow convenient access to the treasure trove of his family history. As a result of the move, David's most valuable possessions survived the fire. The photos of the ancestors that he never met, the clues to the lives of seventy-six relatives murdered in the Holocaust, were sheltered from fire through fate.

For more than forty-four years, David kept quiet about his David-and-Goliath battle to bring Andrija Artuković to justice. Only his closest friends and officials who needed to know were told. To David, having answered to man's law, he is now only accountable to God.

With the telling of this story, David Whitelaw, the teacher, hopes to offer lessons to a world in which antisemitism is on the rise. His family archives contain the primary material for those lessons, the evidence of what life was like before the Holocaust, before wounds were passed down from one generation to the next. Before Artuković murdered in God's name, before children were herded into concentration camps.

The survival of his family archives, which help tell the story David kept inside his own heart for most of his life, seems like destiny, too. This story is a reminder of the predetermining forces of his life.

David's destiny, from the moment he drank in 'mother's milk', was to live the motto: Never Forget. Never Again.

Acknowledgements

This book came about after Michael Jorgensen, an Emmy-award-winning film-maker, approached Kieran LeBlanc, executive director of the Book Publishers Association of Alberta, to ask if she could suggest a writer for a book to accompany a feature film. Kieran recommended me. Michael and I had worked together decades earlier, and we both welcomed a chance to collaborate again. I will be forever grateful to Kieran and her gift for connecting people.

And, of course, I wish to thank Michael for trusting an unpublished author and believing in me. I feel the same gratitude to our agent George Karlov for his tireless and enthusiastic promotion of *The Fierce*. Likewise, Amy Rigg, commissioning editor at The History Press, for her advocacy and gentle guidance, and to project editor Alex Boulton, whose editorial skill strengthened this manuscript. From the outset, I knew I was in safe hands with the entire team.

Thanks also to Ivo Pejaković, Public Institution Jasenovac Memorial Site, for his generous cooperation in locating and supplying photos. Similarly, thanks to the University of Southern California library for providing archival photos. Thanks to historian Robert B. McCormick of the University of South Carolina Upstate for kind encouragement and permission to quote from his work.

I feel indebted to journalists and writers, ranging from the Second World War to the late 1980s, whose storytelling informed my research. My research also benefited from access to thousands of pages of declassified

US government records, thanks to the diligence of the Nazi War Crimes and Japanese Imperial Government Records Interagency Working Group.

I would also like to thank people in Los Angeles who assisted during my three years of research: Dan Laikin of Jewish Life TV for providing office space, Paul Bilski, Mitch Egers, Larry Greenbaum, Suzie Mezei, the Noah family and Michael Tanner. Special thanks to Mitzi March Mogul, whose archival material was a godsend, and Gary Levin, for his generosity throughout the project. Thanks to Debbie Miller Weiss in Brooklyn for the pleasure and privilege of hearing your family's stories.

Every writer leans on friends to lend an ear, read clunky first drafts and provide critical feedback. I'm fortunate that my circle includes Rabbi Mark Blazer, Kathy Collins, Ingrid Fraser, Elinor Florence, Julia Hewitt, Dr Trudy McNabb, Margo McDiarmid, Paula Koponyas, Lauren Spencer and Marguerite Baker. Special thanks to Marguerite, who volunteered her time and prodigious organisational skill to create a Whitelaw family archive. She accompanied me to Los Angeles and sat on the floor of Jewish Life Television's studio for countless hours, day and night, sorting through David Whitelaw's collection of boxes, bags and bins. When she finally stood up and stacked the last of forty-five boxes into place, she had transformed the chaos into a library-worthy catalogue.

I owe a great debt to my husband, Ian Stewart, for offering the gift of his time and talent as a copy editor, technical support and dog walker, as well as his unwavering commitment to this story.

Finally, thank you, David and Edith Whitelaw, for sharing with such open hearts. I can never thank you enough.

Bibliography

Books and Suggested Reading

Blum, Howard, *Wanted!: The Search for Nazis in America* (Greenwich: Fawcett, 1977).

Butler, Hubert, *Independent Spirit* (New York: Farrar, Straus & Giroux, 1996).

Cenziper, Debbie, *Citizen 865* (New York: Hachette, 2019).

Cornwell, John, *Hitler's Pope: The Secret History of Pius XII* (London: Viking UK, 2000).

Eger, Edith Eva, *The Choice: Embrace the Possible* (New York: Scribner, 2017).

Goldberg, Rita, *Motherland: Growing Up with the Holocaust* (London: Halban, 2014).

Kertzer, David I., *The Pope at War: The Secret History of Pius XII, Mussolini, and Hitler* (New York: Penguin Random House, 2022).

McCormick, Robert B., *Croatia Under Ante Pavelić: America, the Ustase and Croatian Genocide in World War II* (London: Bloomsbury, 2020).

Phayer, Michael, *The Catholic Church and the Holocaust, 1930–1965* (Bloomington: Indiana University Press, 2000).

Phayer, Michael, *Pius XII, The Holocaust and The Cold War* (Bloomington: Indiana University Press, 2008).

Pyle, Christopher H., *Extradition, Politics, and Human Rights* (Philadelphia: Temple University Press, 2001).

Newspapers/ Wire Services/Columnists

The Associated Press
Jewish Telegraphic Agency
United Press International
The Guardian
London Times
Los Angeles Times
The New York Times
Israel Today
Long Beach Independent
Long Beach Independent Press-Telegram
Pasadena Independent
Orange County Register
The Tablet, Brooklyn, NY
Milton Friedman's syndicated column, Jewish Telegraphic Agency
Frederic J. Haskin's syndicated column, Information Bureau
Drew Pearson's syndicated column, Washington Merry-Go-Round

Public Records

Arrest Records/Court and Trial Transcripts, David Whitelaw and Michael Schwartz, 1975–1976

Crimes in the Jasenovac Camp; The State Commission for the Investigation of the Crimes of the Occupation Forces and their Collaborators, Zagreb, 1946, translated by Sinisa Djuric, 2003

David Whitelaw psychiatric reports (Coburn, Flanagan, Urbach), Whitelaw Trial and Probation Records

US Department of Justice, Immigration and Naturalization Service vs. Andrija Artukovic, 1985–1986 (Bonaparte, Speare)

CIA/FBI Artukovic file, Volumes 1 and 2, US National Archives

US Congressional Record (House), Vol. 1010, Part 12, pp. 12152–12159, July 29, 1955, The Persecution of Andrija Artukovic

NASA Documentary, *The Flight of Apollo 8*

Websites

Oxford Languages (languages.oup.com/google-dictionary-en/)
USC Shoah Foundation (sfi.usc.edu)